BLACK RELIGION
after
THE MILLION MAN MARCH

BLACK RELIGION
after
THE MILLION MAN MARCH

Voices on the Future

Edited by

Garth Kasimu Baker-Fletcher

ORBIS BOOKS

Maryknoll, New York 10545

The Catholic Foreign Mission Society of America (Maryknoll) recruits and trains people for overseas missionary service. Through Orbis Books, Maryknoll aims to foster the international dialogue that is essential to mission. The books published, however, reflect the opinions of their authors and are not meant to represent the official position of the society.

Library of Congress Cataloging-in-Publication Data

Black religion after the Million Man March : voices on the future /
    edited by Garth Kasimu Baker-Fletcher.
        p. cm.
    Includes bibliographical references.
    ISBN 1-57075-159-5 (alk. paper)
    1. Afro-Americans—Religion.   2. Afro-American men—Religious
life. 3. Million Man March (1995 : Washington, D.C.) I. Baker
-Fletcher, Garth, 1955-
BR563.N4B573   1998
277.3'0829'08996073—dc21   97-32791
                                                                CIP

Contents

PART III: THEMES AS WE TRANSFORM

Black Religion after the Million Man March

Voices on the Future

Almost two years after the October 16, 1995, Million Man March in Washington, D.C., unclear signals abound concerning the future shape of African American religious involvement in the liberation of Black people. On the one hand, it would seem that the March brought together many different kinds of faiths—Christian, Moslem, and even traditional African—to speak publicly on an issue of mutual concern; namely, that of calling Black men into greater responsibility for the condition of our communities. Such a gathering brought leaders of churches, mosques, and various esoteric and largely informal traditional (and even ancient) African spiritualities to pray together, speak together, and respectfully listen to one another's viewpoints. On the other hand, because the "issue" of the March still remains the "leadership" of Minister Louis Farrakhan, his controversial statements and actions continue to dominate reflections about the implications of the March. Without any doubt Louis Farrakhan *is* an issue. Yet allowing Farrakhan to become *the* issue for many African Americans is unacceptable, immoral, and an unconscionable distraction to the pressing issues of unemployment, suppressed dignity, youth violence, drug infestation, and the suppression of public hopes. These issues are not just social or political but are also *spiritual issues in a fundamental sense*. The Million Man March fired the imagination of almost every African American male living in the United States, demanded and caught international attention, and even inspired the predominantly Euro-American and popular Promise Keepers organization to begin taking African American male concerns more seriously.

I could not go to the Million Man March, but I participated in a Day of Absence sympathy celebration at a local church. The Day of Absence ran at the same time as the Million Man March on October 16, 1995. The mission statement of the Million Man March organizers included the following description of the objectives of the Day of Absence:

> We call on those who do not come to Washington, especially Black women, to mobilize and organize the community in support of the

Million Man March and its goals. The Day of Absence is a parallel activity to the Million Man March and a component part of one joint and cooperative project: the standing up and assumption of a new and expanded responsibility by the Black man in particular and the Black community in general.[1]

The sympathy celebration we held at Antioch Missionary Baptist Church in the Pomona Valley involved the joint efforts of an interdenominational group of local ministers. About half of the people involved at our event were women and children. It was a wonderful afternoon of speeches, music, and prayers for our people. It was quite an experience; we left with feelings of bonding, empowerment, inspiration, and a renewed commitment to build stronger bonds of love in our families. In our own way we experienced something quite akin to the experience of those who attended the Million Man March in Washington, D.C.

Black Religion after the Million Man March: Voices on the Future attempts to explore the various currents of frustration, hope, and indignation present among African American males as we reflect upon the impact of that March on our futures. It is a book written by African American religious men and women from our perspectives as persons of both faith and intelligence. As such, it uplifts moments of both celebration and critique and tries to name the *complexity of African American male and female experiences*, rather than attempting to isolate a particular "experience" as singularly representative of all that comprises "Black" manhood and womanhood.

The first part of the book wrestles with conflicting reactions to the March itself. Theodore Walker Jr., professor of social ethics at Perkins School of Theology at Southern Methodist University in Dallas, provides a positive evaluation of the March from the perspective of one not present, particularly in regard to the overwhelmingly negative representations of Black men that motivated some million African American males to travel for a Day of Absence. Walker is interested in articulating the March as "good news"—theologically, culturally, and emotionally—for Black males and Black communities.

Victor Anderson, who teaches Christian ethics at the Vanderbilt Divinity School of Vanderbilt University in Nashville, offers a critical stance toward the March, noting its confused purpose and conflicting signals regarding the inclusion of various kinds of African American males and females; he deconstructs what he calls the "cult of Black masculinity." Anderson is concerned about the unspoken implications of silence on such issues as HIV/AIDS and homosexuality at the March, naming this exclusion as an "abomination of a million men."

The third chapter of the first part is by the book's editor, G. Kasimu Baker-Fletcher, professor of Christian ethics at Claremont School of Theology and Claremont Graduate School in southern California. He engages the issue from the perspective of his writings on creating an inclusive, non-sexist "space" for Black men that he calls XODUS space. Kasimu deconstructs aspects of the

March from the perspective of XODUS theology and ethics, ending with an open-ended ambivalence about its ultimate goals in regard to the transformation and reconstruction of a healthy masculinity.

Part One ends with "Dialogical Interrogations" between Kasimu, Theodore, and Victor. With frankness and an occasional touch of humor, these three African American men seek clarity on their differences.

Having set the tone of difference, the next part of *Black Religion after the Million Man March* tackles one of the most important themes of the March—*manhood*. Several questions will be addressed in a dialogical fashion between Kasimu and the Rev. Dr. Jack Sullivan, pastor of United Christian Church in Detroit in the opening chapter of this section. They will dialogue on the following: What view of manhood was presented at the March, and how does that view support or detract from ongoing ideals of masculinity in African American communities? What kind of masculinity did the March support— one of inclusive male-liberation movements, or one more akin to traditionalist "headship" imperatives typical of most church groups? How were family, womanhood, and the women participating in the March addressed in relationship to manhood?

Anthony Pinn, professor of religious studies at Macalester College in Minneapolis, gives primary attention to how Spike Lee's movie "Get on the Bus" provides a symbolic representation of the call for humanization of males, movement of transformation toward a new realization of masculinity, and resignification of Black males as a diverse and often conflict-ridden group. Pinn utilizes Rap music as expressive of a certain kind of Black manhood and compares the goals of responsibility and healthy relationships gained at the March with these forms of popular cultural maleness.

Salim Faraji, a student at Claremont who participated in the March, adds a unique understanding of manhood drawn from ancient Kemetic (Egyptian) teachings which symbolize the energies of Divinity in a multitude of "gods." Faraji is particularly interested in explicating the spirituality of Heru, one of the pre-eminent divinities of ancient Egypt.

Karen Baker-Fletcher, professor of theology and culture at Claremont School of Theology, analyzes the themes of separate gatherings for women and men "for reasons of health," controversies surrounding lack of women's participation, Alice Walker's positive response, Farrakhan's understanding of power, and cultural ramifications of the March for Black families from a womanist perspective. Baker-Fletcher is particularly interested in promoting a holistic vision of healing and interconnection of human beings with each other and all of the natural order of Creation.

The third part of *Black Religion after the Million Man March*, "Themes as We Transform," presents a multi-disciplinary articulation of various motifs which emerged at the March whose implications far exceed the event itself. The ethical, theological, and philosophical meanings of such terms as: *responsibility, atonement, restoration, reconciliation,* and *renewal* beg for sustained critical analysis in light of future Black religious dialogues. The first three chapters of this part are refined versions of a public conversation on the Million Man March among Lee Butler, G. Kasimu Baker-Fletcher, and Cheryl Sanders which took place in November 1996 at the New Orleans meeting of the American Academy of Religion's Men's Studies Group. Lee Butler, professor of pastoral theology at Chicago Theological Seminary, casts the themes of the March as a "Sermon on the Mall." Butler is concerned about casting the themes presented at the March, and Farrakhan's role, within the framework of African traditional healing rituals, shamanic practices, storytelling cultural indices, and the legacy of Black preachers.

G. Kasimu Baker-Fletcher analyzes the Pledge taken by all the men participating in the March and its ethical-social promises. Kasimu is concerned about carefully sorting among those aspects of the Pledge that actually promote liberation, those which barely confront anti-justice within male and female relationships, and those which might tacitly legitimate injustice within Black families and communities.

Cheryl Sanders, professor of Christian ethics at the Divinity School of Howard University in Washington, D.C., provides a conservative Black Christian response to the implications of the March. She is concerned to move the Million Man March as an event toward its implications as a movement. Further, Sanders elaborates traditional Christian family values as part of her larger theological-cultural interpretation of *exile*, with a view toward reforming immorality within Black communities, which she terms *remoralization*.

Ivory L. Lyons Jr., recent doctoral candidate of the Claremont Graduate School and ordained evangelical Baptist minister, offers an analysis of the possible links between the call for a March issued by Minister Farrakhan and traditional biblical understandings of GOD's calling. Problematizing conventional evangelical theologies of exclusion, Lyons calls for conservative African American Christians to take a more open-minded approach to GOD's activity even in such "unlikely" places as the Million Man March!

Rev. Bessie Collins, U.M.C. minister and doctoral candidate at Claremont, discusses the March as a healing ritual. She utilizes traditional psychological theory as espoused by Freud and Jung in counterpoint to the thought of African American psychologists such as Wade Nobles and Linda Myers to interpret the March and its potential for Healing Space.

Rev. Mary Minor Reed, staff minister at First A.M.E. Church in Los Angeles, shares the sermon "A Ration of Compassion" as indicative of the pervasive ethos of *responsibility and caring for others* that the March represented to those involved in concrete ministry to urban African American young people.

This last part concludes with the Rev. Prof. Cornish Rogers, professor of ecumenics and mission at Claremont, discussing themes of community and ecumenism in relationship to African American religious and socio-political solidarity.

G. Kasimu Baker-Fletcher provides a provocation-cum-summary for the book as a conclusion. Restating the goal of the book in light of the various, sometimes conflicting views of how the March may contribute to future directions for Black religion in the United States of America, Kasimu casts his provocation particularly in light of the radical need for liberation, wholeness, and power in urban African American communities.

The voices in this volume are pastors and scholars, students and teachers, activists and intellectuals, cutting-edge conservatives and radicals, all thinking together. Sermonic discourse is set alongside critical theory, celebration next to stinging criticism. Such is the diversity of voices that informs the lives of African American religious, academic, and activist communities. It is this editor's strong contention that to present reflections and analysis of the Million Man March and its future implications without such contentious display would be an unethical representation of an individual interest. Yet not all of the many voices have been heard, a reflection more of the severe time restrictions brought to bear on bringing this project to an early publishing date than of a particular prejudice on my part against renowned figures who usually are represented in such a volume.

One of the most important voices is not directly heard—that of the Nation of Islam. Unfortunately, while I made several attempts to contact and invite contributions from local and national headquarters of the Nation, I received no response. Having the deepest respect for the ministry of the Nation of Islam and Minister Farrakhan's sincerity, I am hopeful that eventually I may be able to make more fruitful contacts with the Nation for genuinely liberative dialogue and exchange concerning the redemption of African Americans. In the meantime, this volume stands, primarily, as a collection of various Christian and humanist voices challenging Black churches to a deeper prophetic role. Such a challenge hopes to move all persons of faith to consider the March's future implications for Black folk and Black religion.

Note

[1] Haki R. Madhubuti and Maulana Karenga, eds., *Million Man March/Day of Absence: A Commemorative Anthology* (Chicago/Los Angeles: Third World Press/University of Sankore, 1996), p. 136.

Part I

THE EVENT

Chapter One

Can a Million Black Men Be Good News?

A Great Cloud of Witnesses to the Affirmative

THEODORE WALKER JR.

> *Wherefore seeing we also are compassed about with so*
> *great a cloud of witnesses, let us lay aside every weight,*
> *and the sin which doth so easily beset us, and let us run*
> *with patience the race that is set before us.*
> —Hebrews 12:1

Can a million black men be good news? Throughout modern North America, the default answer is no. For modern white America, a self-empowered mass gathering of black men is, by definition, cause for apprehension. And indeed, prior to the Million Man March/Day of Absence (MMM/DOA) in the summer and fall of 1995, when mainstream public media gave attention to the call for a Million Man March, there were no mainstream voices encouraging or predicting a successful march with a good and righteous outcome. Instead, throughout mainstream media, the voices of doubt, "no confidence," apprehension, and discouragement prevailed.[1] Only African American alternative media encouraged and predicted a good and righteous event. (African American alternative media encouraging and predicting a righteous event included the Nation of Islam's paper, *The Final Call*, and other African American newspapers and publications, along with African American radio, television, and Internet broadcasts, and sermons, speeches, and other public appeals at African American churches, bookstores, cultural centers, schools, fraternal and professional associations, barber shops, beauty parlors, restaurants, social clubs, and on street corners and porches.) Most Americans, including many African Americans, were unable to envision the possibility of a million black men being good news. We did not know it could be so.

And now we know better. We now know a gathering of one million black men can be good news because on October 16, 1995, a gathering of more than one million black men *was* good news.

The perpetually good news is: God offers us opportunity for prayer, fasting, confession, forgiveness of sin, atonement, repentance, reconciliation, and

9

responsibility. This perpetually good news was re-presented in Minister Farrakhan's calls for a Million Man March.[2]

The good news particular to October 16, 1995, is this: More than one million black men gathered on the Washington Mall for the explicit purpose of publicly accepting God's lovingly gracious offer. Moreover, millions of others, male and female, in other places and in various ways joined in observing and celebrating this "Holy Day of Atonement and Reconciliation."

Before the March, brothers living in a world relentlessly voting "no confidence" in black men recognized Minister Farrakhan's call for a Million Man March as a vote of confidence. For many brothers living under an ever-present-everywhere vote of "no confidence," this public vote of confidence in black men collectively was itself a first-time-in-many-a-lifetime event.

In dramatic contrast to mainstream images and expectations of the masses of black men, the October 16, 1995, Million Man March produced the largest, most peaceful, most prayerful congregation ever to assemble on the capital grounds. That this was the largest, most peaceful mass assembly in the history of Washington Mall gatherings is an objective fact, a fact reported by Ted Koppel on "Nightline" when he concluded his TV coverage of the Million Man March by noting that this multitude had produced not one criminal incident. Moreover, the subjective witnesses of the returning brothers included reports emphasizing the calm-prayerful-peaceful-joyful-loving spirit of the March.

THE WITNESS OF THE RETURNING BROTHERS

The book *Atonement,* edited by Kim Martin Sadler, includes fifty-one individual reflections by men who attended the Million Man March, and almost all of them bear explicit and enthusiastic witness to the calm-healing-peaceful-loving-joyful-prayerful spirit of that event.[3] The spirit of love and trust was so powerful that one father reported being accidentally separated from his son (age 15) for the whole day and experiencing no worry or anxiety during the day-long separation because he was certain this multitude of brotherly-loving black men would care for and protect his son. And correspondingly, the lost son experienced the same sense of security in the loving embrace of a million-plus keepers of one another. Lawrence Oliver Hall writes:

> My son and I lost sight of each other. There were just so many people. It was hard to search for him. My faith was truly tested. On one hand, as a father I was concerned for my son's safety and well-being, but I knew in my heart that he was going to be all right. My son would be fine in the hands of God and in the company of brothers committed to spiritual renewal and atonement. Everyone was so friendly. No pushing. No cursing. And, oddly enough, I saw no smoking. I did not see my son for the rest of the day, but I knew that I would see him when

the time was right. . . . As I began to walk back to the bus, I saw my son walking toward me. He was smiling from ear to ear. I have never been so glad to see that boy! We started talking, not about losing each other in the crowd, but about our experiences and how wonderful the March had been. My son said that he felt safe and protected by all those brothers. . . . My son had been protected while we were separated.[4]

These witnesses agree in offering hitherto unheard and unimagined descriptions of black men en masse.[5] Here, virtually every witness includes emphatic mention of a peaceful-calm-loving-prayerful-spiritual multitude.

In addition to these and other printed witnesses[6] there are many other public witnesses. After the March, making good news better, the brothers returning from this holy experience came re-presenting what was presented to them: a million-plus votes of confidence in one another and calls for prayer, fasting, confession, forgiveness of sin, atonement, repentance, reconciliation, and responsibility. Frequently they invited non-attending brothers to take the same pledge they had taken—the Million Man March Pledge.[7] At predominantly African American congregations, such as St. Luke Community United Methodist Church (Rev. Dr. Zan Holmes, pastor) in Dallas, Texas (my church home away from home) and Shiloh Baptist Church (Rev. Dr. Gregory Headen, pastor) in Greensboro, North Carolina (my church home at home), and at hundreds and thousands of other black congregations across the nation, returning brothers gave passionate witness to their experiences.

Beyond these many public pledges and witnesses, there are other less public individual witnesses. For example, at a 1996 Kwanzaa/Christmas extended-family gathering at the Roxboro, North Carolina, home of my aunt Matrice Davis Woods, my younger male relatives (generation Xers) who attended the March and my male and female relatives from D.C., all spoke of experiencing a city-wide spirit of peace, love, sharing, purpose, calm, and prayerfulness. Individual witnesses include many witnesses by citizens and residents of D.C. who breathed the prevailing spirit of peace and love. And, most important, individual witnesses include the million-plus witnesses of the individual black men who were there inspiring and being inspired by a spirit of black-on-black brotherly love. Thus, we "are compassed about with so great a cloud of witnesses."

A BLACK THEOLOGICAL WITNESS

The Million Man March is good news for black theology in the following ways: (1) its religious message, as presented in Minister Farrakhan's call for the March, is explicitly biblical and appropriate to black religion; (2) its concern with population-specific social-ethical prescriptions is consistent with black theology, especially with black theology's originating black Christian appropriation of black power/nationalism[8]; and (3) its focus on black men is affirmed by Alice Walker, other womanists, and by black women generally.

Even though Minister Farrakhan confesses Islam, his Million Man March messages are rooted in Judeo-Christian scriptures. Attention to the texts of Minister Farrakhan's calls for the Million Man March reveals a deeply religious understanding of the human circumstance, and 100 percent of the scriptural citations are from biblical texts. These documents include no explicit citations from the Holy Koran.

In the texts calling for a Million Man March, Minister Farrakhan's message to America generally and to Afro-America in particular, and most particularly to African American males, is this: We must come to know our sinfulness, to confess and seek forgiveness from God and each other, and then to repent, to do differently so as to contribute to the realization of a more righteous future in right relations with God, each other, and creation. Except for references to God as Allah and credits to the Honorable Elijah Mohammad, Minister Farrakhan's biblically rooted calls for atonement, reconciliation, and responsibility would "preach" at any black Christian church. The main point of Minister Farrakhan's call for a Million Man March is for African American men in particular to come together in one great assembly seeking "at-one-ment," "reconciliation," and a renewed sense of "responsibility" for one another, our families, and our communities.

Ever since Major Jones prescribed dividing the ethical question,[9] black theology has acknowledged that various populations are called to make appropriately various contributions to the struggle for righteousness. Social ethical circumstances, questions, and answers have significant population-specific aspects. In a manner consistent with black theology's and black power's primary concern with prescribing what blacks should contribute to the struggle for righteousness and empowerment, the Million Man March focused even more specifically on what black men should contribute. The logic and practice of black theology witness in favor of concern with population- and gender-specific aspects of social-ethical inquiry.

Also, from within the great black cloud of witnesses to the affirmative, there is the radical-democratic-Christian witness of Cornel West. West publicly supported the March. He and Rev. Joseph Lowery are listed on The Official Program of the Million Man March[10] as offering statements of atonement and reconciliation. Later, West reports very good news:

> The Million Man March was an historic event—called by Minister Louis Farrakhan, claimed by Black people of every sort and remembered by people around the globe as an expression of black men's humanity and decency. Never before has such black love flowed so freely and abundantly for so many in the eyes of the world. And never before have we needed such respect for each other. . . . Long live the loving and dignified spirit of the Million Man March![11]

A BLACK WOMANIST WITNESS

Black theology today includes black womanist theology. And black womanist theology is much indebted to womanist thought, especially that of founding womanist Alice Walker. In her essay "What the Day Was Like for Me" Alice Walker witnesses to the importance of the March by reporting, "In order to watch the Million Man March I had my tv repaired. It had been on the blink for six or seven months." Walker voices very strong support for the March:

> I think it is absolutely necessary that black men regroup as black men; until they can talk to each other, cry with each other, hug and kiss each other, they will never know how to do those things with me. I know whole black men can exist, and I want to see and enjoy them. . . . I send a prayer to my brothers: that you continue to open to each other and to bless yourselves. Continue to let go of fear. Continue to insist on truth and trust.[12]

Alice Walker's affirmation of the March is highly significant for womanist thought.

Similarly, Geneva Smitherman's essay "A Womanist Looks at the Million Man March" presents an explicitly womanist affirmation of the March:

> As a Womanist I am encouraged by these signs of the Brothers' involvement in our struggle to be free. In the absence of a movement that would provide a space to focus our pain, to analyze it, and devise ways to stop it, our men (and a few of my Sisters too) seemed to have resigned themselves to powerlessness, given up on the ability to make our communities work, and retreated from responsibility to and for Black youth. The Million Man March was a symbolic reminder to Brothers of middle class persuasion not to forget the ones they have left behind. It was an admonition to brothers of "thug life" persuasion to abandon the streets and reclaim their legacy of strength, pride and brotherhood. And it was rejuvenation for all of the faithful who have stayed on the battlefield of the Struggle: the posse is on the way, yall just keep on keepin on.[13]

In "Why Focus on the Men?" Charshee McIntyre offers another black female (and black nationalist) affirmation of the Million Man March:

> I believe that this process had to begin with the most endangered segment of our society, that brothers needed to stand up for themselves in order to stand up for the rest of us, that brothers needed to experience the victory of their Africanness. . . . Yes, we began with the focus on the men to raise our collective consciousness but the struggle requires us all.[14]

And, of course, there were black women at the March. Black women on the program witnessing in favor of the March included Rosa Parks, Dr. Dorothy I. Height, Queen Mother Moore, and Dr. Maya Angelou. Maya Angelou's poem "From a Black Woman to a Black Man" was an especially powerful affirmation.[15] The March's focus on the men was very much criticized in the mainstream media, but, nonetheless, many African American women supported the March.[16] According to the witness of Chimbuku Tembo, that aspect of the March entitled Day of Absence (DOA) was organized by female African Americans supporting the March and prescribing observance of a holy day absent from business as usual. Tembo writes:

> The Day of Absence as a parallel activity to the Million Man March in Washington was a project of sisterhood, community service and social action. In Los Angeles, it was a collective project organized by sisters from various community organizations. . . . We organized around the principle of operation unity. . . . What held us together as "Women in Support of the Million Man March" and "Women Organized for the Day of Absence" was this principle of operation unity, the respect we had for one another as African women, our sense of the historical importance of the project and our desire to see Black men stand up, make and keep commitments to be better persons, build stronger families and struggle to bring into being a just society and better world.[17]

Thandabantu Iversen writes, "The March would probably not have happened had it not been for the many Black women who worked to bring it off."[18] According to the witnesses of many black women, including black womanists, the Million Man March/Day of Absence (MMM/DOA) was very good news indeed.

THE WITNESS OF ONE NOT PRESENT

In the words of Million Man Marcher Thomas E. Wortham III, it was "enough to make a difference."[19] It was even enough to make a difference to those of us observing and celebrating from afar. And, according to the witness of Spike Lee's movie about the March, "Get on the Bus," what is more important than having been there is having been inspired to take responsibility for making new and more righteous differences. The million-plus marchers were called and inspired to march, to seek atonement, reconciliation, and responsibility. Their million-plus witnesses continue to call and inspire others. I was not at the Washington Mall on October 16, 1995. But like many others, I am profoundly moved by these many witnesses. From those of us who were not at the Washington Mall on October 16, 1995, to those of us who were there, then: Thank you and long live the spirit of the Million Man March.

Presently, mainstream media shows little sign of having learned anything from this great black cloud of witnesses. Black men continue to be imagined, depicted, and treated as inherent threats to public well-being, that is, as public enemies.

But things are not the same, especially for a million-plus black men and for those made different by their million-plus witnesses. For those of us previously limited in vision and encumbered by doubt, there is no longer room for doubt. The point has been made beyond reasonable doubt. A million-plus black men can be good news. Not just the exceptional individual black man, not just a Colin Powell, a Michael Jordan, or a Spike Lee, not just well-educated-professional-middle-to-upper-income black men (borrowing language from Cheryl Sanders), not just the Martin Kings but also the Rodney Kings, the masses of black men, upper, middle, and lower classes, old timers, veterans, baby-boomers and generation Xers, students, drop-outs, teachers, preachers, nurses, lawyers, doctors, morticians, security guards, cons and ex-cons, bee-boppers, hip-hoppers, rappers and gangstas, truck drivers, poets and dreamers, the full spectrum including every individual in a million-plus multitude, the masses of black men are capable of inspired-peaceful-disciplined-righteous-loving existence.

As a result of this new knowledge, we are enabled to envision new, alternative, more righteous futures. And we are thereby empowered to pursue new, more righteous social habits and policies, habits and policies not presupposing that masses of black men are incapable of peace and love.

Notes

[1] For discussion of media coverage of the Million Man March/Day of Absence, see essays by George E. Curry, Ismael Reed, Richard Muhammad, Alvin Peabody, and Haki Madhubuti in *Million Man March/Day of Absence: A Commemorative Anthology*, ed. Haki R. Madhubuti and Maulana Karenga (Chicago: Third World Press/Los Angeles: University of Sankore Press, 1996), part 7, "Media, Media, Media."

[2] For the text of Minister Farrakhan's calls for a Million Man March, see the following: Minister Louis Farrakhan, "Minister Louis Farrakhan Calls for One Million Man March," *The Final Call*, vol. 14, no. 4 (December 14, 1994), and on the World Wide Web at http://www.noi.org/FCN/MLFspeaks/marchcall.html. See also idem, "A Holy Day of Atonement and Reconciliation: October 16, 1995," where Farrakhan invites black men to join him "in Washington D.C. to observe a Holy Day of Atonement and Reconciliation," *The Final Call*, vol. 14, no. 22, and at http://www.noi.org/FCN/MLFspeaks/holyday.html; idem, "Why a Million Man March," http://www.noi.org/FCN/MLFspeaks/whymarch.html, where Farrakhan answers the question in terms of the need to show "the world a vastly different picture of the Black male" and in terms of the need for atonement, reconciliation, and responsibility. "Why a Million Man March" is also printed in the National Organizing Committee Packet under the heading "The Vision for the Million Man March" and the National Organizing Committee Packet is reproduced in Madhubuti and Karenga, *Million Man March/Day of Absence*, part 8, "Documents."

"Let Us Make Man" was the title of Minister Farrakhan's speech at the Dallas Convention Center in Dallas, Texas, on April 25, 1994, and my handwritten notes indicate this speech included a call for "one million black men to make the largest march on Washington in the history of America." I did not note and do not recall

Minister Farrakhan identifying a date for the march. In June 1994 Minister Farrakhan "presented his vision of a Million Man March at the first African American Leadership Summit called by Dr. Rev. Benjamin Chavis," writes Cornel West (in Madhubuti and Karenga, *Million Man March/Day of Absence*, p. 98.

³ Kim Martin Sadler, ed., *Atonement: The Million Man March*, foreword by Michael Eric Dyson (Cleveland, Ohio: Pilgrim Press, 1996). The following excerpts witness to the calm-healing-peaceful-joyful-loving-prayerful spirit of this gathering: Ronald S. Bonner Sr. writes of "a God-ordained day" and "a day of Black on Black love being born" (pp. 3, 4). Thomas E. Wortham III writes, "I had never experienced such a warm feeling between myself and total strangers" (p. 13), and, "As I walked around the Mall, I felt a spiritual calmness among the people. Never before had I experienced such a large number of people coming together with such a feeling of peace and togetherness. I knew God had to have a hand in this" (p. 14). Keith Boykin writes of "black men loving black men" as "a revolutionary act" (p. 17). Andre P. Tramble writes of "a spiritual call in divine order" (p. 37), and recalls that "there was a real sense of calm and peacefulness" (p. 38). Hugh Brandon writes, "Black men proudly looked at one another without suspicion or anger" and "Black men looked into the eyes and souls of other Black men, and it felt good" (p. 50). Amoti Nyabongo writes, "The day was very spiritual. I could feel the love, the respect, the warmth, and the compassion transcending one to another. The words 'thank you,' 'excuse me,' 'pardon me,' 'please,' 'take care,' 'peace,' and 'stay strong' echoed across the Mall as we made our way through the crowd" (p. 58). Ronald Cook describes the Million Man March as "a living testimony to the world that we, as African American males, can come together in silence, in prayer, in love, harmony, peace, and joy" (p. 62). Todd L. Ledbetter writes, "Ordinarily I would be wary and guarded in such a large crowd, but there was to be none of that this day. . . . Total unity and singularity of purpose prevailed ..." (p. 68) and "In the aftermath of the March, there was a spirit, a glow that stayed with the participants for days, even weeks" (p. 69). Cleo Manago writes, "We greeted each other warmly. With welcome relief, a connection that waded just below the surface of our pain, we kissed, hugged, and smiled" (p. 74). Manago also writes of black men who "wept in the joy" (p. 76).

⁴ Sadler, *Atonement*, pp. 99, 100.

⁵ The following description of a million-plus black men was generated by visually scanning and sequentially listing terms and concepts from the individual witnesses in Sadler, *Atonement*: black-on-black love, love, connected, spiritual, calm, peaceful, together, loving, religious, healing, spiritual, united, collective cooperation, calm, powerful, loving, united, reunited, spiritual, revived, wanting to do for the community, spiritual, divinely ordered, purposeful, proud, divinely ordered, respectful, calm, peaceful, loving, peaceful, spiritual, united, loving, reverent, courteous, spiritual, peaceful, brotherly, loving, respectful, warm, compassionate, spiritual, silent, prayerful, loving, harmonious, peaceful, joyful, spiritual, united, purposeful, spiritual, loving, brotherly, respectful, sharing, spiritual, spiritual, warm, smiling, hugging, kissing, weeping, joyful, purposeful, renewed, trusting, wonderful, solidarity, spiritual, joyful, blessed, united, loving, at one, spiritual, sweet, divinely inspired, religious, umoja, united, spiritual, friendly, loving, laughing, crying, sharing, forgiving, loving, together, spiritual, respectful, self-respectful, loving, healing, peaceful, unity, prayerful, responsible, blessing from God, redemptive, at one with God, called by God, prayerful, repentant, responsible, and reconciling.

⁶ Madhubuti and Karenga, *Million Man March/Day of Absence*, offers another notable collection of witnesses. Also see Leonard Pitts Jr. (*Miami Herald*), "Million

Man Memories: A Year Later, March Still Drives Us to Action," printed in *The Dallas Morning News* (October 17, 1996), p. 25A.

⁷ The Million Man March Pledge:

I pledge that from this day forward, I will strive to love my brother as I love myself.

I, from this day forward, will strive to improve myself spiritually, morally, mentally, socially, politically, and economically for the benefit of myself, my family, and my people.

I pledge that I will strive to build businesses, build houses, build hospitals, build factories, and enter into international trade for the good of myself, my family, and my people.

I pledge that from this day forward, I will never raise my hand with a knife or a gun to beat, cut, or shoot any member of my family or any human being except in self-defense.

I pledge from this day forward, I will never abuse my wife by striking her, disrespecting her, for she is the mother of my children and the producer of my future.

I pledge that from this day forward, I will never engage in the abuse of children, little boys, or little girls for sexual gratification. I will let them grow in peace to be strong men and women for the future of our people.

I will never again use the B-word to describe any female—but particularly, my own Black sister.

I pledge from this day forward that I will not poison my body with drugs or that which is destructive to my health and my well-being.

I pledge from this day forward, I will support Black newspapers, Black radio, Black television. I will support Black artists who clean up their act to show respect for themselves and respect for their people and respect for the heirs of the human family.

I will do all of this, so help me God (quoted from Sadler, *Atonement*, p. xvii; the pledge also appears in Madhubuti and Karenga, *Million Man March/Day of Absence*, p. 29).

⁸ See James H. Cone, *Black Theology and Black Power* (New York: Seabury Press, 1969). Here Cone's black Christian appropriation of the philosophy of black power yields a black theology.

⁹ Major J. Jones makes "a case for a division of the ethical question" (*Christian Ethics for Black Theology* [Nashville: Abingdon, 1974], p. 15). Jones argues that the descendants of slaves and the descendants of slave owners are both bound by the Christian mandate of love, and this requires each of them to contribute to abolishing the oppressed-oppressor relationship. But differences between the two social locations imply correspondingly different responses (pp. 16-20). Accordingly, Jones finds "the ethical question should be divided" (p. 23), and he understands the "attempt to speak ethically from the black side of the question" (p. 18) to be an attempt at Christian ethics for black theology.

¹⁰ The Official Program of the Million Man March is reprinted in Madhubuti and Karenga, *Million Man March/Day of Absence*, part 8, "Documents." Other documents appearing in this part are "The Million Man March/Day of Absence Mission Statement," written by Maulana Karenga on behalf of the Executive Council of the MMM/DOA; the "National Organizing Communication Packet"; the "African American Father's Pledge," written by Haki R. Madhubuti; and a "Proposal to Establish the African American Fund."

¹¹ Cornel West, "Historic Event," in Madhubuti and Karenga, *Million Man March/ Day of Absence*, pp. 98-99.

¹² Alice Walker, "What the Day Was Like for Me," in Madhubuti and Karenga, *Million Man March/Day of Absence*, pp. 42, 43.

[13] Geneva Smitherman, "A Womanist Looks at the Million Man March," in Madhubuti and Karenga, *Million Man March/Day of Absence*, p. 107.

[14] Charshee McIntyre, "Why Focus on the Men?" in Madhubuti and Karenga, *Million Man March/Day of Absence*, p. 115.

[15] Maya Angelou, "From a Black Woman to a Black Man," reprinted in Madhubuti and Karenga, *Million Man March/Day of Absence*.

[16] See "The Black Woman's Statement of Support for the Million Man March," in Madhubuti and Karenga, *Million Man March/Day of Absence*, pp. 155-56. Also see the "Million Man March National Black Women's Endorsement Roster." Endorsers are Mother Rosa Parks, Dr. Dorothy I. Height, Mrs. Cora Masters Barry, Dr. C. Delores Tucker, Dr. Maya Angelou, Reverend Barbara Skinner, Mrs. Wilma Harvey, Dr. Louise White, Marianne Niles, Attorney Faye Williams, Dr. Mabel Phifer, Dr. Niara Sudarkasa, Mrs. Nadine Winters, Reverend Rossetta Bryson, and Mrs. Marilyn Merry (ibid., pp. 156-57).

[17] Chimbuku Tembo's "The Million Man March and DOA," in Madhubuti and Karenga, *Million Man March/Day of Absence*, p. 125.

[18] Thandabantu Iversen, "A Time to End Privilege," in Madhubuti and Karenga, *Million Man March/Day of Absence*, p. 94.

[19] Sadler, *Atonement*, p. 13.

Chapter Two

Abominations of a Million Men

Reflection on a Silent Minority

VICTOR ANDERSON

I have no doubt that the Million Man March will be regarded as a historical event in African American history and as one of the great experiments in grass-roots mass mobilization. It is perhaps parallel in significance not only to the marches of the 1960s but also to two other social movements: the Garveyite movement, and the formation of the Nation of Islam. To be sure the parallels are more than coincidental. These social movements were led and motivated by religious organizers whose dispositions and messages were charismatic, and a few were also apocalyptic. When compared with the Garveyite and Nationalist Islamic movements, the Million Man March, like these, was programmatically neither revolutionary nor reformist. Rather, each was driven by a conversionist ideology that accents sectarian emphasis on repentance, separation, sanctification, and a summons toward the moral transformation of one's racial self-consciousness. Such religious commitments are deeply entrenched in the moral imagination of African Americans, for they were an inheritance from Protestant, Christian piety long before they were grafted to North American varieties of Islam. Behind such languages of repentance, separation, and sanctification, in the conversionist ideology, is the rhetoric of abomination.

In *Ethics after Babel* (1988), Jeffrey Stout discusses this religious language. I find his analysis helpful and insightful for my purposes in this essay. Abomination provides a way in which communities come to terms with human actions that appear anomalous or ambiguous. An abomination is a moral judgment in which "an anomalous act is more likely to seem abominable where it seems to pose, or becomes symbolic of, a threat to the established cosmological or social order" (Stout 1988, 149). However, the ambiguities surrounding an abomination are judged to be so disruptive that they are understood as the transgression of boundaries that guard cosmic and social order, says Stout (ibid., 150). In a summary passage Stout defines the language of abomination: "In contexts where the anomalous or ambiguous character of an object, event, or act seems to threaten disruption of the natural-social order, rather than promising to knit that order together, the object, event, or act will be abominated" (ibid.).

While many see the Million Man March as a sign of divine grace and promise, for too many African Americans the March imprints on black self-consciousness the abominations of a million men. When beginning with a vow that from this day each man will strive to love his brother as he loves himself, the Million Man March Pledge inscribes on the conscience of every black man a history of self-hatred. It rehearses memories of communal economic failures, violence, drugs, sexual perversions, and misogyny. And it regards all such abominations as the burden of a million black men. Silent among the list of abominations is homophobia. It is on this abomination that I will focus in my critique.

Homophobia is not reducible to the particular accidents and discursive practices of any one cultural group. From my perspective it is no more the particular fault of African Americans than it is a unique characteristic of European thought and culture. According to recent social psychology, homophobia appears to be a cultural phenomenon not only in modern mass societies but also in many traditional societies, including African traditional societies. It is so culture-pervasive that one is tempted to regard it as a "natural" human condition, says Gregory Hereck (1984, 3).

However, it is a mistake to regard homophobia as a natural attitude among all human beings. Rather, it develops in complex matrices of cultural experience that are experiential, social, and political. Therefore, homophobia cannot be reduced to any one matrix (Hereck 1984, 7-8). The many ways that people experience repulsion of others and develop prejudices toward others are not simply explainable in terms of their psycho-physiological reactions to the strangeness of others or to their irrational fears and anxieties about others. Plasek and Allard argue convincingly that such psycho-physiological signs of homophobia are related to social taboos, abominations, associations, and cultural conditions that cultivate both negative and positive effects throughout the culture, including African American cultural life (Plasek and Allard 1984, 23-27).

When I talk of homophobia in terms of negative and positive cultural practices, I am making a logical judgment, not a moral one. Negatively, then, homophobic practices may be maintained for the purpose of "deterring" forms of human association, sexual and social, which some in the community fear are threats to the moral cohesion of the culture. This fits Stout's negative criterion of an abomination. Positively, homophobic practices may "ensure" the cultivation of moral behavior through socialization in proper sexual practices that the culture deems worthy of propagation. In this case, homophobic practices are legitimated through the interest in generativity and justified in the language of abomination.

The point is that homophobia in the black community ought not to be explained simply as if it were a European product transmitted to the culture, as Michael Dyson has recently argued (Dyson 1996, 84-87ff.). Dyson's analysis of homophobia in the black community treats it as a reactive consequence of whites' actions on black cultural life. He does not extend this critique to include the proactive intentions of the black community and its religious leaders to establish African American cultural practices that are as likely as European cultural activities to produce, in the black community, homophobic activities, self-hating practices, and anti-gay discourses. This recognition that homophobia in the black community is a consequence of African Americans' reactive and proactive moral intentions toward cultural generativity goes a long way toward providing a complex moral critique of black homophobia.

Generativity is Erik Erikson's way of explaining the motives behind many of the taboos, sanctions, prohibitions, and moral commitments that a culture seeks to pass on to its progenitors as positive and culture formative practices worthy of dissemination and protection. The Million Man March was, to my mind, a symbolic event that crystallized a set of values that its ideologues regarded as generative. Yet, there is a sense in which all of the values inscribed by the Million Man Pledge can be interpreted through the critical lens of what I have called the cult of black masculinity. In *Beyond Ontological Blackness* (1995), I criticize what I see as a pervasive preoccupation of black intellectuals with the classical, heroic virtues of courage, manliness, strength, self-determination, and racial loyalty in their attempts to establish normative requirements for authentic race consciousness and criteria for the moral valuation of membership in the black community. I try to expose the ways that black cultural studies have defined and evaluated representations of black life in terms of classical masculine virtues.

The cult of black masculinity binds black moral consciousness to a hierarchy of virtues that favors race loyalty and the good of the race over loyalties to gender or sexual self-identification and fulfillment. It favors an unmitigated commitment to race over the claims that an individual's sexual desires, preferences, and orientation make on his communal choices. I also argue that when African American identities are defined morally in terms of the cult of black masculinity, blackness becomes "a totality that takes narrative formations that emphasize the heroic capacities of African Americans to transcend individuality and personality in the name of black communal survival" (Anderson 1995, 15). I also see such a totality signified in the very idea of a Million Man March. That is, the company of those who gathered in Washington, D.C., was not many men but a million Man, One Black Man. I would also hold that cultic devotion to the moral virtues of that Million Man Pledge is as likely to conceal, subjugate, and call into question African Americans' interests in the fulfillment of their orientation and sexual intercourse and love with another black man, just as the cult of black masculinity has historically subjugated black individuality under race consciousness (ibid).

The virtues of black masculinity, which I see delineated in the Million Man Pledge, circumscribe African Americans' gender and sexual interests and provide an overarching depiction of black moral consciousness. The virtues of masculinity exhibit a universality that transcends the particularities of black women's commitments to each other when they are threatened by domestic abuse and violence and encounter sexual harassment by black men. I do not think that it is enough for black men (however many) simply to tell black women that they are sorry and will not do it again. Even if a million men stood together to pledge "I will never again use the B-word to describe any female—but particularly, my own Black sister," Black women have few justifications for regarding such a vow as redeemable after the euphoria of the March subsides and abuse continues. After all, too many black women—mothers, daughters, sisters, and friends—have heard such lines and vows before by millions of men in domestic-abuse proceedings. Moreover, I do not think that the good of redeeming the black heterosexual man's esteem within the black community trumps the preferences of black gays and lesbians for sexual association and the fulfillment of their desire for same-sex unions. Although a million men met in Washington, D.C., to atone for the sins of the community, the March's leaders remained silent about homophobia; no gay or lesbian representative addressed the crowds, no public affirmation of black homosexual love was commended, and no overt sign of acceptance was shown, except the silence of a million men. That is an abomination.

The Million Man March was a symbolic performance of the cult of black masculinity. The "race man" becomes the moral hero of the community. He is strong, self-determined, conscientious, and uncompromising in his commitment to the good of the race in all of his endeavors: in business, in domestic life, in entertainment, and in spirituality. Black presses, magazines, and electronic journals also contribute to the exoneration of the morals of black masculinity and the Million Man Pledge. However, the reality is that many of the intellectuals, politicians, ministers, and lawyers who attended the March are gays. Yet, due to the often discriminatory and alienating experiences that homophobia creates in the black community, their sexual identities became of secondary importance to their public display. The abomination of homophobia in the black community, I contend, renders these members of the black community silent and ineffective in galvanizing the best and most talented members of the community to the Million Man March. The silence among these black male teachers, politicians, physicians, lawyers, ministers, and many in arts and entertainment about the legitimacy, value, alienation, and suffering of black gays and lesbians in the black community is an abomination.

Only recently has the history of homosexuality been developed as a genuine contribution to black cultural studies. The late Essex Hemphill recalls searching the public library for an understanding of his own internal, black, sexual presence in the great Negro novels, the legacy of the black intelligentsia on black consciousness from Du Bois and Garvey to Larry Neal and Amiri Baraka (the so-called new black aesthetic school). He searched for a place in the literature where he enters as a legitimate black subject. He writes: "What was there for me to read in 1969 was in no way affirming of the sexual identity germinating within me. The material regarding homosexuality considered it to be an illness or an affliction, and at worst, a sin against God and nature. . . . The books made no reference to black men that I can recall, nor were there black case studies for me to examine, and in a few pictures of men identified as homosexual, not one was black" (Hemphill 1995, xv). The literature celebrated racial genius—its loves, struggles, and forms of resistance. However, "nothing in those books said that men could truly love one another. Nothing said that masturbation would be comforting. Nothing celebrated the genius and creativity of homosexual men or even suggested that such men could lead ordinary lives. Nothing encouraged me to love black men—I had to learn that on my own" (ibid., xvi).

Given the ways that the virtues of black masculinity inform black moral consciousness, the very idea that black homosexuals can and ought to love and fulfill their desires for same-sex intimacy and unions constitutes a moral emasculation of themselves in the black community. The silence of the Million Man March on this issue does not change my thinking that things are different. Except in the countercultural world of the clubs, alternative restaurants, and the secrecy of their homes and apartments, where they look for and sometimes find one another, the black community continues to regard black gays and lesbians as abominations. Their presence is all too often greeted with suspicion, rejection, rage, and violence.

In *One More River to Cross* (1996), Keith Boykin, a black, gay novelist, writer, and activist, argues that the deadly silence created by homophobia in the black community and rationalized under the moral rhetoric of black masculinity and a Million Man March influences black society at every level (Boykin 1996, 170). He describes the rejection by the planning committee of the Bud Bilikin Parade of a black gay-and-lesbian group in Chicago known as The Ad Hoc Committee of Proud Black Lesbians and Gays. The parade is a historic event that marks the end of the summer and the beginning of the school year in the African American community. The Ad Hoc Committee's application to march in the parade was rejected on the grounds that the limitations of time, space, and manpower restricted the number of groups that would be allowed to march.

The committee filed a second application, this time under the name Diverse Black Role Models. The Bud Bilikin Parade planning committee approved the application. Spokespersons for the black gays and lesbians spoke publicly about the gay contingent in the parade. However, opposition to their marching flooded Chicago black radio stations and the *Chicago Defender,* a major newspaper serving the Chicago black community and the primary sponsor of the Bilikin Parade. Opponents charged the group with "ruining" the parade because it was a family event. Others expressed fears that black drag queens would be marching down Martin Luther King Jr. Drive. Still others expressed suspicion that the black gays and lesbians must be part of a white conspiracy to "divide the black community." According to Boykin, when the committee threatened to sue the *Chicago Defender*, it was granted permission to be a part of the group.

Boykin also attended the Million Man March with an openly gay contingent of several hundred. He comments, "Hundreds of Black gay men and a handful of lesbians joined together in a historic openly gay contingent in the Million Man March, proudly representing the tens of thousands of Black gay men who were there but could not be a part of our group" (Boykin 1996, 16). Boykin, however, never says what he believes to be behind their inability to participate. I am sure that he is right in his judgment of the numbers, but what a curious silence his statement discloses. Had the hundred of thousands who gathered at the March a moral incapacity? Were they gay fathers, brothers, uncles, ministers, blue-collar workers, white-collar elite, teachers, college students whose positions in the black community rendered them unable to participate in the March? Their silence is tragic. Imagine what we could have learned about the black community from their persistent demand to have a representative of their silent class speak to and for them, speakers who could understand their silence and decry the abominations that rendered them silent. No one spoke to the million men about the plight of black gays and lesbians who suffer abuse, murder, and alienation within the community that gave them life and regards them as abominations. No word, but the silence of a million men. Boykin was optimistic about the reception that the black gay contingent felt at the March from the heterosexual throngs. He writes, "October the sixteenth was the first time that many March participants had ever seen Black homosexuals openly, visibly, and unabashedly acknowledging themselves as a part of the black community. Given the opportunity to succumb to peer-pressure prejudice, they took the high road and greeted our participation. They know that the battles for Black liberation requires many soldiers, and in this army, at least, gays are welcomed in the military" (Boykin 1996, 16).

Boykin forgot, however, that in this army the rule of the day is "don't ask, don't tell." However, such silence bears a great cost in the black community. "Despite the welcome extended by March Participants, the organizer and speakers missed two crucial opportunities," says Boykin. "First, to include an openly gay speaker and second to teach Black men how to save their lives in the era of AIDS; prevention was never discussed. Unfortunately, the disease will continue to take a toll on our community so long as Black people and our so-called leaders remain too afraid to address publicly issues of sex, sexuality, and sexual orientation" (ibid.). When are these issues no longer abominations? Again, the Million Man March—its pledge, its speakers, and its silence— is less than helpful in answering this question. The silence about homophobia and homosexuality and its usual association of abominations such as AIDS and herpes is, to my mind, the abomination of the Million Man March. What can be more disruptive and threatening to unity and community than the absence of free, uncoerced speech? Yet no one spoke for our brothers and sisters who suffer discrimination every day in housing, health, and employment. No one spoke for those beaten into silence by harassment, brutality, and fear. And no one spoke for those who lost their lives while walking down community streets with their lovers and friends.

I do not want to leave the impression that the religious lives of African American people are without the possibility of transcendence from the destructive powers of homophobia and the malicious forms of alienation they create among black gays and lesbians. However, transcendence is more likely to come from black religious leaders' and church members' commitments to the human rights of black gays and lesbians than by their pledging personal and spiritual atonement. For black gays and lesbians, homophobia and its destructive power in the black community are not reducible to renewed commitment to the virtues of racial manliness. The issue is justice and peace. Black gays and lesbians certainly welcome the repentance of those black men who, out of deep negative motivations, deny them justice and peace. To be sure, their theologies of redemptive love and grace and their religious language of repentance, separation, and sanctification may help to increase the black community's respect for and commitment to black gays and lesbians. However, the respect and commitment that black gays and lesbians require of black religious leaders do not require theological justifications. As I have argued elsewhere, it is enough that they are the values and requirements of human rights (Anderson 1997).

Black religious leaders participate in many communities of moral discourse where they come in contact with, know, and associate with black gays and lesbians. They know them as their teachers, lawyers, ministers, musicians, bus drivers, bankers, funeral home directors, siblings, uncles, aunts, and so on. My point is that black gays and lesbians are not a degenerative presence in the black community; they are not abominations. They contribute to the flourishing of the black community. Black religious leaders and churches ought to support the good that gays and lesbians seek to fulfill. They ought to give such support not only because God requires it or because black gays and lesbians are valuable resources to the black community but also because what is at stake is nothing less than respecting their needs and human rights.

I can produce a great litany of discriminatory practices against black gays and lesbians throughout the black cultural spheres including arts, entertainment, politics, and religion. However, I am not interested in discrediting black institutions and organizations that have been genuine sites for promoting the social, political, and moral well-being of the black community as a whole. Rather, my interest is to disclose the ways that homophobia in black institutions and organizations perpetuates itself, fostering alienation, harm, brutality, and death within the lives of too many black gays and lesbians who have been judged abominations and excluded from the well-being of the community. In their attempts toward sexual self-fulfillment, black gays and lesbians are often dismissed by their black heterosexual brothers and religious leaders as detractors from the real interests of the black community. Others regard them as aliens, freaks, and a source of death in the black community. And regrettably, for too many others, their demise is of no great loss to the survival of the black community. The Million Man March Pledge never even included, among the primary issues negatively affecting black communities throughout the United States, a vow "to maintain aggressive avenues for the funding and containment of AIDS and other sex-related communal diseases." That would have been a simple act of atonement. To my mind, such silence remains the abomination of the Million Man March.

As a symbolic event in the history of African American mass mobilizations, the Million Man March is less than fulfilling of the spirit and vitality of the historic civil-rights marches on Washington, D.C., in the 1960s. Those marches represented an inclusive claim to the human and civil rights of all African

Americans. A universal message resounded from the speeches of the 1960s. Redemption and atonement were truly communal possibilities on those movements. The Million Man March was a symbolic event. However, what its symbolic significance is will become the critical discourse of many cultural critiques in the future. In the end, I think that each man must account for his own abominations. However, the Million Man March offered no atonement for the hundreds of thousands of black lives lost, brutalized, and alienated by the black community's and its religious leaders' silence about homophobia and homosexuality in our community. That is an abomination.

Works Cited

Anderson, Victor. 1995. *Beyond Ontological Blackness: An Essay in African American Religious and Cultural Criticism.* New York: Continuum Publishing Company.

_____ . 1997. "Deadly Silence: Reflection on Homosexuality and Human Rights." In *Homosexuality and Human Rights.* Edited by Martha Nussbaum and Saul Olyan. New York: Oxford University Press.

Boykin, Keith. 1996. *One More River to Cross: Black and Gay in America.* Boston: Alyson Publishing Inc.

_____ . 1997. "Gays and the Million Man March," In *Atonement: The Million Man March.* Edited by Kim M. Sadler. Cleveland: Pilgrim Press.

Dyson, Michael Eric. 1996. *Race Rules: Negotiating the Color Line.* Reading, Mass.: Addison-Wesley Press.

Hemphill, Essex. 1995. Don Belton, "Where We Live: A Conversation with Essex Hemphill and Isaac Julien." In *Speak My Name: Black Masculinity and the American Dream.* Boston: Beacon Press.

Hereck, Gregory M. 1984. "Beyond Homophobia: A Social Psychological Perspective on Attitudes toward Lesbians and Gay Men." *Journal of Homosexuality* 10/1-2.

Plasek, John Wayne, and Janicemarie Allard. 1984. "Misconceptions of Homophobia." *Journal of Homosexuality* 10/1-2.

Stout, Jeffrey L. 1988. *Ethics after Babel: The Languages of Morals and Their Discontents.* Boston: Beacon Press.

Chapter Three

XODUS or X-Scape?

G. KASIMU BAKER-FLETCHER

African American males live in a time too exhausted to struggle for justice, strangled in the seductive grip of apathy. Our moral hands are awash in the blood of our younger brothers, whose fratricidal appetite has remained unabated since the mid-1980s. It does not matter whether a Black man has a Harvard M.B.A., a police badge, or visually represents a so-called "gang profile"—our consciousness of being Black and male in the United States of America seems invariably to collide with terms like *endangered*, *criminal*, and *vulnerable*. Yet we have refused to roll over and die. In our refusal has arisen a quiet and determined spirit of resistance. Though not quite a mass movement, throughout the land cries have arisen for Black men to stand up and be responsible, accountable men. I call this nascent spirit of resistance a call for "XODUS." The aim of this chapter is to explore the connections between XODUS and the event of the Million Man March. Was the March an XODUS event or merely an "X-Scape" into a misguided fantasy?

XODUS

The call for an XODUS represents a new generation of thinking about the ways in which the take-charge, no-nonsense, rhetorical fire of Malcolm X can be brought together with the militant multicultural envisioning power of Martin Luther King Jr. to galvanize our liberation hopes. XODUS is a yearning for Africans living in the United States to create our own *psycho-cultural and spiritual SPACE* capable of sustaining resistance against self-hatred and nurturing subversive desires for self-affirmation in a land whose everyday practices negate our personhood. Without seeking the validation or approval of European-American authoritative discourses, officials, or institutions, XODUS invokes the mighty creativity of African foremothers and forefathers in their four-hundred-year struggle against domination, degradation, and violence. Without calling for violent political revolution, XODUS urges that our historical moment calls for a renewed sense of *cultural, psychological, and spiritual revival*. It does this by encouraging Black spiritual institutions like Black churches, Moslem mosques, and even less popular religious alternatives like traditional African religions,

27

Buddhism, and New Age spiritualities to become communities engaged in psycho-spiritual *liberation*. Such a stand is critical of religious dogma and practices that encourage detachment, social apathy, or political indifference. Thus while not being overtly political or economic, XODUS believes that psycho-cultural affirmation and spiritual affirmation are the necessary communal bases for engaged multi-generational resistance to oppressive practices.[1]

XODUS may be typified by two metaphors, JOURNEY and SPACE. As a JOURNEY XODUS insists that African American males need to join the call of womanists like Alice Walker, Katie Cannon, Karen Baker-Fletcher, and Emilie Townes (and many others) for a *community affirmation of both men and women included together in the decision making as well as practical work*. Insisting on the liberative aspects of community affirms *the ongoing process of dialogue, criticism, and correction* that makes for genuine inclusion. Yet the JOURNEY of XODUS is not merely a call for dialogue and inclusion of women with men but also a call for a processive and anti-sexist vision of manhood. A JOURNEY cannot be accomplished without some idea of a goal or end. The end of XODUS JOURNEYing is the creation of a new form of masculinity that can celebrate the dialectics of joy and pain, accomplishment and failure, strength and weakness, with poise, grace, and dignity.

In ethical language the end of the course of moral decision making is called the *telos*. The *telos* of XODUS JOURNEY is a rich life too full of relations to be sexist, too active in the struggle to be hateful, and too engaged in saving the planet to be apathetic. Such a *telos* sets forth an ideal of how things *ought to be* for us as males who are African American. Its function as *telos* is to provoke us toward greater realizations of ourselves as moral actors capable of living into our notions of rightness and goodness. A *telos* does not necessarily need to be specified in detail, but it must have clear enough parameters of what can be considered morally appropriate, good, and right actions. In XODUS the means for attaining the end of an inclusive anti-sexist masculinity is accomplished through active practices of anti-sexist ethical choices that include women in the decision-making process of building a genuinely liberative community, deconstruction of ongoing embedded cultural patriarchy both within Afrikan[2] communities and the larger multicultural whole, and resistance leading to reconstruction of holistic forms of masculinity not dependent on the degradation of women for realization. Thus XODUS JOURNEY is a metaphor that both describes XODUS as a *movement of agents toward a telos* and as *purposive ethical practices serving to forward the attainment of the envisioned end*.

The metaphor of SPACE is of equal importance to XODUS in the sense that the movement of XODUS requires recurrent creativity necessary for encouraging inclusive practices. The norms of anti-sexist behaviors and inclusive decision making require self-conscious XODUS males and females to create SPACES in which such practices are normative. XODUS SPACE can take place within the most sexist of institutional spaces—in churches, homes, and work places.

SPACE is a geographical metaphor calling attention to the fact that in order for Black males and females to transform oppressive racist and sexist practices we need to pay attention to the meeting places, rooms, houses, halls, buildings, and other geographies in which our chance encounters can also become opportunities for XODUS re-oriented choices. Ethical problems do not occur merely in textbooks but on floors, grass, and the rocks under our feet. Right and wrong decisions are transmitted in the air. They are affected by the fragrances of a space, the temperature and moisture content of the air we are breathing. Thus to choose to create XODUS SPACE is to decide to resist the pervasive hierarchical patterning of racist, sexist, classist, and homophobic assumptions which dominate our everyday geographies. To do so is to *transform and transmogrify the "everyday" into a liberation moment.*

To choose to be on an XODUS JOURNEY is to be a SPACE-maker. On the JOURNEY of XODUS we find ourselves self-consciously creating opportunities for exercising the choices which manifest XODUS SPACE as a blessing of nurturance and sustaining grace. As it is difficult for those on any journey to travel for long periods of time without rest and recreation, so the XODUS TRAVELER requires the refreshing and revitalizing qualities of an XODUS SPACE to survive. Thus XODUS SPACE is not only an *active transformative creation,* but also *a resting place within the very boundaries of exclusion and oppression.*

XODUS SPACE is coterminous, or at least *inside* the larger space of domination/oppression/subjugation that liberation philosophers and theologians have variously described as a "racist system" (Black Power advocates), the "military-industrial complex of capitalist exploitation" (Latin American freedom-fighters), and "patriarchy" (feminists). Womanists like Katie G. Cannon have noted that Black women experience this space of domination/oppression/subjugation as a series of overlapping and interlocking forms and patterns of oppression. She has also described this hydra-headed system as both "Eurocentric" and "male-normative."[3] Under the influence of womanists like Cannon, I believe that XODUS SPACE is created, sustained, and demarcated within this larger hydra-headed system.

I contend that the Million Man March needs to be evaluated in terms of its ability to forward the JOURNEY and SPACE-making that is XODUS. If one million men (several thousand women and children included) of African descent could gather peacefully at the steps of the Capitol—the symbolic seat of imperial power of the United States of America—we need to evaluate their reasons in line with a clear understanding of liberation. Was the agenda of wrestling with issues of atonement, responsibility, and reconciliation one in which an inclusive and liberative concern for Afrikan communities living in the United States was presented? Was an XODUS SPACE created, nurtured, and sustained? Was the March a momentary incarnation of a larger sustained XODUS JOURNEY on the part of Afrikan males as we search for freedom and self-realization? Or, on the other hand, was the March another example of several abortive attempts by a conglomeration of Black leaders to restart a dead civil-rights agenda? Was it an X-Scape into a romantic reenactment of past civil-rights glory days? Did the March trade sentimental and evocative imagery of former days of Black unity for a substantive program of XODUS JOURNEY? In order to answer these questions more completely we need to define what an X-Scape is in contradistinction to XODUS.

X-SCAPE

XODUS treats with utmost seriousness the power of words to capture the mood, sense, and substance of what they signify. XODUS words resignify traditional meanings to focus the attention of the reader on how meanings of the same word can be transformed to become more relevant for our current concerns. The very term *XODUS* does this. By dropping the first "e" we create a word that *sounds* like the original signifier, *exodus,* but is now applied to the peculiar historical concerns and context of late-twentieth-century–early-twenty-first-century Afrikans. Like the original Hebrew Exodus, we are seeking to name and worship our understanding of the Divine by leaving the space of domination of our oppressors. As those ancient Hebrews required a journey away from imperial Egypt, so we require a JOURNEY away from the psycho-cultural, economic, political, and social space of domination known as "the land of the free and the home of the brave." In *XODUS: An African American Male Journey*, I rather harshly named the space of domination/oppression/subjugation by two neologisms—*Ameri-Babylon,* and the term rappers like Ice Cube initiated in the late 1980s, *AmeriKKKa*. To enter the rigors of an XODUS JOURNEY, to become an XODUS SPACE-maker, is to *self-consciously leave behind those mores, choices, loyalties, values, and norms that most of us make every day within AmeriKKKa in order to create something new*. To create this NEW thing is to begin BE-coming the NEW thing. It is a JOURNEY, a process in which one's intellectual yearnings are part of a psycho-spiritual struggle which gathers in its willful wake our emotions, bodies, and spiritual being-ness. This is an utterly different experience than the momentary high of an X-Scape.

An X-Scape is meaningful ritual of remembrance of our ancestors that has no *telos*. It is a powerful momentary experience that suffuses the emotions with a profound sense of possibility, without providing an adequate program of the aims, direction, and ultimate plans of the leaders. A yearly example of an X-Scape is the various laudatory statements and commercials surrounding the Martin Luther King Jr. holiday in January. Most King celebrations bring together a lovely multicultural "rainbow" of European Americans, Latinos, Asians, and Native Americans with Black Americans to commemorate what is often termed "the achievements" of the Civil Rights Movement under the symbolic aegis of Martin Luther King Jr. While occasionally daring rhetorical challenges are issued by those front-line soldiers who marched with Dr. King, like Jesse Jackson, Joseph Lowry, and Hosea Williams, most of the time the rhetoric is of a shallow and callously ceremonial nature. Engaged dialogue on economic development plans, intensive discussions, and planning sessions on the ways in which the devastated inner-city economic infra-structure can be revitalized are almost never a part of the "celebration." As a result, the radical

Christian militancy, political savvy, and organizational genius of King, the SCLC, SNCC, CORE, and many other active organizations of the 1950s and 1960s are diluted into a nonthreatening, unsubversive recital of Dr. King's speeches. More seriously, the radical visionary quality of King's "I Have a Dream" speech becomes a sound-bite trope for defensive posturing about racial progress and is coopted by those very forces of reactionary politics that are systematically dismantling the very programs King died to create. Most King celebrations are an X-Scape from the corrosive realities of current life, which King lived and died trying to transform. King X-Scapes participate in an ongoing reactive mood toward Afrikans speaking critically about the United States. As such, they are part of a strangling of the determined hopes of most persons of color who live (predominantly) in inner cities.

X-Scape can masquerade as liberation. Many people in the early 1990s wore baseball caps with an *X* on them, perhaps even believing that they were celebrating the life achievements of Malcolm X, but they were not. Rather, they were participating in a commercial venture masterminded by the movie director Spike Lee. Spike wanted to advertise his movie *X* on Malcolm X, so he promoted these caps as a way of getting interest in the movie. The caps took off as a hip-hop fad. Fortunately the movie and the fad prompted *some* serious analysis of the life and teachings of Malcolm X. Serious religious scholars and cultural critics like Cornel West, Michael Eric Dyson, Patricia Williams, and Robin D. G. Kelley contributed creative and critical analyses on Malcolm X during this period.[4] The movie emerged in 1992, the same year that witnessed the April uprising-turned-riot in Los Angeles. Precipitated by the acquittal of brutality charges against four white officers by an all-white jury in predominantly white Simi Valley, the infamous Rodney King beating reveals the depths to which genuine revolutionary rage can be diluted and capitalized into a commercial "hit."

The April 1992 Los Angeles "Event" was a kind of X-Scape from revolutionary action. It was not planned. It had no political goals or aims. Rather, it was the spontaneous explosion of angry poor people over an unjust verdict. Yet the marchers in that event did have a revolutionary chant, "No Justice, No Peace!" But chants without organization wither into street fights with no agenda. The Los Angeles event touched off sympathy events in New York, Toronto, San Francisco, and even Atlanta, but no concerted liberative politics emerged. The watch-line after the "riots" in Los Angeles was "peace and jobs." Even interest in finding ways of bringing those boiling energies into a political and economic framework for justice quickly waned as media attention turned to other matters.

An X-Scape depends on media attention, not careful planning, creative organizing, and long-term revolutionary patience. As soon as the cameras are turned on, X-Scape practitioners whine and complain, howl and moan over injustices, but no plan is put forth as viable.

Genuine XODUS JOURNEY is critical of the masquerade that is X-Scape because to those outside of the long-term concerns of Black peoples the two appear to be the same. Yet XODUS is not widely touted. It moves quietly in fraternities, men's fellowships, churches, and other voluntary organizations. It is the dignified engagement of brothers and sisters who have put their whole lives into doing something positive and uplifting for their local communities. Such grass-roots leaders have neither the time nor the interest in grandstanding in front of television cameras. They are too busy comforting a grandmother who has lost her fourth grandson to either police bullets or a gang drive-by shooting. They are too preoccupied with finding ways to set up economic networks with local businesses for a few worthy young women and men who deserve a chance. They are stretched to their limits of physical, emotional, and psychic strength to be concerned about being on the local evening news with a five-to-ten-second "sound-bite."

THE MILLION MAN MARCH AS EVENT

Reeling from the harsh statistics of Black male incarceration (in 1996 California led the nation with one out of every three Black males between fourteen and twenty-six being either imprisoned, awaiting trial, or on probation), the call for a Day of Absence from our everyday concerns came to all African American males as a powerful imperative. There was a "Must do!" response from deep within the psyches of Black males. The call, even from someone as controversial as Louis Farrakhan, seemed to suggest that "somebody" was willing to do "something" about the confused tangle of perceptions, stereotypes, and overlapping crises that entangle our lives. Trying to demonstrate loyalty to the tremendous bloodshed rampant among the young men in our poorest communities, even New York stockbrokers, well-paid surgeons, and lawyers set aside October 16, 1995, as a hallowed moment to pause.[5] The solidarity of different classes of Black males on that day is a testament to the urgent sense within most Black males that we needed to demonstrate to each other, and the rest of the world.

As an event the Million Man March succeeded not only in capturing the psychic fire of African American males but the attention of an entire world. Would African American males really respond in a massive way to a call by the Minister Louis Farrakhan, one whose public *persona* had been vilified as separatist, anti-semitic, and anti-white. Media conversation framed a new question, Would Black males respond to Farrakhan's call? But Black males seemed to respond to *the call* not the man. Doing so, the Million Man March became a certain testimony of Black men's sense of spiritual and moral urgency *even as they disagreed about Farrakhan.*

XODUS SPACE?

If the Million Man March was a significant liberatory event in the lives of African American men and women, then could it properly be called an incarnation of XODUS SPACE? Insofar as the men who participated in that special

Day understood themselves to be bringing together their bodies, dreams, hopes, and visions of a better tomorrow for themselves, their families, and children in a massive show of solidarity, it was an example of XODUS SPACE. XODUS SPACE is *created by the psychic-spiritual fires of the XODUS TRAVELER*. The spiritual imaginations of hundreds of thousands of African American brothers had been ignited to *do something*. This urge to do something found a community of people awaiting a symbolic enactment of its inner longings. The March provided a focus, direction, and a *geographical destination for localizing and making concrete the aspirations for a better future that lay within so many African American males*.

Even more significantly, if it is true that males seem to be socialized to understand themselves as expressing caring and concern by attempting to "fix the problem,"[6] then the March provided a SPACE to articulate our *mutual concerns for the flourishing of Black communities in crisis*. Men, in such a view, could be interpreted as *active agents of instrumental change,* in the language of ethicists. As moral agents whose bent is toward *activity* rather than *reflection*, such an event as the March provided a SPACE to engage activist energies in a show of strength through numbers. Such a SPACE could be called an XODUS SPACE.

XODUS JOURNEY?

While it is apparent that the March could fit easily into a definition of an XODUS SPACE, it is less clear whether the March incarnated XODUS JOURNEY. While the visions, prayers, and yearnings of a people can literally "create" a SPACE for liberative creativity, XODUS JOURNEY requires a concerted plan toward achieving an end. XODUS SPACE without a clear sense of ongoing commitment and plans set down for recommitment to XODUS JOURNEY can easily fall into the "feel-good"-ism of an X-Scape.

While there were signs of a strong calling for brothers to renounce violence against each other, the women in our lives, our children, and the neighborhoods in which we live, there was not a clear sense of an alternative manhood. These strong callings were couched, in particular, in the Million Man March Pledge. Impassioned prohibitions, however, do not create a *new masculinity*. XODUS JOURNEY is committed to the creation of a *new male*, utilizing the processive metaphor of JOURNEY to emphasize the necessity of *an ongoing, inclusive, open-ended, non-sexist vision*. Though prohibitions against male violence against women, children, and self are predicated on many of the same premises as an anti-sexist discourse, without specifying itself as *anti-sexist*, such prohibitions could be utilized in various ways. While conservative ideologies that bolster patriarchal masculinities as the only *proper* kind would applaud such seeming "neutrality," I see patriarchal patterns of thought, behaviors, and practices as inimical to the entire community. Further, without the March specifying itself as an *anti-sexist act*, it could just as easily accommodate itself to those intent on reconstituting patriarchal masculinities as *the only way to redeem Black males and Black communities.* While conceding that such ambiguity may have contributed to the numerical "success" of the March, I believe that a genuinely XODUS JOURNEY ideal must necessarily criticize this as a dangerous neutrality, one which could be coopted by forces of retrenchment and retreat.

At the same time that the Million Man March provided Black males with an opportunity to participate in the creation of a liberative XODUS SPACE, it did not issue forth a call for ongoing liberative renewal and transformation. It seemed to celebrate itself as it was happening. It was a historic moment conscious of itself as being historic simply because of its impressive numbers without specifying how it was going to affect the histories of all those lives in an ongoing manner.

The Million Man March was a massive demonstration of Black people on the same geographical space[7] and ground hallowed by the presence, voices, and words of the thousands who had been present for Dr. Martin Luther King Jr.'s "I Have a Dream" speech in the August 1963 March on Washington. As such, it could revive the memories of those who remembered, who had participated, or whose relatives had told them about that time. Because it was made more "alive" by the remembered energies of events like the 1963 March on Washington, it carried with it something of the same kind of reminiscent power that grounds the illusory and ephemeral in an X-Scape event. In an X-Scape, the event recalls past glories without providing for ongoing struggle. The Million Man March recaptured some of the fervor of the 1963 march without having been nurtured by the kind of massive revolutionary energies that had led to the fateful march in August 1963.

A MIXED X

The symbol of XODUS has been discussed with a view toward providing a critical interpretive stance toward such events as the Million Man March. What are we left with if we take seriously the two guiding metaphors of SPACE and JOURNEY? We are left with a mixed blessing, something akin to an XODUS SPACE, on the one hand, and an X-Scape, on the other. Perhaps this is what makes the Million Man March such an agonizing yet wonderful representation of the kind of confused historical time in which we are living. Like the March, African American males can do things that have never been done on such a large scale before in our history here in the United States of America. More of us are learning to mentor, support, and encourage one another in professions historically locked away from our yearnings. With all this "progress," however, has come the contradictory indication of a lack of willingness to grapple with the powerlessness of so many. While stockbrokers flourish, most young Black males seem to be falling into increased despair, violence, and nihilism. The March was able to attract both ends of our tortured spectrum, and for several hours one October day in late 1995, it kept both (all) kinds of Black males linked arm-in-arm in a solidarity of possibility.

I believe that it is time for us to rekindle the smoldering fires of the Million Man March. While Minister Benjamin Chavis Muhammad is now speaking about another march in Washington—a million Black families in 1999 or 2000—it is time for the XODUS now.[8] XODUS SPACE requires the energizing, ongoing prodding of the XODUS JOURNEY to be complete. XODUS JOURNEY requires the encouragement, empowerment, and sense of solidarity XODUS SPACE generates. Both are interrelated, interconnected aspects of a holistic liberation of Afrikan males, transforming our sense of self. Both energize male selves to resist patriarchal privileges because of our commitment to a new kind of masculinity. The Million Man March fired the hopes of many more millions than could participate in the Washington event of 1995. Holding together the promise of XODUS SPACE with the challenge of XODUS JOURNEY, we dare to be creators of our future.

Notes
[1] For a more detailed description of the XODUS project, see G. *Kasimu* Baker-Fletcher, *XODUS: An African American Male Journey* (Minneapolis: Fortress Press, 1996); and idem, *My Sister, My Brother: Womanist and Xodus God-Talk*, co-written with Karen Baker-Fletcher (Maryknoll, N.Y.: Orbis Books, 1997).

[2] *Afrikan* is a short-hand term for *all persons of African descent throughout the global Diaspora*. The term is part of the resistant creativity of African-Centered writers in the 1980s, such as Haki Madhubuti, Don Chambers, Jawanza Kunjufu, and Na'im Akbar.

[3] Katie Geneva Cannon, *Katie's Canon: Womanism and the Soul of the Black Community* (New York: Continuum, 1995), 70.

[4] An excellent anthology was edited by Joe Wood, *Malcolm X in Our Image* (New York: St. Martin's Press, 1992).

[5] One of the most unforgettable images of that day (October 16, 1995) was a CNN interview with three men on the Mall. One was a New York stockbroker, one a factory worker carrying his two-year-old son on his shoulders, and the third an unemployed Washington, D.C., resident. All had come to the March.

[6] John Gray, *Men Are from Mars, Women Are from Venus* (New York: HarperCollins, 1992).

[7] Actually, the Million Man March occurred on the opposite side of the Mall from the March on Washington, the Capitol Building side; the 1963 march occurred on the steps of the Lincoln Memorial.

[8] Minister Benjamin Chavis Muhammad spoke in what he called his "last meeting of the West Coast Revival" for the Nation of Islam, April 27, 1997, at the Congregational Church of Christian Fellowship (U.C.C.).

Chapter Four

Dialogical Interrogations

A frican American men seldom dialogue in public in a forum we control. *Black Religion after the Million Man March* is such a forum, a bringing together of our *different* voices. Kasimu, Theodore, and Victor all have fundamentally different responses to the March itself. Yet after proclaiming their own positions, what do they have to say to one another about each other's ideas?

Kasimu: After reading your overwhelmingly positive impression about the March, Theodore, I took another look at the ambivalence that I experienced. Your affirmation compelled me to take a second look at the ways in which black intellectuals (however unintentionally) can become drawn into an abstract reasoning that criticizes in order to demonstrate (to a small circle of academic elites) intellectual "rigor," all the while relegating how "the folk" view an event at the grass-roots level to a lesser place of value. I experienced in this second look a self-critical rebuff from which I am trying to recover. I am *not* saying that your work was *anti-intellectual,* or lacking in critical rigor, but it nevertheless *celebrated both the spirituality and the symbolic meaning* of that day in October 1995. Do you think that my ambivalence about the March was merely an abstract intellectual exercise incapable of generating genuine liberation in our communities? What suggestions would you make to me to strengthen my understanding?

Theodore: No, I do not think ambivalence is a trivial, inappropriate, or unliberating response. Liberating scholarship requires various critical responses: Where there is approximately adequate truth or righteousness, the appropriate critical response is affirmation and maybe even celebration if this is a highly significant truth or ethical guide. Where truth or righteousness is presented, but in a partial and inadequate way, the appropriate critical response is supplementation. Here *supplementation* means adding to inadequate truth-righteousness for the sake of more adequate truth-righteousness, or at least identifying need for such addition. Where there is untruth or unrighteousness, the appropriate critical response is contradiction. Contradiction identifies and subtracts untruth and unrighteousness from our factual and ethical calculations.

Our dialogue displays a range of critical responses: The truth-values of calls for and witnesses to a Million Man March are affirmed and celebrated in my response. Employing his XODUS model, Kasimu affirms and celebrates one aspect of the March (creation of an XODUS SPACE), while finding another aspect of the March (XODUS JOURNEY) to be inadequate and in need of considerable supplement. Hence, his ambivalence. Kasimu's negative criticisms are calls for supplement, not contradictions. The focus of Victor's negative critique is implicitly supplemental rather than contradictory insofar as Victor does more criticizing of silence than contradicting witness. Where the March is said to be abominably silent, Victor adds social-ethical prescriptions for the loving embrace of gay-lesbian existence and for public discussion of HIV/AIDS-related issues. Closely related to Victor's affirmation and celebration of gay-lesbian existence is Victor's contradiction of "classical masculine virtues" and his contradiction of an implicit "cult of black masculinity." Victor identifies no aspect of the March worth celebrating. Celebrations, affirmations, supplementations, and contradictions are critical responses appropriate to liberating scholarship.

Kasimu: Theodore, you described the March as emphatically manifesting a "peaceful-calm-loving-prayerful-spiritual" atmosphere that I would like to call a *Vibe*. Your description of this Vibe suggests that it was generated by a combination of bringing together a multitude of brothers committed to the themes of atonement and reconciliation, on the one hand, and the presence of a Divine Spirit in that Space/Place. While this Vibe revealed an amazing potential for countering, subverting, and overthrowing facile misconceptions about black men generally, I continue to wonder about the ongoing potential for *developing and propagating that Vibe across the country in a massive spiritual-psychosocial fashion*. Can you imagine what that Vibe would be like in a few years if black men throughout the country recaptured and relived it every time we gathered together in a meaningful way? Can you imagine how dramatically we might begin to affirm our potential for cultivating and projecting a Vibe of peace, friendship, and quiet in the midst of the violence and chaos of so many of our lives?

Theodore: Yes, I can imagine such. And you can too. To be sure, Kasimu's XODUS, Victor's *Beyond Ontological Blackness*, and my own *Empower the People* include appeals to such images. Thankfully, the work of imaging a widely shared transforming spiritual "Vibe" is more easily done now that we've seen this Million Man March. Now, unlike before, images of black men as a great multitude of sharing-caring-peaceful-loving-prayerful-spiritual people have a root in recent mass experience.

Many of us easily imagine that regularly recapturing the spirit of that great experience will contribute to the creation of new XODUS SPACES and to the furthering of creative new XODUS JOURNEYS, journeys to previously unimagined places. This is why Cornel West and more than a million others say, "Long live the spirit of the Million Man March!"

I predict many of us will develop the habit of annually observing and celebrating this great witness to an alternative image of black men. And I pledge to join others in contributing to the truth-value to this prediction by actually observing and encouraging annual observances of this new holy day.

Remember, Kasimu, I wasn't there. And I wasn't glued to the tube, to audio broadcasting, or to the Web. For most of the day I wasn't reached by CNN, NPR, BET, BBC, AOL, Prodigy, or any other broadcast media. On October 16, 1995, I was fully attentive to such forgettable concerns. I've forgotten how I spent the day. Broadcast media's first access to me came late that evening when a chance encounter with my non-cabled television created the day's first memorable event—the final minutes of Ted Koppel's *Nightline* report. This was certainly memorable, even inspiring, but I didn't seriously focus on the March until the following days and weeks, when I encountered again and again the joyful witness of returning brothers. A million-plus black men is a sizable percentage of the whole black population, so witnesses were ubiquitous. Mostly I'm describing and criticizing the witness of the returning brothers. Their witness and other witness testify to the "peaceful-calm-loving-prayerful-spiritual" atmosphere you call a Vibe. By the way, Kasimu, were you there? Victor?

Kasimu: No, but I was an avid and prayerful participant in one of the sympathy Day of Absence events in my home neighborhood. I supported the spirit and idea of the March and the Day of Absence.

I guess what really amazes me is that all the religious greetings heard at the March emphasized the holistic kind of peace that comes from the cosmos, GOD, and the potentially powerful and harmonious relationships human beings may have with each other and the rest of Creation. In Hebrew we call it *Shalom!* In Arabic we call it *Salaam!* In ancient Kemetic language it was called *Hotep!* Further, such greetings have always served as a way for various religious groups to focus their positive spiritual energies, thoughts, emotions, and attitudes when gathering for worship. If we look at the March as an example of *invoking blessings of peaceful power*, I think we might come up with a far more positive appraisal of the March (if we believed it to be a negative).

At the same time, I wonder about whether we have wasted that peace-filled Vibe bickering about Farrakhan and his "stuff." What do you think?

Theodore: Public discussion of the Million Man March has frequently followed the path of public discourse about Minister Farrakhan's messages— *criticism via ad hominem.* According to widely accepted rules of academic discourse, criticism directed against the person *(ad hominem)* is misdirected and out of order, even where factually correct. For example, where Minister Farrakhan is said to have said some Jews invested in and profited from the trans-Atlantic slave trade, rather than contradicting this historical claim by reference to historical data, critics usually respond by criticizing Minister Farrakhan himself, saying he is "anti-Semitic," an "apostle of hate." Even if this were factually correct (And it is not correct. Pro-Palestine? Yes. Anti-Zionist? Yes. Anti-Semitic? No. Palestinians are Semitic people. Advocate of hate? No.), this would not falsify historical claims about Jewish relations to trans-Atlantic slavery. Accordingly, the rules of modern academic discourse do not allow criticism of a messenger to function as criticism of the message. Similarly, *ad hominem* arguments concerning Minister Farrakhan cannot function as adequate criticisms of the March, or even of Farrakhan's calls for the March. Fortunately, our dialogue in this book has not "wasted that peace-filled Vibe bickering about Farrakhan and his 'stuff.'" We have not given sustained attention to criticisms of the messenger.

Given the history of much public discussion of the Million Man March, our not being distracted by criticisms of the messenger is a noteworthy achievement. My guess is that the fact that our dialogue is not controlled by white concerns contributes more to this achievement than our loyalty to rules of modern academic discourse.

Victor: Kasimu, my reactions to the Million Man March have been based only to a small extent on my personal reactions to Minister Farrakhan. I understand how much the success of the March depended on the mass media for useful public hype. The best of our public leaders know how to manipulate such hype in order to garner a public hearing and to target their intended audience. It is a mistake and too easy to cast all of one's criticisms of the March solely in terms of one's estimation of Minister Farrakhan. The galvanizing of so many people (here I mean black men and women across age and class levels) is more likely to be the effect of a charismatic religious leader than, let's say, a cool, calculating, policy-oriented public leader, such as was Ron Brown, or perhaps more comparatively speaking, the Reverend Jesse Jackson.

Farrakhan's public rhetoric on race relations, black sexuality, and black economic development is not shocking. His views are consistent enough with the views inscribed on social teachings of the Nation of Islam by the Honorable Elijah Muhammad. I think that mere visceral reactions to Farrakhan without balanced critical thinking about the role that this charismatic religious leader played in this experiment in mass mobilization are unwarranted. To focus negatively on Farrakhan's opinions and beliefs on such public issues as race relations, sexuality, and economic development is a genuine distraction from the importance of these issues to the black community and its need for adequate and progressive leadership. Moreover, notwithstanding what real disagreements I may have with this religious leader's opinions on these large social issues, an adequate public discourse must rise above the strategy that Theodore adequately criticizes, namely, *ad hominem* criticism at the expense of the issues. In good iconoclastic fashion, I think that we ought not give too much credit to a single individual either for the successes or failures of the March. It took an organization to syndicate the many interest groups that met in D.C. The system was larger than the individual. Therefore, I have preferred to look at the effects of the March in terms of its systemic deployment, of which Farrakhan is but one aspect—although an important actor in the performance.

Kasimu: Victor, your work on the March as an example of both the "cult of masculinity" representing itself on a massive symbolic level and as an "abomination" of silencing the real-lived textures of black gay and lesbian oppression *within* black communities is a stunning indictment. I would like to ask you separate questions on each issue. First, while it is clear to me that you intend to subvert overtly misogynist and homophobic representations of masculinity, I am not clear about what comprises your alternative vision of masculinity. Are you arguing for inclusion of a gay masculinity and lifestyle *only*, or are you pressing toward an even more universal understanding of men in relationship to a universal moral discourse? Second, I appreciate your bringing the issue of silencing of gay and lesbian voices to the fore, because I believe that part of my sense of ambivalence about the March arose from the fact of that particular nonrepresentation of black masculinity. I wonder, however, how black heterosexual males can move toward a point of recognizing black homosexuals when their sense of what it means to be a [heterosexual] "man" is so contested and undermined socially. How do males who are unclear (as a group) about their sense of "manliness" open the doors of the Hall of Masculinity to "others" when they are not even sure that they belong?

Victor: Let me respond to your questions by putting together what you break asunder. I think that the two questions you ask are really one, namely, a question about my estimation of black masculinity. Given your own deconstruction of black maleness in *XODUS*, you know as well as any person working in social ethics that the words *masculine* and *feminine* do not refer to anything—no essences and no thing. They are social conventions. This is not to say that they have no work to do as signs. They work powerfully in the same way as do other categories or classifications derived from the Aristotelian metaphysical ontology that has held great influence over our moral thinking in the West. So the real question is not whether I have a vision of masculinity, black or other, universal, exclusive or inclusive. I do not know what it would mean to have a vision of such things.

   I think of the idea of masculinity as a linguistic short-cut, a way of ordering roles, fixing persons' statuses, and arranging bodies, all too often along a hierarchical spectrum that is governed by the principle of gender opposition or negations. Masculinity inscribes a whole set of social obligations and expectations on male bodies of which the grand differential is the penis. This common feature of maleness (except perhaps among transsexuals) means that at least at a minimal level of expectation, black gay males are not the biological, physiological "other" of black heterosexual males. Rather, they show a sexual preference for other males. I think that it is the set of social taboos masked under the category of *masculinity* that morally constrains the sexual desires of black gay males for each other and hinders black heterosexual males from respecting their sexual differences. My postmodern sensibilities reject the constraints of this rhetoric, that is, the rhetoric of masculinity. From my perspective, Kasimu, the moral acceptance of black gays and lesbians requires neither the concept of masculinity, however universally or inclusively you want to construe it, nor theological justification.

Rather, I think it is you who needs to tell me what moral functions the idea of black masculinity is supposed to have in your own deconstruction of black maleness. And, given the concern that Theodore has had throughout his social ethics for highly inclusive and interrelated accounts of African American social problems, I am puzzled why he, like you, regards the objectification of black males as unique social problems—something inconsistent with either of your holistic views of the black community.

Kasimu: Victor, I have based the XODUS deconstruction of both a generalized signifier known as *masculinity* and *black males* specifically on the simple suggestion that Afrikan males can take a significant clue toward subverting dominating forms of being a "man" from what I take to be one of the most important womanist ethical imperatives—*liberation needs the respectful inclusion of all the folk in our communities—women as well as men, the poor as well as middle-class, homosexual, and heterosexual.* Playfully, I suggest you reread *XODUS* and then you might recognize how deeply ironic (and sarcastic) my question about "the Hall of Masculinity" was! Seriously, I am not interested in reconceiving an abstraction known as *masculinity*, or in opening up grandiose, gothic-arched "doors" to a "Hall of Masculinity." But I am deeply concerned with living, breathing, Afrikan, male bodies who struggle toward a spiritually enthused, justice-based, and loving concept of what it means to be a human with a male body.

Abomination in the Bible is used as an indication of a curse as well as to name an abhorrent act or moral decision. By contrast, the word *blessing* is used to indicate GOD's favor and the positive activity of grace in life. While it is clear, Victor, that you have articulated a powerful sense of the abomination of homophobic silencing, I wonder if you could help us to see the "blessing" that you see arising from a more inclusive masculinity and liberative intent for black communities?

Your chapters [Theodore's and Victor's] articulate completely contrasting views of the same event! Theodore's celebration of the "good news" of the march seems radically opposed to Victor's condemnation of the "abomination" of silencing gay-lesbian voices and issues. I want to ask both of you to respond to each other's work in light of your perspectives. In addition, do you see any points where each other's work may have something to contribute to your own?

Theodore: Part of the legacy of the Million Man March is its call for black men to engage in constructive self-criticism. And again, a liberating self-criticism requires affirming and celebrating what is good-righteous about us, nurturing and supplementing what is good-righteous yet inadequate, and contradicting what is bad-wrong. Concerning what is inadequate and wrong about us, we are already very well schooled. All of us know black men are described as more likely to be unhealthy, unwealthy, uneducated, unfree, unhappy, untrusted, unmarried, unloved, unpeaceful, and so on, and so on. That's the ever-present-everyday-everywhere-broadly-cast-same-old bad news. And much of this bad news is explicitly confessed in calling for repentance, reconciliation, and atonement. Victor adds a neglected item to the bad-news list, and in so doing, he calls us to further confession, repentance, and hopefully to reconciliation and to atonement.

The fact that the focus of Victor's critique is more supplementary than contradictory suggests to me that "abomination" may be overstatement. To my ears, *abomination* signifies that which is void of all significant positive moral value and so utterly filled with negative and morally reprehensible values and so deliberately and maliciously evil as to be beyond any conceivable redemption; that is, that which is demonic or satanic, like, for example, a Nazi Holocaust. Thus, to call something an "abomination" is to say the thing is wholly and deeply immoral in all important respects—as distinct from seriously inadequate—that the thing should never have been, that there is nothing worth celebrating, nothing worth affirming or even remembering except with great regret, and that insofar as possible all positive valuing of the thing needs to be condemned and vehemently contradicted rather than supplemented or even endured. Victor's criticisms are not so negative as this. Victor does not contradict all aspects of the March. For example, Victor does not argue that black men have nothing to confess or that black men need to repent of nothing. Nor does Victor argue that black men should not have confessed any of what they confessed and should not have sought repentance, reconciliation, and atonement. Insofar as Victor's critical focus is more supplementary than contradictory, and insofar as Victor may care to admit that the March was not wholly demonic-satanic in all significant respects, "abomination" is probably overstatement.

My questions to Victor are these: Is there something (or nothing) in Minister Farrakhan's call worth celebrating or merely affirming? Is there something (or nothing) in the response of over one million black males worth celebrating or merely affirming? If something(s), what?

Victor: Let me start by answering the question Theodore put to both Kasimu and myself earlier. I did not attend the March. However, the significance of Theodore's question remains unclear to me. That is, it is not clear to me what importance Theodore wants to place on whether either of us attended the March. Is the question relevant to our authority or legitimacy to speak to these issues? I am not sure. My absence was a conscientious one, based on my profound disagreement with the goals and rationales justifying the March. I must also say that I have read Theodore's chapter with great interest, because it is a perspective that greatly balances mine. I think, Kasimu, that you have correctly located the dispositional differences between Theodore and myself regarding the March. And, given your previous question to me, it seems that you, like Theodore, find my talk of "abomination" highly distortive if not an "overstatement," as does Theodore.

Theodore, I think that you are right when you suggest that my use of the word *abomination* has emotive interest. However, I also think that it has a similar effect when biblically evoked by you, Kasimu, as an "indication of a curse as well as an . . . abhorrent act or moral decision," and when you, Theodore, describe an *abomination* as that which is "void of all significant positive value." *Abomination* for you is so utterly filled with "negative and morally reprehensible values and so deliberately and maliciously evil as to be beyond any conceivable redemption, that is, that which is demonic or satanic, like, for example, the Nazi Holocaust." Now, it seems to me that both of your conceptions of *abomination* are emotive. So I do not think that the issue is whether my talk of abomination is emotive. It is at least that.

Neither of you discusses the ways that judgments of moral abominations are themselves relative to a moral judge's taste and preferences. This means that they have a relative standing from any given point of view. I also take it that such judgments, because they are moral, do not comport as neatly to other kinds of judgments or truth-conditions, such as Theodore thinks when he talks about "truth-righteousness" or "un-truth." To a great degree, the differences between my negative assessment of the March and Theodore's positive review depend on what it is we both see as being morally operative throughout the events. To be sure, I have talked about the abomination of silence, but I think that my judgment is balanced by the limiting condition that I place on the term itself. To restate Stout, *An abomination judgment is relevant to anomalous acts that appear to threaten the established order, or acts which appear so disruptive that they are understood as transgressions.* Now, given those limitations, and barring the emotive use of the term, I don't think that my talk of abomination is an exaggeration, as Theodore suggests. However, I hope that it is a faithful and adequate judgment about the omission of a large, often brutalized constituency of the black community from any significant representation in the organization of the March.

Having said that judgments of abomination are relative, I do not mean to suggest that they hold no serious consequences. If a competent moral judge (whether God or a prophet) thinks that an act is an abomination, and where such a judgment is recognized to be cognitively warranted—that is, if one is persuaded that the act in question appears to be or is probably a geniune threat to the established order, or is disruptive to good moral order and ends—then one is morally warranted in altering one's actions by resolving the abomination through some act of contrition, repentance, and the like. Theodore, I think you are only half right when you say that I add to the list of bad things that black men do homophobia and silence about it in the black community, while you want to celebrate the good things done at the March. I would only say that the isolation of black men as unique social problems forces the application of my criticisms of black homophobia to black men as a class, but I hope that the force of my criticism reminds us that *the issues I raise are responsibilities that belong to the whole black community.* Black men in isolation from the whole community cannot atone for any of the sins enunciated in the March Pledge. They certainly cannot atone for the marginalization of black gays and lesbians in isolation from the web of human relations that makes the black community.

If by pointing out that many of the sins that the March imputes to black men can be disclosed by examining the impact that the metaphysical ontology of gender and sexuality has held on black moral consciousness, then my critique is in part faithful to the goal of cultural criticism. My aim is to provide the most enlightening account of not only the positive aspect of black culture but also its dark side as well. Such a disclosure may also evoke in our moral imagination emancipatory strategies for morally guiding our community. And that is the kind of blessing that I can affirm, Kasimu.

Kasimu: How did both of you read the grass-roots reactions of our sisters, mothers, aunts, nieces, cousins, to the March? Did you think that it was important for us to listen to the reactions of women to such massive projects as a Million Man March, or did you believe that women and men should be encouraged to gather separately without commentary, critique, or blessing from each other? This question is important to me because it strikes at the heart of what it means to be *building community* as we become "better and stronger" men. Or do we need to provide more prophetic criticism toward the idea of "building strong men" itself?

Theodore: Sisters who spoke directly to me about the Million Man March prior to October 1995 generally spoke favorably of the March. And more than one sister encouraged me to "get on the bus" and go. After the March, those sisters who spoke with me about the March spoke even more favorably of the March. And more than one sister expressed disappointment at my failure to attend. Perhaps this is more witness to my individual need for repentance than witness to sisterly support for the March. Still, as I read grass-roots reactions, our sisters were generally very, very supportive of the March.

Victor and Kasimu are correct: We need more critical ethical analysis of our conceptions of black male existence. And we all agree, sisterly contributions are essential.[1] To this end, I recommend attention to Iyanla Vanzant's *The Spirit of a Man*. Vanzant is a Yoruba priestess. She writes:

> A spiritual process and spiritual principle exist that, if actively employed, will lead Black men to a state of oneness with your Creator, your inner self, and all with whom you have contact. It is called *atonement*. There must, however, be a readiness and willingness to practice the process and embrace the principles (p. ix).

On the back cover, Na'im Akbar writes:

> Sister Iyanla has given us a first: a Sister's visionary prescription for the transformation of her Brothers. This prescription addresses the unique and special healing of Black men, but it speaks to the health of all men.

Vanzant's text is an important sisterly contribution to a spiritually transformed vision of black manhood.

Victor: I do not know what to say to your last question, Kasimu, except that reactions by black women with whom I relate were mixed. However, I am still somewhat amused by a chant that my sister recounts when she and others met at a church in Chicago to send a bus of black men to the March. The women chanted: "You go, boy, you go, boy. We'll stay home and pray." As she recalled the chant, I got the impression that the women were shouting in relief to be rid of the men for a few days, instead of it being a blessing of their efforts! I recognize that many black women were supportive of the March and did not find their exclusion from the March itself to be a categorical exclusion of women from the major social interests that inspired the March. However, it would not change my mind or my disposition surrounding the exclusion of black women as a class and the marginalization of black gays and lesbians as a class from participating in an event whose meaning was supposed to galvanize the whole black community in support of black fathers, sons, uncles, and mates. Whether Theodore or you evoke a million witnesses, it would not alter my judgment that black men and the social problems that affect their life expectancy and their moral relations cannot but distort our image of their place and their responsibilities within the black community. If such conversations as this one continue as a consequence of the March, then I suppose, Kasimu, I would count *that* as a blessing; yes, Theodore, I would also count such a consequence worthy of celebration.

Note
   [1] In *XODUS*, Garth Kasimu Baker-Fletcher prescribes particular attention to young African American males while emphasizing need for sisterly "criticism and partnership."

Today's TV news reports are filled with scenes of African American males as criminals: arms handcuffed behind their backs, faces pushed down on top of cars or against walls, held under the power of an officer of the law. Such scenes have become so commonplace that they pass for normal occurrences. . . . It is time for all the Black community, from the most highly educated and "successful" to the poorest and most disadvantaged, to begin to shake up the comfortable status quo that is destroying the fiber of self-esteem and self-respect of so many young African Americans, males in particular. . . .

In an era of increasing racial misunderstanding and conflict, and after seasons of urban unrest, it is time for African American Christians and Black churches to respond seriously to the crisis of opportunity and self-image Black males are facing in the dawn of a high-tech, multicultural world. . . . Xodus proposes that African American men need a radical reconstruction of self that values the criticism and partnership of women (pp. ix-xiii).

Bibliography
Anderson, Victor. 1995. *Beyond Ontological Blackness: An Essay in African American Religious and Cultural Criticism*. New York: Continuum Publishing.

Baker-Fletcher, G. Kasimu. 1996. *XODUS: An African American Male Journey*. Minneapolis: Fortress Press.

Vanzant, Iyanla. 1996. *The Spirit of a Man: A Vision of Transformation for Black Men and the Women Who Love Them*. HarperSanFrancisco.

Walker, Theodore, Jr. 1991. *Empower the People: Social Ethics for the African American Church*. Maryknoll, N.Y.: Orbis Books.

Part II

MANHOOD

Chapter Five

Head or Whole?

G. KASIMU BAKER-FLETCHER AND PASTOR JACK SULLIVAN JR.

Kasimu: The Million Man March generated positive feelings about brotherhood and Black men. Accounts by those men who attended the March are filled with glowing commentary about the profound sense of harmony, togetherness, and unity present during the March. One man, Lawrence Oliver Hall, recounted a "feeling of *umoja*, unity, in the air," which he equated with "the presence of the Holy Spirit."[1] A lawyer, Howard B. Brookins Jr., noted that the immense scope of positive feeling and spirituality suggested to him that the March was a "religious experience."[2] His father, Howard Brookins Sr., a funeral home director and retired state senator from Illinois, noted that there was a "sweet spirit" of "respect, unity, and love" that was "evident everywhere."[3] This spirit of unity was manifested by the bringing together of so many different types of religious and civic associations. Thus representatives of the Nation of Islam stood next to Baptists, Methodists, Congregationalists, Masons, and various fraternities (Alphas, Omegas, etc.).

Terms like *umoja* and *respect* carry profound religious significance. They imply a three-way connection between self and GOD, self within itself, and self with other selves. *Umoja*, unity, is the Swahili word Maulana Karenga used as the foundational term for understanding the *Nguza Saaba* or Seven Principles of Kwanzaa (the First-Fruits Festival annually celebrated between December 26 through January 1). Afrikan people cannot arise with strength, confidence, and assurance from the abyss of *downpression* (Rastafarian English for *oppression*) and psycho-social depression perpetrated by race, class, and gender systems of injustice. *Umoja* is a relationship word. It is grounded in relationship with the Divine. As a Christian I call that Divine GOD. Yet the spirit of *umoja* carries us beyond the confines of Christian concepts of the Divine. *Umoja*, at its best, implies *inclusion* and *respect for the many and plural understandings that live and breathe in the hearts of humanity.* As such, to be in *umoja* is to be in a *relationship of respectful unity with GOD,* for the Christian; *Allah,* for the Muslim; *Adonai,* for the Jew; *Nkulunkulu,* for the Zulu; *Nyame,* for the Akan; *RA,* for the neo-Ausarian practitioner; *Shango,* for the Vodun; and so forth. To be in *umoja* is to recognize and respect our *different spiritual groundings even as we stand together—self with self.* But the only way such *respectful unity* can be accomplished is to be in a kind of *self-conscious relationship* (self with self) that believes differences of doctrine, belief, and ritual can be reconciled with tendencies to want to universalize the particular self's way of understanding the Divine-human interaction. That is, a self that can communicate graciously with other selves is one that is *radically in touch with the strengths, weaknesses, and inconsistencies within all of our selves.*

What does any of this have to do with manhood? It seems to me that if the Million Man March is going to have a lasting impact on Black religions, we are going to have to look at the connection between its *spirit of religious togetherness and its view of how men are to be men.* The comments I chose above are a fair selection of commentary by men who attended the March. They suggest to me *a connection between one's sense of religious experience and the respectful gathering of males together for a common purpose.* Is this what we mean by *brotherhood?* If so, how can we begin to reform our ideas about who is our brother in such a way that brotherhood can accomplish healthy goals for the entire community?

Jack: Well, Brother Kasimu, a radical reformation of our understanding of brotherhood is in order. Such a recovery will serve as one of the most important tasks for our generation. I believe that many people in African American communities, and particularly in the part of our community that we call Christian, have embraced and even baptized as legitimate the barriers which keep us disjointed. More often than I want to accept, the status of brother (*Bro,* if you wish) is conferred only on African American males with whom one can identify religiously, politically, economically, educationally, or socially.

When we install and nurture these visible and invisible borders, we signal to other males our acceptance or rejection of them as brothers. This predicament is especially sad when we factor in the systemic evils that seek to downgrade our dignity and hold hostage our humanity. When Rodney King was being brutally beaten by a few corrupt Los Angeles police officers, no one turned up evidence which showed the beating was due to his religious affiliation, or lack thereof. Just a few years ago, when a dear friend and I were questioned by a county police officer in Indianapolis on suspicion of attempted robbery, I do not recall him saying his intrusion on our discourse had to do with our educational achievements or membership in political parties. In both cases the common thread was our blackness and our maleness.

It appears to me, then, that one way for us to begin to reform our understandings of what it means to be a brother is to share our experiences with one another. We must share stories of our pain, such as the ones mentioned above, while at the same time voicing our stories of hope, accomplishments, and progress, because these too are our stories. In so doing, I believe that it will become crystal clear to us that "when you get right down to it," as the Delfonics once put it, we are brothers. Though our religions, skin colors, speaking patterns, and economic levels may vary, we are brothers.

As we share our stories, we will awaken from our long sleep of distrust and animosity to the profound truth that *any religious, social, political, economic,*

*or educational barrier that prevents African American males from working to-
gether for the common good is obscene and should be dismantled.* For me, the
Million Man March achieved this de-construction. On that beautiful October
day the diverse crowd of brothers put aside social and religious lines of demar-
cation long enough to consider the joys and pains of Black life in these United
States and throughout the Diaspora, long enough to pledge to work for more
joy and to strive to eliminate the pain.

True enough, you and I, along with thousands of African American males,
identify ourselves as Christians. Beside us are thousands of other African American males who are Muslim, as well as adherents of other religions. Some are
not religious at all. Yet, even in the midst of our diversity, I believe that *umoja*
is still possible for us. I believe that together we can embrace a common agenda,
one that still seeks the overall advancement of our communities. Each week a
few senior sisters from our congregation and community meet to quilt. I have
watched them for several months and have been amazed at how they take
different types of materials—some shining and new, and others worn and old—
and weave them together with a common thread. Individually, these pieces or
fiber fragments would be discarded; they offer no comfort or warmth. However, when woven together, they form a beautiful quilt offering strength,
warmth, and comfort. In sharing our stories as African American men, we will
discover the common thread that can take each of us with our assets and
deficits and turn us into a *Quilted Community,* diverse and strong, many pieces
yet one body. Have mercy!

Kasimu: I like the symbol of men becoming part of the interconnected threads
which make up a *Quilted Community.* You know, in parts of West Africa it is
the man's responsibility to sew! Even prominent football player-turned-preacher
Rosey Grier demonstrated way back in the seventies how needlepoint and
quilting could be considered manly. At least we were willing to allow a male
like Rosey Grier, who had proven himself to be a "real man" on the competitive field of battle known as football, to sew and do needlepoint without much
fuss. When we bring the metaphor of quilting into a space males inhabit every
day, we challenge conventional understandings of *manliness,* because we tend
to envision those who quilt as "senior sisters," as you said.

Many questions arise for me concerning claims about unity, *umoja,* and
respect for men as brothers when confined to such a massive and singular
event as the Million Man March. What are the ways in which men can be
brothers to one another one-on-one? While such a question may seem silly, I
am responding to the sense that often males really do not seem very adept at
developing long-term friendships of true depth and openness. It seems to me
that males often are fettered by our socialization into seeing one another as
fellow competitors rather than brothers.

The competitor model emphasizes relationships of *mutual self-interest.* Such
a casting of relationship confines the scope of interactions to only those kinds
of contacts that can be mutually beneficial to autonomous, atomized selves.
Thus I can call a golf buddy for a friendly game not because he is necessarily a

friend, but because I want to practice my swing. One can never truly be friends with a fellow competitor but can remain on *friendly terms*—a phrase that has the ring of international relations between two well-armed sovereign nations! Of course, we must also recognize that such "buddy" interactions have often been the screen whereby important business transactions have been sealed— with a "personal touch." The country club as well as the basketball or football game has served as a multi-layered arena of gamesmanship where not all of the points being scored occur on the playing field. Yet one would be sadly mistaken to take *this kind* of buddy as a friend, because as soon as a better deal with more lucrative profits, better positioning, and influence could be had, the buddy is gone! A true friend, on the other hand, is *present* to the other— in good times and bad. True friends are not bound by the shallow veneer of buddiness but by voluntary bonds of affection, trust, empathy, and under- standing. True friends are able to bridge that gap produced by the competi- tive model of rugged individualism, which you wrote about in *Atonement*.[4]

Men, all men, need to learn to be *true friends* with one another. *How do we go about addressing such an issue?*

Jack: Brother Kasimu, I believe that for many African American men, massive amounts of time and energy are spent trying to prove to others around us that "we're the man," which means we are in control of ourselves and our circumstances. Often our interactions with other males are, in fact, character- ized the way you stated: we are on "friendly terms" but not involved in real friendships. When we men gather, seldom do we engage in conversations or acts that would even give a hint that we are not "in charge." I guess that is the way it is with many of us. Some of us need to nurture the image of ourselves as rugged individualists who can recite *Invictus* while singing, "I Did It My Way"! It amazes me that even in Christian communities men will discuss de- tails of a basketball game or a sports/utility vehicle while remaining silent on matters of their hearts, faith, and families. I guess that is what it means to be "cool."

Related to this is the notion of competition. Not only do many of us feel the need to show we are in charge, but we also want to show that we are *more* in charge than those around us. In some cases our relationships change dra- matically when we perceive our "friends" to have outdone us in some way.

However, scores of African American men are, in fact, participating in and enjoying true friendships with other males. These relationships feature less of an individualistic, competitive drive and more of a *creative-true-companion- ship drive*.

This model, that of *creative true companionship*, enables brothers to emerge from the relationship masquerade in ways that can open them to share feel- ings, strengths, and even vulnerabilities while still being seen as a man. When you think about it, should not all friendships possess these qualities? I believe all of us are tired of being asked "How are you doing?" by people who do not even stay around long enough to hear our response. African American men need to be asked this question by other brothers who intend to remain on the scene long enough to hear the response. It seems to me that no friendship should be without this kind of commitment.

Kasimu: What kind of models of male leadership should we be talking about as liberating? There was a mixed message about leadership at the March. On the one hand, the Million Man March was clearly organized and orchestrated by the Nation of Islam. The well-dressed, restrained, disciplined, and courteous ways of the Fruit of Islam [the body-guards Malcolm X created back in the early 1960s] are part of a powerful authoritarian structure in the Nation of Islam led by Minister Louis Farrakhan. While there are some female ministers in the NOI, the image presented by the Nation is one of seamless male authority—from Farrakhan on down. At the same time, on the other hand, under the urgings of [then] Rev. Benjamin Chavis and Rev. Jesse Jackson, prominent African American women also graced the speaker stand of the Million Man March itself. Maya Angelou read a poem saluting Black men, Mother Rosa Parks greeted everyone, Dr. Dorothy Height (president and C.E.O. of the National Council of Negro Women), and Betty Shabazz (wife of Malcolm X/El Hajj Malik El-Shabazz) all addressed the crowd.

What message was sent? Were the men "in charge" while being "inclusive?" Was the embrace of women in a leadership position (on the speaker stand) unenthusiastic, done simply to mollify Black feminist criticism? Or was there a *communal model of leadership and partnership* being offered, a model forged in the many nationwide conversations, meetings, and discussions that Minister Farrakhan held with leaders of various religious, civic, and voluntary associations from 1994 through 1995? The Nation of Islam created a nationwide discussion about the idea of a Million Man March/Day of Absence for an entire year, during which its leaders sought the input, criticism, and blessing of a wide variety of religious, civic, and political leaders in African American communities.[5]

Rev. Cecil "Chip" Murray of First A.M.E. Los Angeles noted that inviting women to come into a "symbolic" role of honor (like a speaker's platform) is much like putting them on a pedestal where they could be viewed as honored, but only in appearance. To be placed on a pedestal, according to Rev. Murray, is not attractive to contemporary twenty-first-century "thinking women," because they recognize that while the rhetoric says "You are so pure, too pure to be dirtied in this struggle," the reality is different. Such "honoring," in fact, manifests women's powerlessness in the actual decision-making as organizations like Black churches and the Nation of Islam seek to "liberate" the community.[6]

An XODUS understanding of a liberating male leadership involves a *communal model of partnership.* What I think the Nation of Islam did in the Million Man March was to seek a *community of men and "prominent" women to provide a symbolic representation of community leadership.* Certainly the numerical success of the March, and the other millions of us who participated in the Day of Absence, suggests that Black folks throughout the land were grateful for the show of leadership and inclusion. An XODUS model of communal partnership, however, would encourage both the Nation of Islam and Black churches *more intentionally to seek ways of including the input and creativity of larger representative groups of men and women.* One cannot make any certain evaluations about the sincerity of the Nation of Islam's motives for a nation-wide discussion of the March. From an XODUS perspective, however, we can strongly encourage representatives of the Nation of Islam intentionally to include a broader coalition of organizations and representatives in the planning stage of future events. If there is to be a Million Families March, then representatives from across the broad spectrum of political leanings, religious beliefs, and class backgrounds must be brought together. I call such an understanding of males in leadership as embracing the *whole* rather than a shallow grab for being the *head* of something—family, church, mosque, or even a movement.

Do you think that the March was an attempt to reestablish the headship model of male authority?

Jack: In all honesty I believe that the March attempted to put forth a model of African American men giving bold, strong, and intentional leadership. Now, it does seem reasonable that some brothers who went to the March believing in hierarchical structures for male and female relationships left with those beliefs intact, not because this idea was preached, but because it was not directly challenged. However, the (eleventh hour?!) inclusion of women and youth to the program for the day suggested that if men are to give leadership with integrity in the 1990s and the days to come, such leadership will not exclude the bold, strong, and intentional leadership of women, as equals. This idea does not negate the need for men to meet together sometimes to share stories. In fact, I did not even recognize the serious need for men to meet together alone until I came to a fuller understanding of why women frequently meet alone. Yet, when asked why we men do get together, our discussions and actions must not be the kinds that "dis" or disenfranchise our sisters.

It seems to me that one of the reasons the March was so widely supported among African American females is that its purpose, in part, was for the brothers to "atone" or make amends for past wrongs and decide individually and collectively to go home and work for the good of our families and communities. We did not meet in order to discuss who would become president of the N.A.A.C.P, Urban League, or our neighborhood associations. In my judgment we met to do a very *Christian* thing, to admit publicly that we had not lived up to the expectations our Holy GOD had for us when we were created. Therefore, we decided that, given the GOD-inspired intentions for our lives, we would return to our homes and communities to do justice and to make things right.

One aspect of African American masculinity that I walked away from the March with was *accountability.* Brothers admitted that we were accountable to GOD, to our families, to our religious organizations, and to our communities. Another facet was *confidence.* How many brothers do we know who have lost any notion that they are persons of great worth and dignity? Every day brothers are slaughtering and being slaughtered as if we were just piles of clay with no divine intention. Many brothers may be decorated with designer clothes but live their lives as if undesigned by a loving GOD. The late Marvin Gaye, himself a victim of this senselessness, sang, "Brother, brother, brother, there's far too many of you dying." How many of us are put down by societal entities and significant others in our lives, both deservedly at times and at times undeservedly? In the midst of all this, the March reminded some brothers and informed others that we are "Somebody!" We were reminded that we are capable of giving respect and being respected. Even more important, we were urged to remember that we are capable of giving love and being loved, of receiving grace and giving grace. Amen!

So then, when I hear brothers in Detroit and other places shout with emotion-heavy voices and moist eyes "Long live the Spirit of the Million Man March," I hear an affirmation that what we had in Washington on Monday, October 16, 1995, was really the Spirit of Almighty GOD, alive and well in clay jars like us, enabling us to be the people GOD intended us to be. The apostle Paul stated it this way:

> But we have this treasure in clay jars, so that it may be made clear that this extraordinary power belongs to God and does not come from us. We are afflicted in every way, but not crushed; perplexed, but not driven to despair; persecuted, but not forsaken; cast down, but not destroyed (2 Cor 4:7-10, *NRSV*).

Kasimu: I was deeply moved by the kind of confession of sins promoted at the March and Day of Absence. I believe that the Million Man March was the first *public* and massive recognition that African American males have participated in abusive behavior toward women, children, and ourselves, along with the promise of reforming our ways.

Males are brought up in our culture (American and Black) to express ourselves in violent ways. As such, when we are mad, frustrated, or even irritated, expressing ourselves in a violent manner is the norm. Beyond pledging that we shall not continue abusing the women in our lives—mother, sisters, lovers, friends, spouses, daughters, grand-daughters, nieces, or whatever form of kin— we need to look at ways in which we may need to reformulate our understanding of maleness to directly counteract the effects of violence. I think that headship views of manhood increase the likelihood of violence and abuse.

In ancient Kemet (Egypt) men and women were educated in the ways of *Ma'at*—a multivalent cosmological and ethical word meaning "truth, righteousness, propriety, balance, harmony, the ordering of one's life-force, and self-control." Self-control was placed last on the list for the very same reason that it is the last "fruit of the Spirit" in Galatians 5:21-24: *it is the most difficult virtuous behavior to achieve.* To be self-controlled, or what the ancient Kemites called "self-mastered" (*geru ma'at*), was to reach the highest level of *Ma'atic* ethical achievement.

If we apply the insight of *Ma'at* to contemporary males we may provide a worthy goal for a new view of masculinity. Instead of worrying about reviving

violent ideals of headship in the family, we might offer a more holistic understanding of male power—self-mastery. Maulana Karenga quotes an ancient
Kemetic proverb:

> Do not order your wife around in her house when you know she keeps
> it in excellent order. Do not ask her "where is it," or say to her "bring it
> to us" when she has put it in the proper place. Watch her carefully and
> keep silent and you will see how well she manages. How happy is your
> house when you support her. There are many men who do not know
> this. But if a man refrains from provoking strife at home, he will not see
> its inception. Thus every man who wishes to master his house, must first
> master his emotions.[7]

Do you think that such a view of self-mastery could be incorporated into a
Christian understanding of manhood? Could such a view help Black men to
aim high and conquer the violence within?

Jack: Brother Kasimu, the concept of self-mastery as outlined in *Ma'at*
forms precisely the kind of cultural lenses that African American Christians,
particularly brothers, must use when reviewing biblical texts, particularly those
which are consistently misused and abused by those who seek to dominate the
minds, bodies, and talents of others. I find it quite interesting that racial violence and subjugation, once considered to be biblically sound during and
after the enslavement of Africans, has been almost universally rejected (100
percent by African Americans!) and viewed as heretical by the church, while
sexism and violence against women still enjoy scandalous support from people
who engage in biblical gymnastics to justify this abuse. Clearly, *Ma'at*'s principles, which complement Christianity as you established earlier, can lead brothers to rethink their need to abuse anyone, especially the women in their lives.
      Along with *Ma'at*, brothers must learn to evaluate the "traditional" bibli-
cal view of male headship and the violence-heavy baggage it often carries
through solid methods of biblical interpretation. Many brothers (and sisters)
engage in a "fast-food approach" to biblical study, in which they embrace a
"God said it, that settles it!" literal method of interpretation without really
probing the texts to learn what GOD actually said! Sadly, this method of
biblical interpretation has led many men to take ill-advised violent actions that
have landed many women and children in shelters, hospitals, and cemeteries
simply because such men concluded they were "the boss." They actually
thought that GOD said they were! Thus the connection between racism and
sexism is clear—they both depend on elevation of some through dehumaniz-
ing others. The fact that much of this is the result of bad biblical scholarship is
astonishing.
      One of the greatest gifts the church could give to many brothers would be
to help them to understand who GOD is, and who they are as African American men—created in GOD's image and likeness, and intended to live in relationship with women, children, and the earth. This new orientation to life can

happen as brothers learn to study with integrity both the Bible ("rightly divining the Word of truth") and *Ma'at*. So then, when encountering biblical texts that stress the headship of men, such as Ephesians 5, brothers will ask about the cultural context of said passages, and what the words like *headship* really mean in light of a Savior named Jesus, who loved the church so much that he allowed himself to be put to death on a cross! Brothers might also run across texts that explain the selfless nature of love as Paul outlines in 1 Corinthians 13. Clearly such biblical teachings justify peaceful, just relationships; they form no basis for violence of any kind. So then, maybe biblical headship means peaceful, sacrificial, and just living in relationship with women in our lives. Maybe it means moving away from "What I say goes!" to "What we say *together* is what goes!"

The church must also help brothers to affirm their African identity through claiming *Ma'at*'s teachings of truth, righteousness, propriety, balance, the ordering of one's life-force, and self-control. The fact that these values so closely identify with Christianity shows that our ancestors possessed God-given pathways to living that were life-affirming and community-sustaining. Now I know that many church-folks reject any linkage between Christianity and African culture, saying, "Don't bring that 'black stuff' in the Church!" Well, in my judgment, it is time for us to get past this form of religious nonsense in order to celebrate God's values as lived on the African continent. Such Godly values are also stressed in *Ma'at*. So then, it is time for Black religionists to reject categorically any life-faith orientations that lead us to declare war on ourselves. The time has come for us to declare a truce, atone for past wrongs, and embrace each other as we lay our physical and emotional swords and shields "down by the riverside" and agree to "study war no more."

Have mercy!

Notes

[1] Lawrence Oliver Hall, "*Umoja!*", in *Atonement: The Million Man March,* ed. Kim Martin Sadler (Cleveland: Pilgrim Press, 1996), p. 99.

[2]. Howard B. Brookins Jr., "The Goal Was Accomplished," in Sadler, *Atonement,* p. 98.

[3] Howard Brookins Sr., "A Sweet Spirit," in Sadler, *Atonement,* p. 95.

[4] Jack Sullivan Jr., "Our Collective Responsibility," in Sadler, *Atonement,* p. 53.

[5] When in Los Angeles, Minister Farrakhan and several NOI representatives met both in a large session at the First A.M.E. Church (February 1995) and with women in order to receive their input.

[6] Phone conversation with Rev. Dr. Cecil "Chip" Murray, May 8, 1997.

[7] Maulana Karenga, *Selections from the Husia: Sacred Wisdom of Ancient Egypt* (Los Angeles: University of Sankore Press, 1989), p. 57.

Chapter Six

Keep on Keepin' On

Reflections on "Get on the Bus" and the Language of Movement

ANTHONY B. PINN

The Million Man March has received a great deal of media attention. A combination of Minister Louis Farrakhan, Benjamin Chavis, and the unprecedented coming together of one million African American men—outside the prison system—was more than mass media could ignore. However, much of this conversation has ignored the religious connotations of the March, limiting the nature of "atonement" to its socio-political and economic consequences. This chapter seeks to correct this oversight by exploring movement or travel as a religiously meaningful symbol.

Enslaved Africans, meeting beyond the gaze of curious whites, presented their concerns for freedom couched in the language of scripture, nature, and existential realities, giving particular attention to the movement of the Children of Israel from bondage into the promised land. In so doing they connected themselves to the Exodus and utilized movement—travel—as the sign or "motion" used to express the larger idea of humanization.[1] The words of countless and unknown slave bards echo this notion of movement as a sign for radical existential transformation:

> You'd better run, run, run-a-run,
> You'd better run, run, run-a-run,
> You'd better run to the city of refuge,
> You'd better run, run, run.[2]

This use of language marks the earliest recorded marker of African American creative imagining that has continued over the centuries. Continued efforts to dehumanize and vilify African Americans makes this manipulation a key form of psychological and physical survival premised upon a sense of self-worth forged in the arena of linguistic battle. And on this battlefield the language of movement has dominated as a sign not only of physical relocation but also of the internal humanization process. For example, beyond the spirituals and blues, one need only listen to the voice of Frederick Douglass, who in his autobiography says:

Only think of it; one hundred miles straight north, and I am free! Try it? Yes! God helping me, I will. It cannot be that I shall live and die a slave. I will take to the water. This very bay shall yet bear me into freedom. The steamboats steered in a northeast course from North Point. I will do the same; and when I get to the head of the bay, I will turn my canoe adrift, and walk straight through Delaware into Pennsylvania.[3]

In addition to narratives such as Douglass's, much of the physical and symbolic significance of movement is embodied in the underground railroad's lore. This notion is further developed with respect to the mass migration of African Americans into southern and northern cities during the late nineteenth and early twentieth centuries.[4] With the underground railroad, spirituals, and so on alive in the language, imagination, and literature of African Americans, it is no wonder the language of movement continues to serve as a major sign or symbolic representation of humanization.

Black cultural production over the years has provided many additional examples of movement as sign or symbolic representation of substantial epistemological and ontological change. Most recently, the language surrounding the Million Man March and accompanying cultural production, such as Spike Lee's "Get on the Bus," provide examples of this. I suggest that the language of Lee's film provides images of movement as metaphor denoting the epistemological and ontological "shift" urged by Minister Louis Farrakhan. I develop this thesis by briefly discussing three things: (1) pre-movement epistemological and ontological considerations, such as the notions of manhood that the March seeks to alter; (2) the desired outcome of the March, for example, humanized existence complete with a stronger sense of accountability and responsibility for community affairs; and (3) steps outlined in "Get on the Bus" as the enablers for (2).

PRE-MOVEMENT REALITIES

African American male identity is much more complex than mass media depictions would have us believe. It is at once a very "American" creation, in keeping with dominant social perceptions and attitudes, and a strike against the status quo and its rigid (and rather unobtainable) standards of maleness. There is a history to this dichotomy. The abuses faced by African slaves are well documented in numerous other sources and will not be rehearsed here. Hence, suffice it to say that both African males and females in what was to become the United States were denied participation in "standard" family structures and social roles; and slaves who forgot these boundaries faced beatings, mutilation, or death. It was not until after the Emancipation Proclamation that large numbers of African Americans could seriously (not necessarily safely) construct their own notions of masculinity and femininity, based, of course, on both an embracing of white American social norms and a reaction to these very norms. Within Black communities seeking to carve out a space within the larger community, the struggles of Black women for recognition and personhood were combined with a similar quest on the part of Black men.[5] With time, this quest often resulted in a struggle not only with white America but between Black men and Black women, the former arguing that Black women participate in and benefit from the position of Black men, and the latter arguing against efforts to demonize women as "work horses" and castrators.[6] Those of us who have come of age in the postmodern world are most familiar with this tension as it develops in efforts to construct identity during the 1960s. That is to say:

> In the beginning, the civil rights movement had served to confirm masculine as well as racial assertiveness, but when it began to break down, that old nightmare of impotence no doubt resurfaced. . . . By 1966, the movement had taken a decided turn—to the North. There, manhood was measured by wages, oppression had no face, and powerlessness no refuge. And in the North, the exhibitionism of manhood was not mitigated by the strength of Black institutions whose most vital resource was women. Both Black men and radical-chic White men—women, too— applauded the machismo of leather-jacketed young men.[7]

Yet such understandings of masculinity and its forms of expression were not new. To the contrary, African American folk tradition and musical production are full of these statements and endorsements of manhood as the ability to dominate and control one's environment. One need only listen to the stories of Stagger Lee's exploits to see the historical continuum. And these attitudes continue beyond the 1960s as evidenced in action and cultural production. The lyrics of many rap songs, for example, attest to this "macho" construction of maleness:

> Old Busta ass nigga talkin' bull shit,
> don't know I'm the wrong nigga to fuck with.
> Git lit or hit up by the doctor [Dr. Dre]
> A nigga that breaks em off properly
> Real G so don't doubt it
> I'm the one doing it while these other niggas talk about it.
> And if motherfuckers come at me wrong
> I straight put my .44 desert eagle to his
> motherfucking dome.[8]

Although the role of racism, sexism, heterosexism, and other forms of oppression cannot be forgotten, the role of this warped—and American—notion of manhood in the destruction of life and values within African American communities cannot be ignored. That is to say, African American males play a role in the demise of African American life through the harmful and irresponsible ways in which they exercise their "manhood." A sense of accountability and responsibility, a recognition of this fact, is vital if African American communities are to develop in healthy ways. In the words of Minister Louis Farrakhan, atonement is necessary.

MOVEMENT: THE GOAL

Is this "movement" unique? Hardly. What distinguishes this March or movement—symbolic and real—is the lack of agreement on its merit. The underground railroad or crossing the River Jordan as movement toward freedom and democracy are embraced by most. Yet Farrakhan and Chavis's call for movement toward responsibility—humaneness—was considered suspect because of media depictions of these two figures. Yet it is arguable that in the late twentieth century only someone of Minister Louis Farrakhan's stature— like him or hate him—could bring it about. With the dilemma of Black leadership continuously exposed by figures such as Cornel West, how many within African American communities could muster the movement of one million African American men? In the words of Henry Louis Gates Jr.:

> Farrakhan's peculiar mixture of insight and delusion would be a matter of mainly academic interest if it weren't for his enormous populist appeal among black Americans—an appeal that was clearly demonstrated in the 1995 Million Man March. That occasion has been widely seen as an illustration both of Farrakhan's strengths and of his weaknesses. "If only somebody else had convened it," the liberal-minded are prone to say. But nobody else—not Colin Powell, not Jesse Jackson—could have.[9]

Farrakhan called for a physical movement to Washington, D.C., on October 16, 1995, as a symbolic or metaphorical gesture denoting a changed sense of self, an embracing of responsibilities—in short, a humanization process. This call seems in keeping with the historical agenda of the Nation of Islam, the religious organization developed by the Honorable Elijah Muhammad and currently led by Farrakhan. For example, the Honorable Elijah Muhammad, in *Message to the Black Man in America*, describes the agenda that foreshadowed this movement to Washington:

> We must begin at the cradle and teach our babies that they must do something for self. They must not be like we, their fathers, who look to the slave-makers' and slave-masters' children for all. We must teach our children now with an enthusiasm exceeding that which our slave-masters used in having our forefathers imbed the seed of dependency within us. We must stop the process of giving our brain power, labor and wealth to our slave-masters' children. We must eliminate the master-slave rela-

tionship. We must educate ourselves and our children into the rich power of knowledge which has elevated every people who have sought and used it. We must give the benefit of our knowledge to the elevation of our own people.[10]

This was, ideally, a call to humanization, a call to accountability and responsibility for one's actions and mistakes. It, ideally, was to entail attitudinal movement away from harmful notions of masculinity that deflect one's responsibility to self, friends, family, and community. All of this was symbolized, placed within the metaphor of movement: away from harmful ways of being in the world, to Washington as site of change, and back to home with new ways of operating and renewed commitment to transforming the world. This is all expressed in the Million Man March Pledge, part of which reads:

> I, from this day forward, will strive to improve myself spiritually, morally, mentally, socially, politically, and economically for the benefit of myself, my family, and my people. I pledge that from this day forward, I will never raise my hand with a knife or a gun to beat, cut, or shoot any member of my family or any human being except in self-defense.[11]

MOVE: THE TRANSFORMING ACT

What follows is explicitly grounded in certain methodological considerations present from the very beginning of this essay and that I must briefly confess. I rely on a loose interpretation of Victor Turner's triadically structured ritual process—separation, liminal period, and reintegration—as the framework for thinking through Lee's film.

In *Ritual Process* Victor Turner builds upon Van Gennep's three-phase notion of ritual (separation, liminal period, and reintegration). In so doing, Turner suggests that the ritual process involves a movement or transition "in and out of time." That is, those participating in ritual activity involve themselves in a transforming process consisting in the movement from a societal present (things as they are) into a period of ambiguity and back into a reconstituted societal present (an existence premised upon new insight, abilities, and responsibilities). During the liminal or ambiguous period, society recognized through hierarchies and structures is juxtaposed to some type of *communitas* (that is, a system of relationships based upon equality and commonality). As Turner illustrates, this process is discernable in a variety of communities. There is present here an interplay between social existence and the possibility of better—*communitas*.[12]

With all of its problems, addressed elsewhere in this volume, the value of the Million Man March, the call to atonement, is found not in the D.C. gathering per se but in the process of getting there—the liminal period of alteration. This, I think, is nicely presented in Spike Lee's "Get on the Bus." That is, this film captures the movement toward humanity—*communitas*—entailed in community building; as such, it serves as a symbol or sign for the March's attempt epistemologically and ontologically to "move" Black men in liberating directions.

To begin, I must admit—after viewing it five times—that I think this film is some of Lee's best work. I am in full agreement with the reviewer who said:

> Spike Lee's "Get on the Bus" follows 12 African-American men as they travel from L.A.'s South-Central toward the Million Man March in Washington, D.C. The men, in Reggie Rock Bythewood's script, are strategically deployed to exemplify the diversity of, and the fissures within the black community. . . . Like the march itself—which is only briefly glimpsed—"Get on the Bus" is conceived as a challenge to black men to take accountability for their lives. A sermon wrapped in a road movie, at its best it can stir the soul.[13]

Although problematic in that Lee does not successfully move beyond some of the stereotypical depictions and provincial attitudes present in early work, it is still a tremendous effort—from initial financing arrangements through production. And in all honesty, Lee should not receive all of the blame for the film's less-than-ideal moments and attitudes. Some of this, I'm sure, results from the historical event and the personalities he seeks to capture. In a real way the film presents—although in a jagged manner—the often uncomfortable complexity of African American life; it is quite clear over the two hours that all African American men *are not* the same. This community is far from monolithic and phobia free.

As the cast of characters begins to board the bus (Turner's moment of ritual separation), headed to the Million Man March, this complexity begins to surface. The need for humanization—or atonement, as Farrakhan puts it—is unmistakable, and this bus ride presents the opportunity for transformation. Oddly enough, they gather in the parking lot of the First African Methodist Episcopal Church of Los Angeles, a church within the first Black denomination in this country and a church historically committed to the "uplift" of African Americans. And in addition to this symbolism, they embark on this transforming journey aboard the "Spotted Owl" bus. We are later told, as most of us already gathered, this owl represents, as do the Black men within it, an endangered species. The colors of the bus are yellow, black, and green, which bring to mind Marcus Garvey and his efforts to instill within African Americans a sense of self-respect capable of sustaining positive and transforming actions.

All the participants seek to ride into history, to be a part of something "big," but they do this for a variety of reasons.[14] What are these men separating themselves from? What is the nature of their existence, their current and pressing realities? What are the circumstances motivating this journey? Although not the first passenger aboard the bus, we begin answering these questions with Evan Sr. and Evan Jr. (a.k.a "Smooth"). The former is a father who gave life to a child he was ill-equipped to care for; he spent much of his life running, as many do, away from his responsibilities. And Evan Jr., his son, has been convicted of a misdemeanor and has been ordered by the judge literally to be bound to his father (by a chain) for seventy-two hours. Evan Sr. decides to take his son on this journey in order to present him with life options—a sense of accountability and responsibility for one's actions; underlying this is a desire to bond with his son, to insert himself into his son's life, to atone for his misdeeds.

Two gay males board the bus—Kyle and Randall—bound for the Million Man March. They are leaving a context in which it is detrimental to acknowledge publicly one's lifestyle and whom one loves. Kyle and Randall found that heterosexism and homophobia affect the ways in which they respond to each other, yet both recognize that these issues are intimately connected to issues of race and class and that the March affords an opportunity to respond to these issues in the company of other concerned African Americans. For them, this ride means a claiming of their space and rights within Black America. But this will not be an easy journey, in part because of the aggressive homophobia of another passenger—Flip (Philip Carter), an actor from Los Angeles who in vulgar ways questions the right of "faggots" to ride the bus and participate in the March. The reasons for the actor's participation in the March are vague at best, but he does function as a "ghetto" gadfly, sparking conversation and touching ideological soft spots. In a more overt way, Flip, in essence, represents the sense of homophobia earlier embodied in figures such as Eldridge Cleaver and others who presented the quest for manhood in macho terms.

Notions of homophobia are never sufficiently addressed. A reevaluation of African American manhood must also entail a rethinking of who men are "permitted" to love. The film's attempt to address this falls short in that the resolution comes through a violent encounter between Flip and Kyle. Kyle, one is led to think, achieves respect and "manhood" for himself and Randall through winning his physical fight with Flip. One problem is resolved only by creating another—black-on-black violence. This is a John Wayne-ish move inappropriate for a community already on the verge of destruction because of both externally imposed and internally enacted violence.

Flip's comments are not limited to Kyle and Randall. He also addresses issues of biracial relationships, the racial and cultural sensibilities of biracial children, and colorism. Gary Rivers, a police officer from Los Angeles is the butt of Flip's remarks concerning racial purity. Gary, on the other hand, is interested in contributing to progressive action that fosters a sense of accountability and responsibility for actions taken. Jamal, an orthodox Muslim and ex–gang banger, desires participation in efforts toward unity and harmony within Black communities; this is Allah's call on his life. Xavier, a UCLA student, brings his camcorder and tapes the interactions on the bus. He chronicles the events for us, and it is often through his lens that the audience participates as voyeurs. Xavier (or "X") invites the audience into the transformative conversations and, in this way, urges the viewers' own growth. The bus driver, George, is the conductor who negotiates the movement sought by all of these men. "Pop" or Jeremiah (the biblical imagery of the prophet is important here but cannot be discussed) is the *griot*; he tells the history, points out moments of success, and criticizes failure. He is personally leaving a context of surrender to the status quo—a lifetime of opportunities sacrificed on the alter of illusionary security. Pop understands this as his opportunity to step out in an act of daring and growth.

Others are aboard the bus, but these are by far the more significant characters, all seeking in some way to move beyond social contexts marked by racism, classism, homophobia, colorism, black-white relations (for example, Black/Jewish interaction), and heterosexism. Boarding the Spotted Owl bus entails a separation from these conditions and the beginning of a period of liminality—between-ness.

Once the bus pulls out of the parking lot the liminal period begins, a period of uncertainty and fluidity during which issues are rehearsed, bonds forged, ceremonies learned and enacted. Fears and hopes are expressed without regard to how that information might be used later. Suspicion and guardedness are suspended. And issues are discussed and fixed using central elements of Black oral tradition, such as signifying and the dozens. The agenda for these men is to establish the agenda, to set the ground rules, to prepare for what will take place once Washington is reached. This liminal period is a purging process, a readying the self for transformation, for profound alteration—for *communitas.*

As part of this process there is an effort to create homogeneity or a monolithic reality in which all Black men on the bus agree as to the basic parameters of acceptable behavior. In the words of Victor Turner: "It is as though they are being reduced or ground down to a uniform condition to be fashioned anew and endowed with additional powers to enable them to cope with their new station in life."[15] On the surface, this might appear a useful tool. But it is dangerous. Take, for example, the exchange with a short-term passenger on the bus—Wendell Perry, a Lexus dealer from Memphis, Tennessee.

In Memphis, the Spotted Owl pulls into a rest area, which allows for further discussion of white reaction to the Million Man March and, more specifically, Minister Farrakhan. As a result of heated conversations on the bus combined with some accurate and inaccurate depictions of Farrakhan, the Jewish bus driver refuses to continue with his duties. Inside the restaurant conversations develop regarding the agenda of the March and the status of Farrakhan as a leader of African Americans. Evan Sr. corrects many of the misperceptions, summing it up with this remark: Pro-Black feelings and desire for selfhood are not by nature anti-white feelings.

As they are preparing to reboard the bus, Wendell Perry asks for a ride to the March. His motive for attending, as he initially presents it, seems legitimate from the perspective of the others. However, once the bus is moving again, Wendell shows himself to be a republican who is contemptuous of "niggas," whom he considers lazy, lacking in ambition, and economically wanting. He denies racism as a significant factor in the failure of many African Americans to achieve recognizable success. In an effort to create the consensus often present in the liminal phase, Wendell is thrown off the bus. Granted, many of his remarks are extremely offensive and suspect, but no more so than the rantings of Flip. Consensus is sought, but is it useful or even possible? Can an appreciation for diversity and difference develop through the suppression of uncomfortable difference? Is left of center the only ideological and political position for African Americans? These are just some of the questions posed by conversation on the bus; and, based on this, perhaps the only possible consensus is a recognition of diverse opinion as grounded in the multiplicity of experiences. This philosophical stance, developed during the liminal period, provides the transformation necessary for reentering social space in fruitful ways. As the bus leaves Washington, the viewer is to understand this transformation as real and ultimately leading to renewed life and healthy options for a larger community based upon mutual respect, communication, and commitment.

This transformation must happen in an unlikely way because some never make it to the March; on this bus, Jeremiah passes away and the men spend their time in the hospital. Lee rightly points out that transformation did not center around physically gathering in Washington. In fact, the transformation must occur outside the speeches and greetings. It must occur during the journey—through the conversations, encounters, and moments of reflections housed on the many buses, in the planes, trains, and cars as folks encounter folks. The process is redemptive. Ideally this is what happens, but the good feelings generated by a film quickly fade.

FINAL THOUGHTS

Farrakhan and the other organizers of the March envisioned an evaluation of Black manhood promoting renewed accountability and responsibility for the condition of African Americans. Was this achieved? What does Lee think?

Overt areas of problematic Black male behavior are at least subtly critiqued, as is evidenced in the response of the travelers to the more overtly offensive remarks of Flip. Relationships between men and women that are healthy and nurturing are quickly promoted through Gary's remarks regarding his respectful relationship with his girlfriend, Jamal's relationship with his girlfriend, and George's relationship with his wife. Abuse and infidelity as markers of masculinity are denounced. Manhood within the film also requires responsibility for one's family, mentoring and guiding one's children constantly and consistently. Showing, openly and frequently, concern, compassion, and love is embraced. The transformation of the two Evans is a marker of this. Yet there is something ambiguous and "spotty" about the bus conversations; after all, only so much can be done in two hours. So we are left where we started: What does it mean to be a man, an African American man? Perhaps the answer rests somewhere in the process of asking the question, of moving from old ground toward new.

Notes

[1] One of the best treatments of the spirituals is John Lovell Jr., *Black Song: The Forge and the Flame; The Story of How the Afro-American Spiritual Was Hammered Out* (New York: The Macmillan Company, 1972).

[2] Ibid., p. 267.

[3] Frederick Douglass, *Frederick Douglass: The Narrative and Selected Writings*, ed. Michael Meyer (New York: Random House, Modern Library College Edition, 1984), pp. 74-75.

[4] For information on the language of migration see, for example, Griffin, *What Set You Flowin'* (New York: Oxford University Press, 1994).

[5] The brevity of this essay does not allow for a detailed discussion of these issues. However, additional information is available in sources such as Paula Giddings, *When and Where I Enter: The Impact of Black Women on Race and Sex in America* (New York: Bantam Books, 1984); Richard Majors and Janet Mancini Billson, *Cool Pose: The Dilemmas of Black Manhood in America* (New York: Touchstone Books, 1992); Anthony Pinn, "Gettin' Grown: Gangsta Rap Music and Notions of Manhood," *The Journal of African-American Men*, vol. 2, no. 1 (Summer 1996), pp. 61-73.

[6] On this latter point see, for example, Michelle Wallace, *Black Macho and the Myth of the Superwoman* (New York: Verso, 1990; New York: Dial Press, 1978).

[7] Giddings, *When and Where I Enter*, pp. 314-15.

[8] Dr. Dre., *The Chronic* (Los Angeles: Interscope Records, 1992).

[9] Henry Louis Gates Jr., *Thirteen Ways of Looking at a Black Man* (New York: Random House, 1997), p. 145.

[10] The Honorable Elijah Muhammad, "Help Self: What Must Be Done with the Negroes?," in *Message to the Black Man in America* (Chicago: The Final Call Inc., 1965).

[11] Printed in *Atonement: The Million Man March*, ed. Kim Martin Sadler (Cleveland: Pilgrim Press, 1996), p. xvii.

[12] Victor Turner, *Ritual Process: Structure and Anti-Structure* (Ithaca, N.Y.: Cornell University Press, 1969), p. 96.

[13] David Ansen, review of "Get on the Bus," *Newsweek* 128/18 (October 28, 1996), p. 74.

[14] Overarching all of this is a sense of divine destiny, providence. However, this is of limited importance for the participants. Sure, they pray, but for those other than two Muslims and an elderly gentleman, it is an act of ceremony. This points, I believe, to the often symbolic importance of religious organization and language; it provides a way of speaking to circumstances.

[15] Turner, *Ritual Process*, p. 95.

Chapter Seven

Walking Back to Go Forward

SALIM FARAJI

> *When the history books are written in the future,*
> *somebody will have to say, "There lived a race of people,*
> *black people, fleecy locks and black complexion, people*
> *who had the moral courage to stand up for their rights.*
> *And thereby they injected a new meaning into the veins*
> *of history and civilization."*[1]
> —Reverend Dr. Martin Luther King Jr., 1955

I attended the Million Man March as an act of renewed commitment to my wife, Monica, my two daughters, Nailah and Yaa Asantewaa, my extended family, and the wider African American community. The March represented a symbolic call for the unity and solidarity of African American men in this country. The March also provided the impetus for an international awakening announcing to the African Diaspora and the world that Africans in the United States are awake. I experienced the March as healing, inspiring, and rejuvenating. I felt a continuity with our ancestors. I knew I was inextricably woven in the African sacred tradition of struggle, resistance, and triumph in the United States. The reality of one million African American men holding hands, singing, praying, crying, and embracing one another was overwhelming. The stereotypical image of the machismo, insensitive, violent, aggressive, gangsta, basketball slam-dunkin' Black man was shattered. On that day we expressed qualities of spirituality, cooperativeness, and mutual affection.

This chapter seeks to interpret the Million Man March as an invitational ritual designed to reengage African American men collectively in the liberative processes of resistance and renewal in African American communities throughout the United States. I utilize the ancient Kemetic (Egyptian) deity Heru as a hermeneutical archetype for explicating the central focus of African American spirituality. I will also briefly highlight the lives of men who represent the diversity of religious and political perspectives in the African American community. Through my personal interaction with these men I have encountered the vivacity and vitality of Heru. Our variegated religious self-understandings are held together by our common historical legacy of resistance and renewal.

CURRENT CHALLENGES

Dr. King's words indicate to us that although African American religions and spirituality represent a diversity of practices and perspectives, theological and doctrinal tenets, history will declare the African sojourn in the United States as a liberative quest for human dignity, freedom, and self-definition. However, the African freedom movement in the United States cannot be confined solely to the utopian goal of "making history." Our struggle has also been defined by more immediate aims such as survival, physical security, and the assertion of our unique humanness without the fear of repercussions. Nearly thirty years after the assassination of Dr. King and thirty-two years after Malcolm X's assassination, African American communities have succumbed to a lewd culture of individualism, materialism, and consumerism. The consequences of such rancid behavior have produced a climate of extreme narcissism coupled with an unadulterated display of wanton relativism. The proliferation of illicit drugs, alcohol, tobacco, and firearms in our communities has created an environment that stifles our collective growth and the emergence of revolutionary possibilities.

The hedonism prevalent in our communities is propelled by a Western-sanctioned international capitalist "underground" drug economy that fuels itself upon avarice, exploitation of the powerless, and military containment of potential adversaries. The rapper Ice Cube alludes to this reality in the rambunctious "rap cut" "Gangstas Make the World Go 'Round." Ice Cube isn't referring to the street hip-hop gangstas who unwittingly attempt to emulate the gangstas on Wall Street and in corporations. Ice Cube is exposing the U.S.-led elitist conglomerate of international capitalists that controls the global economy for its own expansion and aggrandizement. Ice Cube suggests a resistance tactic of beating the oppressors at their own game. He is correct in assuming that the accumulation of economic power and capital is essential in establishing social, cultural, and political autonomy; however, without spiritual maturity, discipline, and strategic planning these efforts are rendered futile.

In recent years African American men have been the victims of self-inflicted *and* externally perpetrated atrocities due to the inter-dynamics of white supremacy, mental genocide,[2] and economic disenfranchisement. Many African American men function in a precarious state of anomie, completely alienated from the struggle and triumphs of their own resistance and liberation movements. These men operate as functional amnesiacs divorced from an African historical consciousness.[3] African American men who find themselves in the quagmire of the illusionary accoutrements of middle-class status often mistake individual success for collective empowerment, shallow opportunism for authentic progress. As a result of this historical void they lack a sense of urgency, mission, and purpose. Without these essential qualities, attaining an education, providing for our families, nurturing healthy relationships, securing viable incomes, and contributing to our communities become mere drudgery. Therefore potential leaders in our community advance and reinforce the deterioration of African American communities throughout the United States.

As we embark upon the twenty-first century we enter the threshold of a pivotal historical moment. We must decide whether we will bring into fruition Dr. King's historical forecast that we "had the moral courage to stand up" and thrust "new meaning into the veins of history and civilization." On Monday, October 16, 1995, the Million Man March provided the opportunity for African American men to realign themselves with the magnanimous tradition of African American spirituality of resistance and renewal.

THE RITUAL

In what fashion was the Million Man March an invitational ritual designed to reengage African American men collectively in the liberative processes of resistance and transformation in African American communities throughout the United States? During the months prior to and after the Day of Atonement and Reconciliation, many organizations both secular and religious within the African American community debated and questioned the utility of such an event. During a dialogue with one of my peers, Reverend Bessie G. Collins, Ph.D. student in theology and personality at the Claremont School of Theology and Womanist theologian, it was revealed to me that the Million Man March's effectiveness was found in its ritualistic dimension. Simplistically understood, ritual consists of inviting the Divine to commune and intervene in our mundane affairs. In his book *Ritual: Power, Healing, and Community*, Malidoma Patrice Some' discusses extensively the purpose for engaging in ritual in traditional African societies. *Rituals are always a matter of restoring balance and equilibrium in community;* what goes wrong in the visible world is only the tip of the iceberg. So, to correct a dysfunctional state of affairs effectively, one must first locate its hidden area, its symbolic dimension, work with that first, and then assist in the restoration of the physical (visible) extension of it. Visible wrongs have their roots in the world of the spirit. To deal only with their visibility is like trimming the leaves of a weed when you mean to uproot it. Ritual is the mechanism that uproots these dysfunctions. It offers a realm in which the unseen part of the dysfunction is worked on in ways that affect the seen.[4]

The Million Man March was a mass ritual that summoned African American men to experience the therapeutic power of atonement and reconciliation. The fragmentation and despair of our communities required an exercise in acknowledgment and confession of wrongs and the mending of community brokenness and failed promises. The nature of the March declared that the source of African American men's societal dilemmas is spiritual bankruptcy. This is evident when we note the manner in which the March commenced. Prior to the presentation of speakers, Islamic prayers were offered in Arabic, a Christian prayer was given, a libation was poured to honor our ancestors, there was a drum invocation and a moment of meditative silence. These practices invoked the divine and created an atmosphere in which spiritual healing could take place.

The Million Man March signaled a call for reinvigorating what Cornel West calls "combative spirituality"[5]; that is, a warrior spirituality in defiance of all elements and forces that obstruct the formation of genuine personhood, family, and community. A spirituality of resistance necessitates the exercise of non-oppressive leadership, courage, responsibility, discipline, and accountability— all of which are impossible to cultivate in men who are intoxicated, or engaged in abusive behavior. The Million Man March sought to alleviate the debilitating condition of apathy and obstinacy among African American men.

In the Million Man March mission statement[6] the terms *recommitment, renewal of commitment, expansion of commitment* and *the renewal and expansion of responsibility* are stated at least a dozen times. The mission statement is fundamentally about resistance and renewal for the purpose of initiating liberation and transformation in our communities. The mission statement echoes the themes of resisting evil and establishing truth and justice, or, what the ancient Kemetians (Egyptians) called MAAT.[7]

A REACTIONARY IDENTITY

Victor Anderson, professor of Christian ethics at Vanderbilt Divinity School and author of the book *Beyond Ontological Blackness,* cautions African American men against restricting their identity formation to the processes of resistance and liberation. There is a fear that an identity construction based upon "struggle" is simply a reaction to white supremacy, enslavement, and dehumanization. Anderson views such an identity as lacking in autonomy, self-creation, and the possibility of transcending those intimate and opposing forces. This reactionary identity amounts to what Anderson calls "the blackness that whiteness created."[8] Anderson argues that African Americans have moved into an era of "Postmodern Blackness." "Postmodern Blackness" refers to the complexity of African American identity along the lines of race, gender, sexual orientation, and educational level. Anderson argues that it can no longer be assumed that African Americans represent a socio-cultural monolith. The African American experience cannot be essentialized under the quixotic notions of unfulfilled rhetoric about liberation and Black consciousness. Anderson comments:

> Talk about liberation becomes hard to justify where freedom appears as nothing more than defiant self-assertion of a revolutionary racial consciousness that requires for its legitimacy the opposition of white racism. Where there exists no possibility of transcending the blackness that whiteness created, African American theologies of liberation must be seen not only as crisis theologies, they remain theologies in crisis of legitimation.[9]

Anderson is correct in cautioning African Americans against restricting our identity to reactionary impulses. Human cultures and societies do not thrive only by engaging in negation of inimical forces, but, more important, they prevail when they are able to propagate by adhering to self-created visions of progress. I suspect, however, that Anderson is narrowly defining our resistance tradition to the unique geographical context of Africans suffering in the United States. Liberation and justice themes are and have been significant elements of African spirituality in both antiquity and contemporary periods. Therefore, our liberation tradition cannot be limited to "the blackness that whiteness created." It is more accurate to view our tradition as arising out of the indefatigable surge of the human spirit to be free. This inherent spiritual quality found within human beings transcends the historical contexts in which we operate. In Christian theology Jesus confronts and defeats the quintessential evil, death. During his ordeal on the cross he suffered pain, agony, and brokenness. In his struggle the forces of the enemy were neutralized and transcended. In Jesus, eternal life was restored. His resurrection is the very epitome of resistance and renewal.

Basing the formation of our collective spiritual identity upon the processes of resistance, liberation, and renewal is active. This continuous project was deemed an imperative in classical African cultures. In ancient Kemetic ethical philosophy this process is called replacing IFSET (disorder, falsehood, injustice) with MAAT (truth, harmony, justice).[10] Our resistance tradition is not limited to this historical moment, for it is connected to the perennial process of establishing a sane and just world in all places at all times.

HERU

In ancient Kemetic theological traditions the deity Heru (called Horus by the Greeks) is the icon and archetype of resistance to evil and the inauguration of justice in the world. *African American spirituality has traditionally embodied this classical African deity.* Heru is most popularly known within the Ausarian (Osiris) mythological tradition. He is the son of Auset (Isis) and the avenger of his father Ausar (Osiris). Throughout ancient Kemet's history Heru took on multiple forms and expressions. This is due to the fluidity and multivalency of ancient Kemetic religion. The deities or *neters* were not gods in the sense of being singular, separated entities. Rather, the deities/*neters* represented forces and intelligences at work in creation and the universe. Depending on the function that a particular *neter* was ascribed to, its expression—and therefore its form, symbol, and mythological traditions—could change. More brilliantly, a deity could maintain a multiplicity of forms, expressions, and symbols simultaneously. For example, three popular forms of Heru found in Kemetic texts are Heru-Ur (Heru the Elder), who is depicted in the form of a man with the head of a hawk (and also a lion with the head of hawk); he usually wears the crowns of the South and North united. The second is Heru-P-Khart (Heru the Younger), whom the Greeks called Harpocrates or Hippocrates. He is depicted as a child with a lock of hair on the right side of his head and with a finger in his mouth. The third is Heru-Behutet, who represents the form of Heru that was triumphant over the archenemy Set.[11] In the Ausarian mythological tradition we detect the multiple forms of Heru being submerged within a central Heru figure.

It is the form of Heru within the Ausarian mythological tradition that provides an interpretative framework for explicating African American spiritual traditions.[12] The most popular rendition of the Ausarian myth comes to us through the Greco-Roman intellectual Plutarch in his book *Osiris and Isis*.[13] There are more ancient versions of the myth found in the Pyramid texts and the literary Ramesside version.[14] The myth is also made reference to in the *Per Em Heru (Egyptian Book of the Dead* or *The Book of Coming Forth by Day)*. The most ancient depiction of a Heru figure was discovered in 1898 at the Temple of Heru at Hierakonpolis. This discovery was the famous Menes-Narmer palette, an engraved stone commemorating the uniting of the two lands, lower and upper Kemet, and the establishment of Kemet's first dynasty. The stone displays two images, one showing Menes wearing the white crown of upper Kemet as he defeats his enemy, and the other image depicting him wearing the red crown of lower Kemet as a falcon positions itself overhead.[15] The Heru-Falcon was associated with a king who was fearless and just in ancient Kemetic society.

In order to understand properly the contemporary applicability of Heru to African American spiritual tradition, I will present a brief synopsis of the Ausarian myth in order to identify the role of Heru. There are three central cycles to the Ausarian myth: the murder and revivification of Ausar; the protection of Heru by Ausar's wife, Auset; and the ultimate victory of Heru over the evil force of Set.[16] Ausar is the just and righteous king who rules the land with equanimity and fairness. Ausar is murdered and dismembered by his evil brother Set. Set assumes authority in the land and ushers in an era of chaos, oppression, disorder, and falsehood. Auset searches for her slain husband and through her power brings him back to life. In the process she is impregnated and gives birth to her son, Heru. She protects Heru in the marshes of the Nile from Set and from the bites of scorpions and snakes. When Heru becomes a man, he struggles against Set and resists his evil rule. After several battles Heru ultimately defeats Set with wisdom and guidance from the deity Tehuti (Thoth). Heru is declared ruler of the Day and his father, Ausar, becomes ruler of the Underworld. In the *Per Em Heru* (*The Book of Coming Forth by Day*) Heru is a central figure in Kemetic funerary theology. The deceased or aspirant may only come to Ausar by way of Heru. And even then, the deceased or aspirant's life must be in accordance with MAAT.

In the Temple of Edfu in upper Kemet reliefs have been discovered on the walls that reveal a dramatization of Heru's triumph over Set.[17] The Temple of Edfu was built during the Ptolemaic period. Heru during this period was the symbol of resistance and revolution against the Ptolemaic invaders of North Africa. Kemetic temples, like Black churches in the United States, served as enclaves of subversive activity and nationalist resistance. Outwardly, the indigenous people of Kemet appeared to appease their Ptolemaic rulers; in their clandestine communities, however, they were anticipating the emergence of a Heru freedom fighter. The Ptolemies were identified with Set, the archetype of evil. H. W. Fairman comments on this matter:

> When, therefore, "The Triumph of Horus" was performed each year it was not a mere archaic, religious exercise, it was not solely an occasion for fun and jollity, it was a political act fully understood by the Egyptian audience. All knew the defeat of Seth by Horus ensured that ultimately not only Egypt's enemies beyond her frontiers but also her foreign rulers should be defeated. Hence the play was designed to be performed in public, before as large an audience as possible.[18]

As late as the period of Roman occupation of Kemet the religious practices and hieroglyphic symbolism continued to exert tremendous influence in the Nile Valley. It was also during this period that a Palestinian sect would rise to prominence and would later be known as the Christian movement. The early Christian movement gained momentum in the Nile Valley and would be organized, structured, and given a systematic theology in Africa during the first four centuries of the common era. Many of the indigenous Africans of Kemet were congenial toward the early Christian movement because it was viewed as a vehicle of resistance to Greco-Roman imperialism. The Greeks and the Romans had long coopted many aspects of Kemetic religion, rendering it ineffectual as a force of resistance. Heru continued to be an icon and symbol of resistance in Roman-occupied Kemet. Marvin Meyer and Richard Smith identify Jesus with both Bes and Heru.[19] Jesus in all probability was perceived as a Heru figure by the Kemetic Christians—the Copts.[20] The Kemetic people had long been awaiting a revolutionary figure to initiate a resistance movement in the same manner that the ancient Hebrews had been awaiting a messianic figure.

In this brief historical overview of Heru I have attempted to highlight the key elements of this *neter* in Kemetic history. My goal was to provide a substantial example of the historical longevity of liberation and resistance traditions among African people. African American spirituality of resistance is not a unique occurrence dangling on the appendages of racism-defined history. In fact, we see that liberation has been a constant theme of African religious traditions in both antiquity and contemporary history.

HERUIC MANHOOD

Heru provides an excellent interpretative model for articulating the unity-in-diversity of religious expressions found within the African American spiritual tradition. The qualities and characteristics of Heru represent the unifying core of the various religious identities represented in African American life. It is the qualities of Heru that unite African American churches, African American Islam in all of its variations, Rastafarianism, traditional African societies, Kemetic societies, and the Marxist, Nationalist, and Pan-Africanist elements in our communities. Heru as an interpretative icon holds together both religious and secular movements in the African American community. All of these groups throughout their history or at certain periods in their development have served as vehicles of resistance to Euro-American domination. More important, they have also affirmed African peoples' humanity and provided alternative ways in which to engage and interpret reality. Without a doubt all of these groups were represented at the Million Man March. Despite differences, the spirit of Heru summoned African American men together for a day of "Atoning and Reconciling Manhood." This was the initial step toward the process of realigning ourselves in the African American tradition of *Heruic Manhood.*

In the formative years of my life I was reared in an African American Baptist Church in West Philadelphia. Most of the members of this church, including my family, were migrants from the South. The church's worship and preaching tradition was centered in Southern African American folk culture. In this church I experienced "hand clappin'," "foot stompin'," and classic African American oratory consisting of call and response. The retention of Africanisms was quite evident in this church. It was common to witness members enter into a trance or possessed state through the Holy Spirit. There was frequent dancing and singing of spirituals and gospel music.

In Philadelphia as well as in many other cities, Christianity is not the only significant religious institution in the African American community. This has been especially true since the decline of the Black Power and Civil Rights movements. There are vibrant and active religious communities representing Islam, Hebrewism, traditional African religions, ancient Kemetic spirituality, Rastafarianism, and the ancient Oriental religions. I have been exposed to and tutored in the theological perspectives of the myriad of religious traditions in the African American community. I am therefore not solely a product of African American Christianity. I am also a product of African American religions, a composite religious tradition anchored in a spirituality of resistance and renewal.

HONORING HERU TODAY

I want to highlight briefly the lives of men who represent not only various religious and political perspectives in the African American community but who also revealed to me the spirit of Heru. I have been positively influenced by a countless number of Heruic men in my life, all of whom I am greatly indebted to. The following list of Heruic men represents those who have initiated me into new phases of my life:

Dover Carter. My grandfather was an ordained deacon in a Baptist church. He organized for the NAACP in Georgia during the 1940s.

James Carter. My father is an ordained deacon in First United Baptist Church in Philadelphia. He taught me the values of hard work, perseverance, and family.

Rev. Cecil Gray, Ph.D. A minister in the United Methodist Church, he introduced me to the study of African-centered scholarship and world religions. Rev. Gray is a key facilitator of student movements at Penn State and Temple University.

Suliaman. An orthodox Sunni Muslim, Suliaman introduced me to the study of Islam, Holy Qur'an, and Sufism. I attended my first *Jumaa*[21] with him.

Brother Sekou. A priest of Obatala in the traditional African society of Yoruba Egbe in Philadelphia, Brother Sekou ignited in me a political consciousness and introduced me to the spiritual culture of the Yoruba religion.

Ur Aua Tehuti Kamau. A priest of Ausar in the Ausar Auset Society, he introduced me to African ritual, divination, and shamanistic practices. He also introduced me to ancient Kemetic philosophy and history.

Elias Farajaje-Jones. Farajaje-Jones is an ordained priest in the Eastern Orthodox Church and an initiate in the religion of Santeria. A long-time activist in gay, lesbian, and trans-gender communities, he introduced and sensitized me to the perspectives of gays and lesbians in the African American community.

William Stoner (a.k.a. Sababu Uhuru). Stoner is a revolutionary nationalist and Pan-Africanist I met while at Penn State University. He prompted me to think critically and to use my knowledge and education to benefit the African Diaspora.

There have been other African American men who have personally influenced my view of African American men as Heruic leaders, such as Molefi Kete Asante, W. Wilson Goode, Cain Hope Felder, and Rev. Willie Richardson. Not all of these men agree, nor would they claim to be perfect in their respective spheres of life. However, each man has embodied the qualities of Heru.

THE FUTURE

The future of Black religion in the United States must take seriously a theological synthesis of liberation theology and theology of religions perspectives.[22] In particular, African American churches must begin to view themselves within the matrix of African American religions.[23] Liberation theology has historically responded to the urgent issues of suffering and injustice. Liberation praxis becomes more vital when we consider that many of the oppressed in African American communities and the African Diaspora negotiate their life struggles through non-Christian religions. Religious pluralism is a reality within the African Diaspora. This fact should not inhibit the various religious traditions represented in the African Diaspora from working collaboratively to heal African people. African American churches, with their historical and pervasive influence, can play a significant role in establishing constructive Pan-African

American religious unity. Operational unity is increasingly important, because as we enter the twenty-first century Africa will become the continent with the largest number of Christians in the world.[24] It is important that the African Christian Diaspora contribute to the further development and progress of African people of all religious traditions. In turn, those elements in the African American community who function in "conscious circles" (that is, nationalists, Marxists, Pan-Africanists, traditionalists) outside of African American churches must embrace the church and contribute to its mission in our communities. It is important that the various religious communities engage in continuous dialogue in order to develop a broad perspective for effecting change in the African American community.

In this chapter I have sought to reference the classical African *neter* Heru as an archetype for interpreting the purpose of the Million Man March, and the tradition of liberation spirituality in African American religions. Indeed, the future of Black religion in the United States rests upon our shared commitment to embody Heru even as we honor our diversity and distinctiveness.

Notes

[1] Vincent Harding, *Hope and History: Why We Must Share the Story of the Movement* (Maryknoll, N.Y.: Orbis Books, 1990), p. 126.

[2] See Dr. Bobby Wright, *The Psychopathic Racial Personality* (Chicago: Third World Press, 1986). Wright coined the term *menticide* referring to the psychological assault on African people's mental capacities by white supremacist distortions of reality and history.

[3] See Amos N. Wilson, *The Falsification of Afrikan Consciousness: Eurocentric History, Psychiatry, and the Politics of White Supremacy* (New York: Afrikan World InfoSystems, 1993). Wilson argues that alienation from African history in combination with Eurocentric interpretations of history creates historical amnesia in African people.

[4] Malidoma Patrice Some', *Ritual: Power, Healing, and Community* (Portland, Oregon: Swan Raven & Company, 1993). Some' was raised in a village in Burkino Faso, West Africa. He is initiated in the ancestral tribal traditions and is a medicine man and diviner in the Dagara culture. Some' holds three master's degrees and two Ph.D. degrees from the Sorbonne and Brandeis University.

[5] Cornel West, *Prophetic Fragments* (Grand Rapids, Mich.: Eerdmans; and Trenton, N.J.: Africa World Press, 1988), p. 43. West utilizes this phrase in his discussion of how African American spirituality in general and Black churches in particular served as a reservoir for the development of resistance strategies against Euro-American oppressive forces.

[6] Maulana Karenga, "The Million Man March/Day of Absence Mission Statement," in *African Intellectual Heritage: A Book of Sources*, ed. Molefi Kete Asante and Abu S. Abarry (Philadelphia: Temple University Press, 1996), pp. 780-90.

[7] See Maulana Karenga's discussion on Maatian ethics in "Towards a Sociology of Maatian Ethics: Literature and Context," in *Egypt Revisited*, ed. Ivan Van Sertima (New Brunswick [USA] and London [UK]: Transaction Publishers, 1989).

[8] See Victor Anderson, *Beyond Ontological Blackness* (New York: Continuum, 1995).

[9] Ibid., p. 117.

[10] See Karenga, "Towards a Sociology of Maatian Ethics: Literature and Context," p. 373.

[11] See E. A. Wallis Budge, *The Gods of the Egyptians*, vol. 1 (New York: Dover Publications, 1969), pp. 466-99.

[12] See Na'im Akbar for an Afrikan-centered psychological interpretation of ancient *neters* in reference to African American experience (*Light from Ancient Africa* [Tallahassee, Fla.: Mind Productions and Associates, 1994]). Akbar focuses on Isis and Osiris in his analysis, saying that contemporary African Americans *are* Isis searching for the pieces of the dismembered Osiris. Dismembered Osiris represents the fragmentation of African Americans due to enslavement, cultural annihilation, and ongoing practices of white supremacy. I focus, by contrast, on Heru in order to uplift historical traditions of resistance.

[13] J. G. Griffith, "Plutarch: De Iside et Osiride," translation and commentary (Swansea, 1970).

[14] Stephen Quirke, *Ancient Egyptian Religion* (New York: Dover Publications, 1992), p. 64.

[15] See J. G. Griffith, *The Origins of Osiris and His Cult* (Leiden: E. J. Brill, 1980), pp. 15-16 and 121-22. See the introduction of the section entitled "Resistance and Renewal," in Asante and Abarry, *African Intellectual Heritage: A Book of Sources*, p. 587. See also "The Lost Pharaohs of Nubia," in Van Sertima, *Egypt Revisited*, p. 91.

[16] Quirke, *Ancient Egyptian Religion*, p. 67.

[17] H. W. Fairman, trans. and ed., *The Triumph of Horus* (Berkeley and Los Angeles: University of California Press, 1974).

[18] Ibid., p. 33.

[19] Marvin Meyer and Richard Smith, eds., *Ancient Christian Magic: Coptic Texts of Ritual Power* (HarperSanFrancisco, 1994). This is a remarkable collection of translated Coptic magical texts from the Roman period in Egypt. These texts reveal the continuance of Egyptian religious practices during the emergence of Egyptian Christianity. Bes was an ancient deity symbolizing neo-natal, pleasure, and happiness. By the Greco-Roman period Bes had been reinterpreted to become solar deity in affiliation with Heru.

[20] Gerald Massey, *Ancient Egypt, Light of the World*, vol. 2, ed. Charles Finch, M.D. (Baltimore: Black Classic Press, 1993). In his Appendix Massey highlights over two hundred similarities between Heru and Jesus.

[21] *Jumaa* is Islamic worship.

[22] Paul Knitter, "Toward a Liberation Theology of Religions," in *The Myth of Christian Uniqueness: Toward a Pluralistic Theology of Religion*, ed. Paul Knitter and John Hick (Maryknoll, N.Y.: Orbis Books, 1994).

[23] For extensive characterization and analyses of the composite and plural nature of African American religions, see *The Encyclopedia of African American Religions*, ed. Larry G. Murphy, J. Gordon Melton, and Gary L. Ward (New York: Garland Publishing, 1993); see also *African American Religion*, ed. Timothy E. Fulop and Albert J. Raboteau (London: Routledge, 1996).

[24] Howard Clark Kee, *Christianity: A Social and Cultural History* (New York: Macmillan, 1991), p. 757.

Chapter Eight

"All God's Chillun Got Trabelin' Shoes"

Womanist Wordings on the Million Man March

KAREN BAKER-FLETCHER

Yes You Are:
You are mother's darling Negro child
With eyes so dusky brown and lips so full and round
And hair so tenderly caressing
As it hugs and twines around my hungry fingers
But you must know, now soon,
How cruel the world may be to you
You must know, now soon,
That brownish tints are Heathen tents
That bar you in both night and day
From free development and lifelong play
And, I must tell you slowly now
Before you walk, before you talk,
Before your eyes are dimmed
With stabbing tears
That drive their code of fears
Into your gaping ears
You are mother's darling Negro child
Your soft, clear eyes are very black
Your dark, warm skin is very black
Your textured hair is very black
And there is beauty, sublime beauty,
In this black and you and I must find it
We two, together—together we must interweave
An armor strong for you—so strong that none of
Life's deep horrors, no nightmares shall leave a dent
Upon your mighty shield, because you are mine
                                    Yes you are!

—Superia Fletcher
Sixteen years old
Early 1930s

The above poem was written by my deceased mother-in-law many years before she became a mother. It was only after many miscarriages that she finally bore a child, which she wanted so much, well into her thirties. The child she bore and raised became the man I married. Born at a time when we were "Negroes," this manchild, as she called him, and his mother would become *Black*, the word she deals with so much in this poem. Together they would grow to celebrate African and African American history and culture. Every year we take out the hand-carved Kwanzaa kinara (candle-holder) this Swahili-speaking mother purchased in the 1960s, long before Kwanzaa was widespread. She raised a son who would learn not to wear armor but the power of the spirit, a power that not only shields but fights back. I thank God for this woman who raised my partner, because she raised a man strong enough to love a strong woman. His mother was a strong woman who worked, wrote, drew, painted, and taught while her husband worked, planted corn, magnificent apple trees, pine trees, and tomatoes. They did the housework and cooking together. Together they raised a man who could be a partner with me, as they were partners. I am thankful that they raised a man who knows from the witness of childhood experience the meaning of true equality, mutuality, and love.

As I sat at home watching the Million Man March on television, October 16, 1995, with my daughters, one just a few months old, my partner, Garth Kasimu, and our son attended a church service celebrating the event. I found out later that the whole family could have attended the church service if we had desired. Why? I suspect because in the thinking of most everyday, local, traditional Black churches "all God's chillun got trabelin' shoes," as the spiritual goes. The purpose of the church service was to stand in prayer and solidarity with all those men, a few women, and a few children who had boarded the buses so they could put on their traveling shoes and make their spiritual, atoning, reconciling, political, and economic sojourn to Washington.

Millions of African American men, women, and children honored this Day of Absence, standing in spirit with those who marched and stood shoulder to shoulder, chest to back, leaning on one another when their bodies were weary. Many of us nationwide abstained from buying and selling that day. On the face of it, the Million Man March was about Black men. At the heart, it was about strengthening entire Black communities. Most moving for me was the sight of *at least* a million Black men gathering together to name themselves and rededicate themselves as *men* committed to love of self, love of brothers, love of women, children, and community. I was moved by their willingness to listen to all kinds of truths, including truths from women and children, mothers and daughters, as well as sons, peers and grandfathers.

Especially moving was the young girl who reminded men how they should treat little girls, that they are not to molest or abuse them. I was pleased that commitment not to engage in acts of child abuse and domestic violence was part of the Million Man Pledge. The young girl recited her piece with strength and conviction. Her delivery was not only a necessary challenge to men and the larger community but a source of deliverance and empowerment for any child confronted with or confused about abuse. I was pleased that as a community we are beginning to find ways to address these issues in public and atone for them.

Maya Angelou's delivery of poetry, ending in words about "a going on people on the rise again" was equally moving. But I found the little girl most moving because she was like an empowered young Maya. It took Maya Angelou years, well into adulthood, before she was able to write out and speak out about child sexual abuse. What a testimony to Maya Angelou's life, I thought, that today this little girl can stand up and protest the types of abuses that muted Angelou as a little girl. Will muted girls today, I wondered, see this and feel encouraged to speak up and speak out? How far Angelou's message has come, I thought, that little girls today can speak before men about previously unspeakable issues. How transforming it would be if we could hear more of this in our places of worship, in Sunday school classes, in scripture-study classes. What a special day, I thought. Why can't we have more days like this one, where men, women, menchildren, and womenchildren speak in simple honesty, breaking silence about the wounds that hinder us so we can sojourn to healthier space? Speaking this way is a kind of exodus out of our self-imposed bonds of oppression that hinder us from fully claiming spiritual and socio-political freedom. To sojourn in this way is indeed to sojourn into what Garth Kasimu Baker-Fletcher calls "XODUS SPACE." It is a space of freedom to be who we really are as our most loving selves in community.

I disagreed with Angela Davis's monolithic, all-encompassing description of the Million Man March as sexist. I wondered if she was speaking from her wounds of the 1960s and 1970s rather than listening to what Black men are trying to do today. My own response was to hope, wait, and see what Black men wanted to make atonement for. Most Black women in the community were positive about the March and were supportive of it as an opportunity for growth and healing. While a few Black women have criticized the March for being a million *man* march and not a "million Black people" march, like Alice Walker I support an occasional gender-particular sojourn for healing and whole-ness as long as the final goal is to work in solidarity with entire communities, male and female.

Efforts at community healing are incomplete if participants do not first engage in some particular self-healing. I have no use for Black men who have not healed themselves trying to heal the community. When we don't take responsibility for self-healing, we spread disease to our communities. I suspect this is the reason why a disappointing number of leaders of color have suc-cumbed to bribes, whitened their faces, turned to the god of materialism, stolen money from their constituencies, and seemingly turned heart and hand away from communities they started off serving.

In her second definition of *womanist*, Alice Walker explains that a womanist is "not a separatist, except on occasion for reasons of health."[1] From a womanist perspective, it makes sense that Black men should be separatists, occasionally, for reasons of health. Meditating on men's issues, men's problems, and men's need for repentance, forgiveness, and renewal is a movement toward health for Black men that directly affects the entire community if commitments are kept. Black men need to focus on their own needs for growth and healing on occasion just as Black women need to focus on theirs. Only then can we work more effectively with one another. Occasional male or female pilgrimages can be healthy and strengthening, if we remember our goal is to become healers sojourning in partnership with entire communities. I find it contradictory, hypocritical even, to suggest that we women need our women's retreats, political summits, healing agendas, and so on, but that Black men should not have theirs. I know some may say, "Well, Black men are always separating themselves." But looking at the March, it was a different kind of separation— a separation where men began taking off their masks and tried to be real with each other rather than strut and show how big they were. While I disagree with Davis's decision not to support the March, I think there were some helpful results from the criticisms of Black feminists like Angela Davis. The critical commentary of such feminists provoked and elicited some helpful clarifications from Black men about the meaning, purpose, and structure of the March. Organizers were able to clarify the purpose of the March as an opportunity to talk about repentance, dreams, respect for men *and* women, honoring of children and elders, commitment to spiritual growth. This was done in public space, on national television with witnesses of all genders and ages. Before such a cloud of witnesses, Black men made their pledges spiritually naked.

Growing up in a family with a strong and proud patriarchy, I rarely remember any of the men admitting before women and children that they were wrong or needed to work on some issues. I got the clear impression, shared by many other women, that men believed they were supposed to be in charge, in control, strong at all times, and unfailing in their knowledge. But being that way is a heavy burden leading to an unhealthy "Superman" syndrome. The Superman syndrome is every bit as problematic as the Superwoman syndrome Black women struggle under. Both crazy ideals are impossible to live up to, requiring us to be superhuman, damming up wells of genuine mutual creativity for renewing life. It was a breath of fresh air to witness men being honest about their weaknesses and discussing how to live healthier lives for themselves, families, and communities. We all need to do that sometimes in our lives. We all need days of atonement.

Why were some of us women so afraid of the Million Man March? I don't think it was for unfounded reasons. It had to do with painful experiences of betrayal. We wondered if we would be betrayed again. Some assumed we would be. Some wondered why our men could not march together with us. Perhaps we were afraid that if they focused on their own pain, they might forget our pain, fail to recognize us who stand beside them every day. Perhaps we were afraid they would blame "the Black Woman" for all of their problems, as many activists did during the 1960s and 1970s. Writer-activists like Ishmael Reed still retain a derisive tone against women who are critical of Black men, as is evident in his response to feminist criticisms to the March in his essay "The Message and the Messenger."[2] While it is appropriate for him to question the accuracy of criticisms, he needn't do so by dismissing Black feminist criticisms as frivolous and trivial. We need more listening and less name-calling. I wish both Reed and Davis could have communicated more constructively, asking more questions before making flat, dismissive accusations. In the end, the March was not about big-name individuals, who have the privilege of dismissing one another in print and on television. It was about masses and masses of Black men coming together in love of self, God, and community. It was about the masses of women and children who proudly, prayerfully supported them.

The critical questions about the need for a male-female community march raised by Black feminists are good ones. Such a march, however, should not have replaced the Million Man March. I am glad it did not. I think we need many different kinds of marches—some for men, some for women, some for both. I am pleased that a Million Family March is in the works. I hope it includes all kinds of families—single, extended, nuclear, adopted, and so-called pretend families that people put together when the biological ones are far away or too unhealthy to remain in. But I would not have wanted to attend such a family march before men attempted new levels of awareness about who they are, naked in spirit before their communities. That's one of the effects of the Million Man March. I hope that men maintain the level of honesty they reached at the Million Man March during the Million Family March. I hope they go even deeper. I hope they don't snap back like rubber bands into controlling behavior. I admit that I suppose some of them probably will.

I can't say that I am keenly impressed by Louis Farrakhan, but I've stopped looking for man-gods, so that's all right. We need to move beyond the expectation that people who carry mantles of leadership walk on water. None of them do. He is one of the few men in America who, for better or worse, speaks honestly enough to draw one million Black men together. As Cornel West points out, the fact that the leadership was collaborative, with Ben Chavis, Jesse Jackson, Maulana Karenga, and other diverse Black men on board in the leadership, drew men who have strong disagreements with Farrakhan but supported his idea. As West put it, "In casting the demonstration as 'Farrakhan's march,' the mainstream media want to shift the focus from black pain to white anxiety."[3]

My most pressing questions about Farrakhan are out of respect for Betty Shabazz's suspicions about his participation in Malcolm X's assassination. I don't know if Farrakhan had a direct role. He says he did not. He has apologized for the crass comments he made about Malcolm as a young man. But I cannot dismiss Malcolm's widow's suspicions that Farrakhan's words set a tone of violence. Women's feelings, thoughts, words, are so easily dismissed that I cannot cast Betty Shabazz's feelings to the wind. Nevertheless, she attended and spoke of the March, demonstrating her support for the community values voiced there. I am stung by recent events in which one of Malcolm and Betty Shabazz's daughters, Qebillah Shabazz, was accused of planning a hit on Farrakhan. I am pleased that Farrakhan refused to press charges, showing compassion for the pain of Malcolm's widow and children. I am pleased that he chastised political attempts to feed on and manipulate that pain. I take Farrakhan's gestures of compassion as actions of repentance for the harsh words of his youth. But the painful effects of words spoken long ago and the events that followed are generations long, affecting even the grandchildren. Recently, Qebillah's son was so troubled, so angry about being sent to live with his grandmother while his mother tried to get help for self-healing, that he burned his grandmother's home, eventually causing her death. Violent words, as well as violent acts, against Malcolm have created feelings of betrayal, rage, and abandonment in three generations of one of our most beloved families.

Whether Farrakhan was directly involved in Malcolm's murder or not, the death-dealing words he spoke about Malcolm were so callous, so reprehensible that three generations of a family have been wounded to the quick. Violence, whether in acts or words, has such long-lasting effects on a family. The childhood rhyme "sticks and stones shall break my bones but words shall never hurt me" is a self-defensive non-truth. Farrakhan's words about Malcolm as a traitor deserving death were as lethal as the act of Malcolm's assassination. That someone said it and that it came to be suggest the power of words, the strength of curses, the willingness of somebody to act on death-wishing sayings. This is at the heart of the Jewish community's anger at Farrakhan's carelessness with the power of words. I see Farrakhan as a man with a powerful, often-careless rap, a man with potentially healing power who has not always been fully aware of or responsible with the reality of power.

Power is always double-edged. Power requires more wisdom than young men often have and that old men often gain too late. It can curse as well as bless. That's why it's important for Black men and women to move closer to the group-centered model of leadership that was advocated by civil-rights activist Ella Baker during the Black Freedom Movement. We saw the beginnings of such a model implemented during the Million Man March. I hope the Million Family March will involve group leadership by men and women, grass-roots and middle-class, which was Ella Baker's ideal.

The Million Man March is a large idea that takes a multitude to implement. The same holds true for the Million Family March. And that's good, because the best ideas come from a source of strength larger than ourselves. I see Farrakhan as a tragic leader, deeply flawed, who does important work by getting Black men off the streets and into more committed, responsible lives. I am glad that entire communities have implemented some great ideas under his flawed but ever-present leadership. Great ideas are implemented not by individuals but by the community, by people like the repentant gang-bangers at the Million Man March who were forthright about who they were, who they had been, and who they wanted themselves and others to become.

Alice Walker writes of her impressions as she sat before her television, which she rarely watches, on October 16, 1995:

Soon there was a young man who reminded me of John Lewis (years ago, of SNCC), who was exhorting his brothers to "go home" and take on the ills of violence and cocaine. It was a refrain that took me back to the March on Washington of 1963. At that march I sat in a tree listening to Martin Luther King Jr. asking us to go home and take on the problems. There is the most revolutionary advice that can be given.[4]

Walker writes that as someone "who has been thrown out of the black community several times," she was heart-warmed to see Jesse Jackson, Ben Chavis, and Louis Farrakhan assert their right "to stand together on issues so large" that everyone of us will have to work to keep the boat afloat. "I did not feel left out at all," Walker comments. She finds it "absolutely necessary that black men regroup as black men." Until they learn to talk, to cry with, and to kiss each other, she explains, they will never know how to do those things with Black women. She sees the March as a movement toward wholeness, knows that "whole black men can exist," and wants to see and enjoy them.[5]

In considering what really stands out for her about the March, Walker writes that it is

> the children, most of all. The articulate, poised, and impassioned young boy and the brave, thoughtful, and serious young girl who asked fervently to be *seen* as children, protected, respected, and affirmed by black men. Queen Mother Moore, too old and weary by now even to talk, still reminds us that, for our suffering and the stolen centuries of our lives, we deserve reparations. Rosa Parks, Jesse Jackson . . . Louis Farrakhan. Who would have though he'd try to teach us American history using numerology? I was intrigued. Who even suspected that his mother was West Indian, and that he could not only honor her by recalling her wry humor but share her spirit with us by uttering her Jamaican folk speech? This was the man nobody wanted black leaders to talk to? It seemed bizarre.[6]

To me, that's the reality of life. When we are doing what's most important, being our most honest, working at healing ourselves, it's bizarre. No one falls into the neat categories we like to place them in to make navigating our world easy. At bottom we human beings, we Black Americans, are complex, unpredictable, capable of the worst and best of what it means to be human. Our children teach us, remind us about, reveal to us the simplest, the deepest, the most important truths about us adults and what it means to be a child and to love a child. The elders teach us, remind us about, reveal to us the deepest, most important truths about how to know and love ourselves. The imperfect, most controversial, tragically flawed leaders touch our hearts and minds in ways we least expect. Our prejudices, prejudgments, and assumptions fall to the ground like rose petals from a rose bush so that like the rose bush we can stretch taller, grow lushly, and reach further toward the sun.

I was glad that Ben Chavis said a few words. Ben Chavis is a leader on the issue of *environmental racism,* his term for describing the disproportionate dumping of toxic wastes in Black communities and other communities of color. I wish he could have said more about environmental racism. I wish he could have made commitment to resisting environmental abuses in Black communities, where toxic wastes are dumped disproportionately, part of the Million Man Pledge. Chavis made such ground-breaking work on environmental racism as leader of the Commission on Racial Justice of the United Church of Christ during the 1980s. We all need to take his findings very seriously and support environmental justice as part of a national platform for the Black community. We don't talk about environmental issues enough in our communities. Part of our healing requires reconnection to the earth, but we cannot do that when the land we live on and our children play on has dangerous levels of toxins. There is good reason why Black children have disproportionate amounts of lead in their systems, for example. High levels of lead are problematic in our communities not because of neglectful parents but because of neglectful industries and landlords.

It is good that so many of our marches are at the Nation's capital, outside, on a grassy mall with a reflecting pool and trees. With all the marches of justice and healing, the millions of feet that have sojourned and stood on that soil, I suspect it reverberates with blessings and wisdom. I suspect it reverberates with the power of our ancestors, who were brought to the same mall for sale as slaves. I wonder if it also cries out for its own justice as rocks, land, trees. We need to remind one another, regularly, that our communities and land are in threat of dying together. As communities of color are becoming increasingly aware of the connection between economic and environmental justice; we are developing hundreds of small, grass-roots organizations to demand not only jobs, but safer jobs with higher industry environmental standards and safer air, water, earth in our neighborhoods, free from lead dust and other toxins.

We have so much to struggle for in our struggle for justice. Sometimes it does not all get said. As Walker reminds us, Black men still have much work to do in the area of homophobia.[7] There is unwillingness to wrestle with diverse experiences of sexuality and different orientations in human sexuality. Much listening, much learning still need to take place. Sexism needs to be broached ever more profoundly. Heterosexism needs to be addressed. If "all God's chillun got trabelin' shoes," will there be healing during the Million Family March for gays and lesbians who have been estranged and rebuffed by their families? Will we begin to give strong voice to the fact that many of our men, women, and children are dying from AIDS because, heterosexual and homosexual alike, we avoid discussing sexuality in our families? Will we begin talking about the fact that AIDS is a *human* disease, not a *gay* disease, and that it is no respecter of sexual orientation? Who will feel included as family? Who will feel excluded? Which health issues will be named? How will the community address the multicolored, multitextured tapestry of issues before it?

In the end, it is love that needs to grow, the capacity for love in each and every one of us, to love one another in all of our difference and diversity. All God's children have traveling shoes. But if we don't travel with love for each and every one of God's children in our hearts, we will not go very far. Our sojourn will get sidetracked and stunted. Our healing will be incomplete, our blessings as small as our hearts and minds. Our task is to grow large hearts, large minds, reconnecting with earth, Spirit, and one another. Black religion must grow ever deeper in the heart.

Notes

[1] Alice Walker, *In Search of Our Mothers' Gardens* (New York: Harcourt, Brace, Jovanovich, 1993), preface, pp. xi-xii.

[2] Ishmael Reed, "The Message and the Messenger," in *Million Man March/Day of Absence: A Commemorative Anthology*, ed. Haki R. Madhubuti and Maulana Karenga (Los Angeles: University of Sankore Press, 1996), pp. 129-33.

[3] Cornel West, "Why I'm Marching in Washington," in Madhubuti and Karenga, *Million Man March/Day of Absence*, p. 37.

[4] Alice Walker, "What That Day Was Like for Me: The Million Man March, October 16, 1995," *Anything We Love Can Be Saved* (New York: Random House, 1997), p. 109.

[5] Ibid., p. 111.

[6] Ibid.

[7] Ibid., 110.

Part III

THEMES AS WE TRANSFORM

Chapter Nine

Sermon on the Mall

A Pastoral Theological Look at the Million Man March

LEE H. BUTLER JR.

> *Jesus went throughout Galilee, teaching in their synagogues and proclaiming the good news of the kingdom and curing every disease and every sickness among the people. So his fame spread throughout all Syria, and they brought to him all the sick, those who were afflicted with various diseases and pains, demoniacs, epileptics, and paralytics, and he cured them. And great crowds followed him from Galilee, the Decapolis, Jerusalem, Judea, and from beyond the Jordan. When Jesus saw the crowds, he went up the mountain; and after he sat down, his disciples came to him. Then he began to speak, and taught them.*
> —Matthew 4:23–5:2, NRSV

INTRODUCTION

Jesus, the carpenter from Nazareth of Galilee, actualized a phenomenal second career at approximately the age of thirty. From this developmental perspective, Jesus' presentation of himself to John to be baptized in the wilderness was an action motivated by personal crisis. His calling, accompanied by a sense of being driven, heightened his awareness of danger as well as the hopefulness of possibilities associated with changes in life. The events that immediately precede the Sermon on the Mount text can similarly be interpreted to suggest that the social conditions and challenging life circumstances that directed Jesus to public ministry also inspired a nation to respond to its communal crisis. Those persons who gathered on the mountain experienced a calling accompanied by a sense of being driven to have their spiritual longings fulfilled.

This wandering, ascetic preacher proclaimed an empathic message of peace and love to the poor, but to the religious aristocracy he proclaimed a venomous message of judgment for their apathetic behavior. Everywhere Jesus journeyed men and women from every strata of society gathered to experience his charisma. The curious and committed, the seeker and saved gathered as he sat on the mountain sharing the words of understanding and hope with those willing to be present for hours as listeners.

Jesus was called a miracle worker, profound teacher, exorciser, healer, prophet, drunkard, sinner, and the Son of God. Those present on the mountain as his kerygma of blessing went forth probably thought him to be all of the aforementioned identifiers—a preacher is, after all, a multidimensional figure. This is especially true of one who comes as a second-career preacher; and just like Jesus, his first disciples—fishermen, tax-collectors, aristocrats, and those suspected of being revolutionary assassins—were all transformed into second-career preachers. His twelve hand-picked messengers were not the last to be transformed from the moderate to the profound through a religious career change, nor were they the last to be criticized for their transformative world view.

Considering this legacy, it should not be a surprise that the late-twentieth-century leader of the Nation of Islam, Minister Louis Farrakhan, is radically critiqued as a second-career preacher. He is loved and hated—admired for promoting love through self-respect and accused of promoting hate through anti-semitic and anti-white rhetoric. Even so, on October 16, 1995, African American men gathered and stood for hours just to hear this man. Simultaneously, millions of television viewers sat in awe of the scene and were riveted by his message. No matter what one thinks of the man and his message, Farrakhan is an example of the "religious-cultural-social-political synthesis"[1] that is characteristic of Black religion.

Millions were enthralled as he delivered his message to the crowd gathered on the Mall in Washington, D.C. The Sermon on the Mall, as I have identified his Million Man March message, will go down in history; Louis Farrakhan's name will ever be associated with the event for its organization and his message. Reflecting on the legacy of the Black preacher and the Black church as the mobilizer of the Black community, how is it that this religious figure has commanded such authority among Christians and non-Christians alike?

THE AFRICAN HEALING TRADITION IN AMERICA

When a traditional culture meets a colonial or imperial culture, the traditional culture has two choices. It can either choose to become a resistance culture, or it can choose to assimilate and become like the colonizer. While in some cases this may seem like a subtle difference, the distinction is quite significant. If the choice is to become a resistance culture, the most significant traditions and practices enter into an evolutionary process for the purpose of survival. That evolutionary process could so disguise the expressions that when observed by the uninformed, one could conclude total assimilation has occurred. In those instances the most adequate understanding is not assimilation, which results in a loss of identity, but accommodation, which suggests multiple levels of appropriation through an intrepid blending of past and present.[2]

The most significant community dynamic that shapes all relational interactions within the African American community is the "call-and-response." This dynamic, which is characteristic of Black worship, is the hallmark of Black preaching—that is, the sermonic "call" of the preacher and the participatory "response" of the congregation. The sermon is one medium whereby the gathered community becomes present to the One Spirit in a transformative moment. These same dynamics are also employed on a smaller scale where the psychotherapeutic process is more narrowly defined. Regardless of the size of the gathering, from pastoral care and counseling perspective, the preacher is identified as a healer.

One of the issues pertaining to the healing attributes of the preacher has to do with the issue of liminality. I agree with Robert Moore's[3] critique of Victor Turner's understanding of liminality and community. Unlike Turner, Moore concludes that liminal space is a transformative communal space that is mediated by the ritual elder. In Moore's understanding, the transformative noncommunal space typically identified as liminal, because of the radical separation from the familiar, is actually liminoid space. This space tends to be manipulated by power-hungry persons who are selfishly motivated to do something other than promote communal integration and wholeness. When the collective community is engulfed by liminal space through the process of call-and-response, all of life is experienced relationally through the connections of person-to-person and person-to-sacred. The preacher prompts the people to respond to the movement of the Spirit as he or she actively pushes back the forces of evil through prayer and preaching.

In order to better appreciate the healing power of the African American preacher, the division of shaman and priest must be seen as a false dichotomy. Although shamanism is not the label that is used, shamanic traditions and practices are seen as an integral part of the priestly function within the African American ministerial tradition. An important interpretive key on this matter is African spirituality. This concept is not dependent upon dualistic thinking. There is no separation between the sacred and secular, and roles are determined by functionality. The cosmological view is causal rather than random. Bruce Jackson notes that folk medicine has two branches: (1) natural folk medicine, and (2) magico-religious folk medicine. The first involves the use of herbs, plants, minerals, and animal substances for healing. The second involves the use of charms, holy words, and holy actions for healing. Jackson further notes that within the African context the two branches were often combined. He also comments, "What is curious about the American situation is that the second aspect survived."[4] The Bible and the cross became the charms, healing instruments, and divining tools of the African American, although there are those who have chosen to maintain the traditional elements as instruments.

THE LEGACY OF THE BLACK PREACHER IN AMERICA

If we are to understand the charismatic appeal of Minister Louis Farrakhan, it first must be acknowledged that he is a Black preacher. His delivery is sermonic, and he does occasionally "tune" and "hoop." He encourages, albeit controlled at times, the "call-and-response" characteristic of Black worship. Even the event was organized around this principle. This gathering was not prompted by a simple invitation; a *call* was issued that resulted in a communal, participatory *response*.

Within the African American communal tradition, the sermon is perhaps the most powerful conjuring[5] tool. As such, the sermon is a healer's technique. Nurturing the legacy of the African American oral tradition, the sermon engages God for the purpose of transforming the community's encounter with evil. The design and delivery of the sermon are as important as the content of the message—the rhythms, intonations, and words carry the power of transformation. It combines the spirit power of the shamanic tradition, the *griot* storytelling tradition of the community at large, and the hermeneutical and homiletical skills of the literary religious tradition creating a rhetorical charisma that makes the sermon a matchless oration. Due to the prominence of community as the source of identity, care and counseling have tended to be group processes occurring within the context of worship.

The African American community as an oral culture emphasizes the spoken word, as opposed to a literary culture, which emphasizes the written word. This results in the preservation of cultural values and norms as an oral record rather than through written documentation. The oral tradition also carries with it an attitude of flexibility rather than the rigidity so often associated with literary traditions. Because the oral necessitates communality for its context, community remains the central descriptive of African Americanism. Consequently, oral tradition is foundational for the superstructure known as Black preaching—"the preaching cure."

Our survival as Afrikan people has been ensured by our capacity for accommodating culture within variant contexts. As a result, three shamanic roles remain prominent within the African American community: healer, prophet, and reconciler. The power of all three roles is rooted in communality. African shamans preserve communal relationships by functioning as conflict experts, that is, healers and reconcilers. They detect the active agents of conflict situations and then intervene to control or to resolve the conflict. The prophetic role is proclamation, sometimes through divination, empowered by the spirits for guiding listeners to a transformative moment.

The second dominant feature of the oral tradition and culture is storytelling. It is an art form that has constituted the library of thoughts, feelings, values, and history. Because of its historical impact upon the culture, it is perhaps the most effective pedagogical tool. Of course, within the sermonic tradition that point is unquestionably gospel! If you are not able to "tell the story," it is not a sermon, and you are not preaching. Within West African culture, the storyteller is the *griot*. The *griot* was the custodian of the covenant because the *griot* was the keeper of the communal legacy. In addition, the *griot* at work actualized communality through the use of call-and-response and established sacred space through the actual retelling of the story.

> Since storytellers, or griots, focus mainly on the history of their people, ancestors are usually the principal subject of a particular chronicle of the past—the ceremony framed, as it were, by the listeners gathered around the storyteller. Depending on the demands of the narration, they either listen or, on signal from the storyteller, become active participants.[6]

As for the final component that contributes to the legacy of the African American oral tradition, the roles (or offices) of the shaman and the *griot* were integrated during the emergence of the Invisible Church during Antebellum slavery. According to Sterling Stuckey, African institutions and African priests were brought to America in large numbers and, unrecognized by whites, found their places in a variety of communal contexts. This is where the contemporary African American religious leader finds his or her nexus with African culture. The African priest and *griot* were reborn in the United States through a transformative, accommodative act of preservation and evolution. The African priest dispensed psycho-spiritual, social, and physical healing, and the *griot* recited or sang about origins, attitudes, and relationships. Through their integration, the African American preacher transforms ordinary space into sacred space by means of the sermon and the sermonic "hoop." *Hooping* is the melodious articulation that evidences the presence of the Spirit in the preaching cure and prompts the gathered to experience and give testimony of the Divine Spirit in their own lives. It is within this sacred space, created by the sermon, that the malevolent powers that would consume the soul are rendered powerless.

Those are the roots that sustain, encourage, and lead preachers to believe that the groanings of their spirit and the words they proclaim are generative words, healing words, prophetic words, inspirational and transformative words. Therein lies the reason why Archie Smith understands preachers to be folk therapists and ethical prophets concerned with psychological and spiritual wholeness, and for the moral and social dilemma.

> The traditional preacher has felt commissioned to address the congregation's collective moral integrity, alongside its external strength in the form of social-political empowerment and freedom. Not infrequently, these compound tasks have united in one person the role of a theological ethicist, a social activist, and a therapeutic practitioner in the community.[7]

As a result, the shamanic *griot* of the contemporary African American community is embodied in the preacher. Through the incorporation of the literary religious tradition, the preacher systematically interprets scripture, history, and culture with the hopes of expanding the sacred space of the community. In diagnosing the health of the community, the preacher confronts the chronic ills of racism, discrimination, injustice, economic crisis, hopelessness, and family dysfunction.[8] Standing between the destroyer and the people, the preacher must gaze upon suffering, divine the truth, and be "a bold prophet, a doer, a speaker of truth—no matter how bitter or confrontational, or unpopular that truth may be."[9] Because the African American preacher is expected and encouraged to proclaim a word that is expressive of the sacred communal theme of freedom (and we know biblically and psychologically that the "truth makes us free"), the preacher must have the creativity and flare to mobilize the community and immobilize opposing forces, thereby restoring health to the community.

FARRAKHAN, THE MUSLIM PREACHER

By expanding the historical context to include all of the influences that have contributed to the formation of the African American and the African American preacher, we discover, along with Gayraud Wilmore, that the phenomenon of Black preaching as prophetic oratory or shamanic storytelling is the fusion of African spirituality and biblical religion. Also, acknowledging that African Muslims brought to North America during the Middle Passage constituted as much as 20 percent of the resident population on large plantations changes the entire scheme. Whereas the Muslim influence did not survive as a vital religious force during Antebellum, its import remains a permanent part of our psychic legacy. This is perhaps why the "proto-Islamic" movements, as they are referenced by Lincoln and Mamiya, have had such phenomenal success during the twentieth century.

An interview with the Rev. Jesse Jackson appeared in the *Chicago Tribune* during March 1996. Here is one question he was asked: Why do you think Nation of Islam leader Louis Farrakhan's appeal is so strong in the Black community? The Rev. Jackson responded: Because Farrakhan addresses, in a very pointed way, the pain and alienation many Blacks feel. The context of his message is that one of every two Black children is born and bred in poverty and has no access to health care. We are born sicker, with less access to education and jobs. We die earlier. There are 200,000 more Blacks in American jails than four-year colleges. So he addresses that reality, and it is a reality that should be changed.[10]

In the words of the Last Poet, Abiodun Oyemole, that pain and alienation has resulted in "grenades in (our) eyes, death is (our) prize. Peace will arise, destroying the lies." Because the eyes are thought to be the windows of the soul, our rage is seen in our eyes as bombs waiting to explode. Farrakhan focuses his attention on that rage and seeks to transform it through faith, discipline, and self-respect. By doing so, he creates angst within certain sectors that identify his ministry as having the potential of mobilizing the existential rage of the community to extend a separatist agenda through armed conflict.

The harsh realities of the African American community direct Minister Farrakhan to establish a safe and sacred space for African Americans through the ethos of nationalism. He is regularly criticized for his methodology, but ethnic identity and separation are always central to nationalism, regardless of the group that employs a nationalistic approach. A critical concept that drives nationalism is segregation. Implicit is the sense that contact with otherness is overwhelmingly destructive.[11] Nationalism begins with self-acceptance, even if at the expense of another. Due to the oppression experienced by African Americans, the thrust of Black nationalism is to confront the issues of color prejudice and racial identity. In fact, it was "Malcolm X and the Nation (of Islam that) are credited with the primary ideological foundations that led to the development of the concepts of 'black power,' 'black pride,' and 'black consciousness' which stirred black youth and reverberated all through the civil rights movement of the period."[12] The ultimate concern is to transform the community from despair into an ancestral hope.[13] Following the tenets of nationalism, Farrakhan skillfully crafts his sermons.

THE SERMON ON THE MALL

Many proponents of the Million Man March have voiced that there must be a separation between the man and the March. Yet, how is it that 400,000 to 1.2 million African American men actually responded to the call of Minister Farrakhan by meeting on the Mall in Washington, D.C., on October 16, 1995? The common tactic has been to say that the significance of the event was more profound than the single voice of Minister Farrakhan calling to African American men across the nation. Farrakhan addressed the notion of separating him from the March in this way:

Brothers and sisters, there is no human being through whom God brings an idea that history doesn't marry the idea with that human being no matter what defect was in that human being's character. You can't separate Newton from the Law that Newton discovered. Nor can you separate Einstein from the theory of relativity. It would be silly to try to separate Moses from the Torah, or Jesus from the gospel, or Muhammad from the Quran. . . . (You are saying Farrakhan) you have a defect in your character. Well, that certainly may be so. However, . . . I have never heard any member of the faith of Judaism separate David from the Psalms because of what happened in David's life. And you never separated Solomon from the building of the Temple because he had a thousand concubines. And you never separated any of the great servants of God. So today, whether you like it or not, God brought the idea through me. And He didn't bring it through me because my heart was dark with hatred and anti-semitism. He didn't bring it through me because my heart was dark and I'm filled with hatred for white people and for the human family of the planet. If my heart was that dark, how is the message so bright, the message so clear, the response so magnificent?

However, if it is impossible to separate the voice of the man from the event, as it is with so many other like situations, then it must be concluded that the man and the marchers were engulfed within the sermonic space of "sacred time." The Mall was populated by those who had a strong sense of personal and communal crisis, a longing for spiritual renewal, and a desire for collective transformation. A mood was generated through intonation as much as word choice. On that day Washington became sacred space and the Mall became hallowed ground.

In classic Black sermonic analogy Farrakhan proclaimed, "I'm not telling you I'm a psychiatrist, but I do want to operate on your mind"; and "I come in the tradition of the doctor who has to point out with truth what's wrong." The clarion call of the day was 2 Chronicles 7:14: "If my people, which are called by my name, shall humble themselves, and pray, and seek my face, and turn from their wicked ways; then will I hear from heaven, and will forgive their sin, and will heal their land." Like a therapist, he called the kinship together to discuss concealed feelings and publicly make peace between brothers and sisters. He called, and we responded. Central African healers have a range of knowledge on matters such as familial lineages, the origin of villages, the relationships among clans, the roles and psychologies of each member of the community, along with past, present, and potential conflicts. These healers, therefore, work on three levels: ancestral tradition, familial relations, and cultural context.[14] Minister Farrakhan's Sermon on the Mall covered all these areas. Like a traditional healer, on that day he sought to heal, to transform, and to reconcile. He even included in his sermon an invitation to sit and talk with members of the Jewish community.

> Perhaps in the light of what we see today, maybe it's time to sit down and talk, not with any preconditions. You got pain, we got pain too. You hurt, we hurt too. The question is, if the dialogue is proper, then we might be able to end the pain, and ending the pain may be good for both of them, and ultimately good for the nation. We are not opposed to sitting down. And I guess if you can sit down with Arafat, where there is rivers of blood between you, why can't you sit down with us, and there's no blood between us? You don't make sense not to dialogue. It doesn't make sense.

FROM XODUS TO "XING" THE JORDAN

A sermon, as the preaching cure, is a liberative, transformative sound and word that establishes a sacred space, psycho-spiritual renewal, and a reconciled existence. Farrakhan referred to this through his hermeneutical identification with the biblical Exodus story. He interpreted that story as prefiguring the suffering and deliverance of the African American.

> Now the word *Exodus* means, departure, a going out, a way out. What did we come to Washington for? We didn't come to Washington to petition the government for a way out of here, to find a way out of our affliction, but a way out of something bigger than our affliction.

The liberative, transformative space that I am suggesting is created by the sermon has been identified by Garth Kasimu Baker-Fletcher as "XODUS SPACE"—a space named, owned, and maintained by the bold and persistent creativity of the Afrikan self. XODUS is the movement that carries a new sense of African American masculinity in honor of Malcolm X. "The 'X' in his name signifies the unknown, the lost the 'dis-remembered' past that may finally be claimed as an essential aspect of one's self."[15] In spite of the remembered animosity between Malcolm X and Louis X, Farrakhan's appeal is not totally independent of the El Hajj Malik El-Shabazz legacy.[16]

While the projected macho image was, perhaps, an organizational undercurrent of the March, macho was an image that the March tenaciously sought to transform. This could have been the case due to the attitude of *permanent separation*. Attitudes of separation have a way of growing to include new categories of "otherness." In this instance, women became an "other" to be separated from. While the call was for a temporary separation for the purpose of atoning, it points to a deeper ideological principle of inequality. Minister Farrakhan declared, "(I) called men. Why did (I) call men? Because in the beginning, God made man. And if we are at a new beginning, we got to make a man all over again, but make him in the image and likeness of God." The mission statement of the Million Man March called for men to be present on the Mall and called women to a Day of Absence.

> We call on those who do not come to Washington, especially, Black women, to mobilize and organize the community in support of the Million Man March and its goals. The Day of Absence is a parallel activity to the Million Man March and a component part of one joint and cooperative project: the standing up and assumption of a new and expanded responsibility by the Black man in particular and the Black community in general. Women are in the leadership of the Day of Absence without exclusion of men, as men are in the leadership of the Million Man March without exclusion of women. And both activities are equally essential.[17]

Although we can sometimes get in the way of what is good, the Spirit has a way of speaking through our weakness. The XODUS SPACE created on the Mall by the spirit of brotherhood and friendship was heightened by Farrakhan's sermonic XODUS calling. His persistent message is what Baker-Fletcher identifies as "the prophetic summons to leave the sinful Space of Euro-domination, and to wake up!"[18] The March was an XODUS moment witnessed by the entire planet. It was a moment when our false perceptions were cast from our yesterday, and we experienced a new hope for the Life of Promise. Introjected perceptions of ourselves have us cautiously distant and afraid of one another. Anytime we approach one another, even if only in passing, there is the conscious assessment to determine, not whether the person is dangerous, but to assess just how dangerous the other is. The XODUS SPACE of the March brought all who were present, and many who observed, to a new experiential consciousness. We experienced the psycho-spiritual liberation that only comes through an encounter with the Divine. Only on this day, it was clear that the Divine was experienced and revealed through affectionately engaging self and another. This occurred among those who rarely, if ever, affectionately engage anyone, least of all, women.

The Sermon on the Mall brought us, once again, to the river. We transcended our psychic pain from our legacy of "Xing" the Atlantic and our eyes were opened to new possibilities. We witnessed a miracle and now give testimony to the experience. We saw hands transformed into offering baskets as money was passed in all directions. We saw the group perceived to be the most violent on the planet courteously moving about where there was standing room only. We saw marchers connected, standing shoulder to shoulder for six to eight hours. We saw traditional African American solidarity among those who have been segregated by contemporary society; that is, Christians, Muslims, Hebrew Israelites, atheists, and agnostics all stood connected to one another. Our XODUS SPACE gave us a vision of the fulfillment we will experience by Xing the Jordan. Even now, we look back in wonder at October 16, 1995. My prayer is that we will march on.

Notes

[1] Joseph Mitsuo Kitagawa, *The Quest for Human Unity* (Minneapolis: Fortress Press, 1990), pp. 1-2.

[2] Drawing on the work of Albert Raboteau, Theophus Smith writes that there are traceable continuities of perspective between the historic West African and the contemporary African American. The two broad areas that provide the basis for such continuities are located within religious experience: beliefs and practices. "In this instance the beliefs concern spiritual beings, and the practices comprise magical and ritual performances. The first area (1) not only involves beliefs per se but includes of course communications and relationships with divine or divinized beings. Raboteau's catalogue of such beings comprises (a) a "High God" or "Supreme Being," alongside (b) a pantheon of lesser deities or secondary gods, and also (c) a world of spirits and (d) a cult of ancestors. The second area (2) constitutes a system of practices involving (a) magic so-called, which in Africa is intensively related to (b) medicine, and also involves (c) witchcraft and counterwitchcraft, and (d) divination. Integrating those practices and augmenting them are (e) ritual performances that incorporate such acts as drumming, singing, chanting, or 'incanting,' dancing, and—most conspicuously—spirit possession and ritual sacrifice" (Theophus Smith, *Conjuring Culture: Biblical Formations of Black America* [New York: Oxford University Press, 1994], pp. 36-37).

³ Robert Moore, "Space and Transformation in Human Experience," *Anthropology and the Study of Religion*, ed. Robert Moore and Frank Reynolds (Chicago: Center for the Scientific Study of Religion, 1984), pp. 126-43.

⁴ Bruce Jackson, "The Other Kind of Doctor: Conjure and Magic in Black American Folk Medicine," in *African American Religion*, ed. Timothy E. Fulop and Albert J. Raboteau (New York: Routledge, 1997), p. 420.

⁵ I use the term *conjure* in the same sense as Smith. "Conjure is fundamentally magic. It is first in consideration the magical folk tradition of black North Americans. Its practitioners have traditionally performed their craft in order to heal or harm others by the operation and invocation of extraordinary powers and processes. More concisely and comprehensively stated: conjure is a magical means of transforming reality. Here the term 'magic' is best understood as one system, among humanity's more primal cognitive systems, for mapping and managing the world in the form of signs. Rather than consider such phenomena merely irrational or marginal, to be relegated to the unintelligible realm of the supernatural or to the heterodox realm of the occult, I follow contemporary scholars who regard magic as a primordial and enduring system of communication—as a form of 'language.' But it is obviously not simply speech or expression. Rather, magic is ritual speech and action intended to perform what it expresses" (Smith, *Conjuring Culture*, p. 4).

⁶ Sterling Stuckey, *Slave Culture: Nationalist Theory and the Foundations of Black America* (New York: Oxford University Press, 1987), p. 14.

⁷ Smith, *Conjuring Culture*, pp. 162-63.

⁸ James H. Harris, *Preaching Liberation* (Minneapolis: Fortress Press, 1995), p. 3.

⁹ Ibid., p. 5.

¹⁰ Jerry Thomas, staff writer, "'On the Record' with Jesse Jackson," *Chicago Tribune* (Sunday, March 13, 1996), sec. 2, p. 3.

¹¹ C. Eric Lincoln, *The Black Muslims in America* (Trenton, N.J.: Africa World Press, 1994).

¹² C. Eric Lincoln and Lawrence H. Mamiya, *The Black Church in the African American Experience* (Durham, N.C.: Duke University Press, 1990), p. 389.

¹³ "Black nationalism is more than courage and rebellion; it is a way of life. It is an implicit rejection of the 'alien' white culture and an explicit rejection of the symbols of that culture, balanced by an exaggerated and undiluted pride in 'black' culture. It involves a drastic reappraisal not only of present realities but also of the past and future. Black nationalists revise history (or correct it, as they would say) to establish that today's blacks are descended from ancestors, from powerful and enlightened rulers and conquerors" (Lincoln, *The Black Muslims in America*, pp. 41-42).

¹⁴ David Augsburger, *Pastoral Counseling across Cultures* (Philadelphia: Westminster Press, 1986), p. 281.

¹⁵ Garth Kasimu Baker-Fletcher, *XODUS: An African American Male Journey* (Minneapolis: Fortress Press, 1996), p. 5.

¹⁶ "The attraction of Islamic movements to black males may be due to several reasons, among them the legacy of the militant and radical black nationalist Malcolm X has been a profound influence on these young men. As a culture hero, Malcolm X was seen as the uncompromising critic of American society. Another reason is that the Muslims project a more macho image among black men" (Lincoln and Mamiya, *The Black Church in the African American Experience*, p. 391).

¹⁷ Organizing Committee, *The Million Man March/Day of Absence: Mission Statement* (Chicago: Third World Press, 1995), p. 15.

¹⁸ Baker-Fletcher, *XODUS*, p. 6.

Chapter Ten

Keeping the Promises of the Million Man March

G. KASIMU BAKER-FLETCHER

In the increasingly insecure racial environment of North America, the Million Man March of October 16, 1995, has come to symbolize the ambivalence of our post–civil rights era. African American men came pouring into Washington, D.C., the seat of the imperial power known as the United States of America, by the hundreds of thousands in search of a vision of hope and a theme to hang our deferred dreams upon. Longing for unity, some 800,000 to a million and a half African American males made a powerful statement of our capacity to come together for a "Day of Absence" from our work places, our careers, but not from our families. There was no ambivalence in *that* message. Black men came neither because the Honorable Louis Farrakhan asked them to miss a day of work to demonstrate their support for his agenda nor to grant him the mantle of "Head Negro in Charge," as the mass media believed. Rather, African American males came because they wanted to affirm some sacred sign of life in the valley of the shadow of deadly misrepresentation known as the "land of the free and the home of the brave." More important, the March came to represent a way for Black men to make a very public Promise to ourselves, our families, our lovers, and the nation at large that we had arrived at the mature place of public self-critique. Yet making such a Promise, under the long-winded shadow of Minister Farrakhan's controversial rhetoric, revealed the deeply entrenched socio-political and economic disempowerment of men too harried to care about the convener of such an important event. For most, the Event, and getting there, became a kind of search for a "Holy Grail" of public spiritual responsibility—a search so deeply embedded in our psyches that even the most gifted orator could scarcely have articulated its meaning with words.

I want to examine the *Million Man March Pledge* taken by all of the brothers after the two-and-a-half-hour sermon delivered by Minister Louis Farrakhan. Standing by itself, it is an amazing document, because it lists nine pledges and one final prayer. There is a kind of mystical "secret" even to this arrangement foreshadowed in Farrakhan's strange introductory remarks, in which he elicited the numerological significance of the number "1" next to the number

"9." He noted that both the Jefferson and Lincoln Memorials are "19 feet high" but did not note that both were crafted by architects familiar with Masonic allusions to ancient Egyptian numerological "secrets." He hints at such when he noted the following:

> What is so deep about this number 19? Why are we standing on the Capitol steps today? That number 19! When you have a nine, you are womb that is pregnant. And when you have a one standing by that nine, it means that there's something secret that has to be unfolded.[1]

What an unusual statement to make about the Million Man March, its location, and the participants! Could it be that Farrakhan was prophetically suggesting that these men and women were literally standing in a place bursting with a meaning whose secrets were about to be revealed, as a woman is pregnant with a child soon to be born? While Farrakhan's long speech perhaps did more to *obscure* the meaning of atonement and why God had called so many to that Event, I think that the nine pledges and concluding vow to God might actually be the ongoing unfolding of meaning that the March represented. The March, to continue interpreting this numerological "secret," was the pregnancy Event of a new, and different kind of manhood, a foreshadowing of the birth of a responsible and public Black masculinity. If this is indeed what the *Million Man March Pledge* represents, then let us note whether the nine pledges suggest a comprehensive enough theological, ethical, and social transformation for genuine atonement to occur.

MAKING THE PROMISES

The first pledge notes that *"from this day forward I will strive to love my brother as I love myself."* The allusion to the Golden Rule, "Love thy neighbor as thyself," is overt, but narrowed and specified toward loving *my brother*. Why this narrowing? What is suggested? Brothers pledging to love fellow brothers was the spiritual tone of the Event. It was the unspoken "given" that was suggested by having a Million *Man* March—that African American men needed to come together in a massive way. Brothers pledging to love one another is a public commitment to caring for one another, supporting one another's needs, striving to reach out with compassion, and doing all this in order to affirm that mystical bond known as *love*. For a million men to say this pledge together in 1995 is to represent to the nation, and to ourselves, that all the terrible statistics about fifteen- to twenty-five-year-old Black male homicidal violence against each other must not be the final word spoken about Black males living in the 1990s USA. In a very real way, the first statement of a new and responsible African American manhood had to be the assertion of our ethical duty to love one another and ourselves. A duty is an obligation supported by a priori principles—whether theologically articulated, philosophically expostulated, or merely an unconscious *urging* bubbling out of the depths of our psyches.

Loving our brothers . . . which ones? Are *all brothers* included in this pledge? Who is included, and who is left out? Specifically, which brothers are deemed *worthy* of being included in this circle of ethical concern? Don Belton interviewed independent film maker Isaac Julien and poet Essex Hemphill in his book about Black masculinity. As creative gay men whose art represents and extends "the range of black gay men's identity,"[2] it is clear that Black gay men were clearly disturbed by what they perceived to be a "silencing of differences" that masks outright hatred for the gay "difference." In particular they noted that gay Black men would not be invited to speak at the March (the interview took place before the March), and that only "men who are considered safe" would be asked to address the gathering. This was offensive to Essex Hemphill, in particular, who noted that while the call for such a march was "historic," it would also be a demonstration of a pseudo-"unity." Instead, he cited bell hooks's call for *communion* rather than unity, because "the root meaning of communion suggests that our union is based on a willingness to communicate with one another."[3] Is such a criticism *fair?* It helps us focus on the co-mingling of social ideals of *unity* and the rhetoric of *love* that many Afrocentric leaders have used to silence and overtly condemn the "difference" that homosexuality poses. Molefi Asante, Haki Madhubuti, and Maulana Karenga—the great triumvirate of contemporary Afrocentrism—have all condemned homosexuality as inimical to what they have perceived to be "genuine" Afrikan-centeredness. Since Madhubuti and Karenga were featured speakers and organizers of the March, I believe that the fears of Black gay males about not being extended concrete ties of genuine love and respect are fair.

I spend a great deal of time with this first pledge because it forms a kind of microcosm of the other pledges, and because it reveals the ambivalence of inclusion and exclusion that marked the March from its inception. One cannot make such an unconditional call for love and be believed if one's track record and commentary has already excluded various brothers along the way. Farrakhan's name continues to be tied to the lethal and threatening rhetoric that heightened tensions between Malcolm X and the Nation of Islam just before his assassination, and rumors still abound about the extent of his direct involvement in that death. Was Malcolm X Farrakhan's brother? Farrakhan's rhetoric still excludes Ashkenazic Jews from the circle of so-called genuine Judaism and challenges Judaism in general. Since many Jews are also of African descent, are Black Jews included in the circle of the pledge's love? Such questions are not meant to negate the positive impact of Black men calling for love of each other and of ourselves, but rather to interrogate who our "brother" is according to Farrakhan and the March organizers. At the same time, one needs to affirm the distinct possibility that the message of other-love and self-love has transcendent wings fully capable of carrying it beyond the original (perhaps narrow) intentions of the original framers.

The second pledge promises *"to strive to improve myself spiritually, morally, mentally, socially, politically, and economically for the benefit of myself, my fam-*

ily, and my people." Striving to improve the self from the holistic point of view is a quest as ancient as the ancient Kemetic ethics preserved in the *Husia*; Karenga notes that in the "nine petitions" (again, that number!) in *The Book of the Moral Narrative* that living out the principles of *ma'at* (truth, justice, and righteousness) is "the foundation of both the natural and social order."[4] Striving to improve the self in all realms of activity has also been a part of African American Christian historical tradition—from Ida B. Wells-Barnett and the Club-Women (including Anna Julia Cooper) to Booker T. Washington. Striving to improve one's self implies that one recognizes room for improvement and growth. Part of atonement (something this essay will not spell out as elaborately as Minister Farrakhan did that day) is not only recognition of failure and taking responsibility to right wrongs, but also is the ongoing sense of moving toward a moral/spiritual, and in this case, material goal. This second pledge makes clear, as does the first, that the self and others are to be connected from the start, and that the improvement of self must be linked to the improvement of family and community.

The third pledge promises to *"strive to build businesses, build houses, build hospitals, build factories, and enter into international trade for the good of myself, my family, and my people."* Perhaps Minister Farrakhan is most respected in Black communities for his leadership on issues of economic and infrastructural renovation. Black folk admire the savvy and perspicacity of Black Muslims, selling their bean-pies, hawking the *Final Call*, opening and maintaining excellent restaurants, and so forth. Throughout the public ministry of the Nation of Islam (NOI) in our communities the rehabilitation of the most despised criminals, the most disenfranchised elements of our people, has been accomplished by turning self-destructive and predatorial behaviors into business professionalism. Predatory criminals have been transformed into *homo faber*—human beings the Makers. This pledge also suggests the third principle of the *Nguza Sabaa*, *ujima* (collective work and responsibility). It suggests that the task of *building* is one that must be done as a *collective work*. As a Christian I believe that we must also remind people that many (most) of the Black universities, as well as most of the new private schools and day-care centers in our communities, are church-sponsored and church-developed. African American churches need to revitalize our sense of helping folk build their lives, their work places, and their homes. Part of the restoration of our *Imago Dei* ("image of God") must be developing concrete programs to help channel our energies into building (re-building) our communities.

The fourth pledge begins a cycle of concrete promises aimed at taking responsibility for wrongful acts. It promises *"from this day forward I will never raise my hand with a knife or gun to beat, cut, or shoot any member of my family or any human being except in self-defense."* Islamic law shines forth here. This is not a blanket call for unconditional nonviolence but for a restraint of violence. It silently admonishes the Christian call to "love your enemies" while simultaneously condemning the rampant violence promoted by gangs in "da Streetz" (as Rappers say). But is it enough? Is it enough to restrain the viciousness of Uzi guns and the callous brutality of policemen who continue to gun down our sons at an alarming rate? There is room here for reasoned and passionate debate about doctrines of unconditional love in relationship to dogmas of self-defense. What is their proper relationship? Perhaps such a pledge demands a new dialectic, one which balances the Christian challenge to "rise" to love unconditionally with the Islamic demand for the reasonableness of self-defense. While such a dialectic cannot be worked out in this writing, both sides could agree (from taking this pledge) that casual and lethal harm of another human being violates ethical standards, period. The clause "except in self-defense" is an exception, not the rule.

The fifth pledge makes the promise that *"from this day forward I will never abuse my wife by striking her or disrespecting her, for she is the mother of my children and the producer of my future."* This is an amazing public confession of wife-abuse which Black men voiced on the steps of the Capitol. Never in the history of the United States have Black men as a group publicly admitted in front of other groups—particularly in the media presence of European Americans(!)—that we have been abusive to the women in our lives. It is a limited call, however, and in its limitation invites a terrible criticism, which I am compelled to address. It addresses "wives," and not "women" in general. It does not address lovers, girlfriends, or dates—all very real relationships that are open to abusive treatment by males toward females. It narrows the ethical concern to a "wife," and then *defines* her in the very traditional way as "mother" and therefore as "producer of my future." There is a terrifying self-orientation in this construction that disturbs and offends even as it also initiates public discussion about wife-abuse. For me, the restricted "liberation" of this pledge reveals a traditional and conservative attitude—stemming from both ortho-dox Christianity and Islam—concerning which women are to be honored. Wives are to be honored because they *belong* to a fellow Muslim or Christian male. Other women, not immediately "under" a man, are not addressed, and thereby are rendered invisible. What happens to such women? I fear that they remain outside of the circle of newly redemptive behavior because of their invisibility. This pledge reveals for me the great work necessary in Black theol-ogy and various liberation philosophies to begin addressing such issues of male attitudes and behaviors toward all women. My own work in *XODUS* is an initial step in that direction, but it is by no means the last word on this issue!

The sixth pledge addresses sexual perversion—incest and pedophilia— say-ing, *"from this day forward I will never engage in the abuse of children, little boys or little girls, for sexual gratification; I will let them grow in peace to be strong men and women for the future of our people."* When I heard this pledge I was stunned because it deepens the scope of issues publicly confessed as Black male irresponsibility. Perhaps Alice Walker smiled, for she brought this issue to our national attention in *The Color Purple* years ago and was vilified royally by the so-called righteous protectors of Black maledom like Ishmael Reed. Now we have "committed" the "unpardonable sin" of "airing our dirty laundry"—just like Sister Alice Walker did over ten years ago! Is it "okay" for us to do it now because we are doing it together, a million strong, and "taking responsibility for it?" Or should we question why Alice Walker and other vilified Black female artists who have spoken/written/sung/drawn about this issue were not even publicly thanked for bringing this painful issue to the forefront? Whenever we confess our sins we ought to give thanks for those who helped us recognize that we were sinning in the first place. Such patterns of perversion must be broken in order for the shattered social fabric to be restored through prayer and counseling.

The seventh pledge addresses the issue of disrespect of women, promising to *"never again use the 'B' word to describe any female, but particularly, my own Black sister."* Decrying derogatory language against women is an important step toward confronting male disrespect of women, because language houses the active intent, thought, and meaning resident in the speaker. To speak in an insulting fashion about women reveals a hidden hatred and lack of human regard for women. Black men have an ambiguous relationship to derogation of women, represented most forcefully in the Rap lyrics of the late, great Tupac Shakur. Tupac's language about women ranged from the emotionally uplifting and poignant paean to his mother (and all single mothers in general), "Dear Mama," to a wide range of insulting casual references to women as sexual objects, sexual predators, and money-grubbers. Without using *his* words, it is very clear that this pledge addresses the Tupac-type of brother who can uplift and express genuine respect for his mother in one moment, while in the next let loose a tirade of hurtful and disrespectful rhetoric against all (other) women. Again, this extension of the notion of a woman being *owned*, of *belonging* to a man, is not really addressed in this pledge. "My own Black sister" sounds like a congenial form of taking responsibility for an Afrikan woman, except that it also suggests a notion of ownership masquerading as *belonging*. Black women and men need to have a public discussion about the boundaries of belonging for each other. Is *belonging* best understood as "belonging," in which we exist, we "be," in a relationship of desire, eros, longing for each other? Or is belonging a legalized form of being somebody's property? I believe that we ought to affirm the former even as we work to undo the hegemony of the latter.

The eighth pledge promises *"from this day forward that I will not poison my body with drugs or that which is destructive to my health and my well-being."* This pledge extends the promise of "no harm" developed in previous pledges to the physical body. Black bodies, male and female, have been the sites of casual violence and exploitation since we arrived in the hulls of slaveships. As the chattel or property of other human beings, we learned to look at our own bodies as instruments to be used. An instrumentalized view of the body exacts a heavy price in psychic pain. Valuing our lives, we withstood the whips and chains in order to preserve enough life-force to pass on our hopes and dreams of a future day of freedom. Now, over a hundred years after being legally freed, the patterns of exploitation ingrained over the centuries have locked many out of the so-called mainstream of opportunity and economic access. Without reflection, in desperation, many of us have turned to the escape of drug-induced fantasies, poisoning our bodies and corroding our ability to get help for ourselves. Yet drug addiction cannot be broken until the addicted come to the place of recognizing their addiction. Personal responsibility for addictive patterns is incumbent for the process of atonement to take place. This is why this particular promise is so moving and silently requires our prayerful support.

The ninth pledge fulfills the *Nguza Sabaa*'s fourth principle, *ujamaa* (co-operative economics) by stating *"from this day forward I will support Black newspapers, Black radio, Black television. I will support Black artists who clean up their act to show respect for themselves and respect for their people and respect for the heirs of the human family."* Here is a challenge to the African American community to become more attentive to, aware of, and consciously intent upon supporting Black-owned and Black-run businesses. Yet it is also a challenge to Black artists (read in particular *Rap Artists*) whose lyrics, videos, and music often express a message of self-denigration, disrespect of Black people, and an overall disregard for humanity. Certain examples of gangsta rap certainly qualify for such charges, as memories of a certain Eazy-E song, which said, in effect, "Can't trust niggaz, niggaz ain't sh_t, Don't listen to me, I don't give a f_ _ k!" Such lyrics bespeak a pointless, harmful, and ultimately self-destructive nihilism. However, the pledge leaves the door open for supporting various other Rap artists, like Salt-N-Pepa (whose music often uplifts the dignity of women, "Sistahs doin' it for ourselves!") or soul/Hip-hop songsters like Boyz-to-Men, and so forth. What it calls for is cooperative support for community-run and community-responsible artists and businesses.

The "1" standing next to the "9" is a vow: will do all this, so help me God." We take vows on special events, the most common being that of marriage. What is subtly suggested here is that this event has the sacramental significance of a marriage, but what or who is being married? The full significance escapes easy definition, but perhaps the marriage is that of ourselves with our families and communities. Perhaps an even more apt analogy would be that of a recommitment of vows service of a couple who have been married for many years. By taking responsibility for our sins and participating in a public ritual of confession, perhaps African American males were retaking our birthright-vows to the community of our origin. Such a vow unfolds a mystery of relationship deeper than the pain, stronger than our faults, and more lasting than our individual weaknesses. The critical question would be whether the public confession of such heinous crimes as incest, domestic abuse, and pedophilia requires recommitment, or therapy![5]

KEEPING THE PROMISES

Sentiments about whether the Promises have been kept or not depends on who one asks. Womanist scholar Geneva Smitherman has written about the fact that there was an immediate and noticeable dampening of violence in Detroit. She rejoiced in the enlivened spirits of the men who returned to her hometown and noted how in Atlanta Thomas J. Miller "turned over management of his company to his wife" in order to become a full-time volunteer for the Southern Christian Leadership Conference.[6] Ben Chavis, speaking one year later in an interview with Bryant Gumbel of *The Today Show* (October 16, 1996), proudly declared that gang violence was "down significantly" but did not cite any figures.

Later that same day on CNN, Minister Farrakhan noted the same thing, emphasizing that long-term projects have been reinvigorated. In Los Angeles large churches, such as First A.M.E., noted that the men who came back from the March had a "fire," that they "literally shone with a new aura of commitment," which has translated into greater participation in the various community-uplift projects that have made F.A.M.E. a genuinely "famous" church.[7] So it can be said without a doubt that, at least on small, local levels, the March provided a potent impetus to go back home and get involved.

On the other hand, many committed men and women in the community have been critical of the March's lack of a clear political agenda, failure to capitalize on the overt political momentum generated, and unclear signals sent from the symbolic leader, Minister Farrakhan. In particular, Farrakhan remains an enigmatic presence, confusing friend and foe with an extended international tour in the summer of 1996 that included photo-ops hugging Moammar Khaddafy and embracing Saddam Hussein. Farrakhan's rationalization included an appeal for autonomy based on his status as the leader of a religious movement, the Nation, but many of us (myself included) wonder at both his wisdom and his timing. No other human being in the history of the United States of America—not even Dr. Martin Luther King Jr.— has brought a million people to the steps of power in our country. Why Farrakhan has walked away from taking responsible steps to ensure the permanent import of this socio-political Event eludes analysis or understanding. Some have speculated that perhaps he did not have an agenda beyond demonstrating that he had such power. Such a demonstration, without follow-up, implies an unbridled egoism that runs counter to the community-orientation of the Norms uplifted in the *Pledge*. Farrakhan's enigmatic, fiery rhetoric continues to amaze, perplex, and astound even those of us who want to give him the benefit of the doubt. Time will tell . . .

In the meantime I want to suggest that the Promises of the Million Man March require a yearly Ritual Enactment in order to remain meaningful to the liberation of our community, particularly its males. Black Churches could easily incorporate the *Pledge* into the various men's groups that have sprung up in the last five years.

These Promises would also be read in the mosques and temples of other faiths, binding the African American male liberation movement to an ecumenical, interfaith spirit completely foreign to the heavy Christocentrism of the predominantly white, Promise-Keepers. The Million Man March needs to become a Million Man Movement, overtly, without apology. There is enough creativity and fire in the hearts of brothers still inspired by that magnificent October day in 1995 to ignite something more permanent than a one-time Event. Finding ways to reenact, recite, or even *create* a Ritual that ensconces the *Pledge* into our religious life would be one sure way in which the March could both remain meaningful as a memory and begin to develop meaning as a ritual. Is such a suggestion risky? Only if we are afraid that God (or Allah) has already and *only* "spoken" in times past, and that any revelatory call from the Divine must not be controversial! If Farrakhan is a problem for many churches as the "prophet" of this occasion, we need to remember how Isaiah shocked his listeners by insisting that the king of Babylon, Cyrus, was "God's anointed" to bring about the liberation of captives. Perhaps God has chosen this "unlikely one" as a way of awakening the sleeping Christian churches!

Finally, like the wise rabbis after the great Destruction of the Second Temple in the first century of our common era, I see the deepest "promise" suggested by the Million Man March as a kind of *decentering strategy of home sacredness.* Such a strategy, like the celebration of *Shabbat* every Friday night in the homes of practicing Jews, implies that keeping the spiritual fires "lit" in our lives must be done in our individual homes. The March may yet be enshrined as that first moment of awakening, inspired by the cleansing initiation of a massive act of repentance. As such, the March could be remembered as that *kairotic moment* when we, as brothers, created a massive XODUS SPACE,[8] escaped the psycho-cultural, economic, and spiritual "captivity" of AmeriKKKa, and then took that Awakening back to our homes, our wives, our sisters, our brothers, and our children. In the privacy of our homes we have been given the challenge of creating liberating, sacred "SPACE."

Farrakhan's hint about the Million Man March being a *pregnant moment* is essentially correct, but now it is time to help a newly born massive African American male movement take shape. We must incarnate the promises of the March by creating XODUS SPACE. Such SPACE is holy because in it we recognize God's preeminence, favor, and presence. Such a SPACE is sacred because we remember that our very bodies are "the Lord's temple" and that we are to keep ourselves purified from poisons, chemical and spiritual. Such a SPACE is healing because we can create a "communion" (as bell hooks says) of love, difference, and acceptance. Such a SPACE, for me, will have to include all kinds of differences *within our community*, as well as acceptance of the wondrous differences that make us all God's children living on one Earth. Such a SPACE goes beyond the event of the March because it calls the Cosmos to bear witness to our responsible cries for compassion, justice, and caring—for ourselves, our community, and the very dust underneath our feet. As Children of both Dust and Spirit[9] we are also God's children, by whatever Name we call the Divine. Such a SPACE is indeed WHOLLY HOLY . . . separate from the profane separativeness, hierarchies, and exploitative practices which contaminate spirits, bodies, water, earth, and air with pollution. And yet this WHOLLY HOLY XODUS SPACE is also a *habitus,* a place to live in . . . comfortably. With head, hands, heart, and uplifted voices we can "sing a new song" to God, and create a New Day.

Notes

[1] Louis Farrakhan, "Day of Atonement," in *Million Man March/Day of Absence: A Commemorative Anthology*, ed. Haki R. Madhubuti and Maulana Karenga (Chicago: Third World Press/Los Angeles: University of Sankore Press, 1996), p. 10.

[2] Don Belton, "Where We Live: A Conversation with Essex Hemphill and Isaac Julien," in *Speak My Name: Black Men on Masculinity and the American Dream*, ed. Don Belton (Boston: Beacon Press, 1995), p. 209.

[3] Ibid., p. 213.

[4] Maulana Karenga, *Selections from The Husia: Sacred Wisdom of Ancient Egypt* (Los Angeles: University of Sankore Press, 1984), p. 29.

[5] All quotations from *The Million Man March Pledge* are taken from Madhubuti and Karenga, *Million Man March/Day of Absence*, p. 29.

[6] Geneva Smitherman, "A Womanist Looks at the Million Man March," in Madhubuti and Karenga, *Million Man March/Day of Absence*, p. 106.

[7] Conversation with Jane Galloway and Rev. Mark Whitlock of F.A.M.E.'s Renaissance program, November 1996.

[8] This expression, as well as other following expressions, flow from my work in *XODUS: An African American Male Journey* (Minneapolis: Fortress Press, 1996). The object of such rhetoric is literally to open up a rhetorical SPACE wide enough to provide genuine liberation for African American women and men—together, as a community.

[9] An allusion to Karen Baker-Fletcher's original naming of human beingness as connected to both the "dust" of Earth and the sacrality of God's "Spirit" in our co-authored book, *My Sister My Brother: Womanist and Xodus God-Talk* (Maryknoll, N.Y.: Orbis Books, 1997).

Themes of Exile and Empowerment in the Million Man March

CHERYL J. SANDERS

To begin I must express my appreciation to both Lee Butler and G. Kasimu Baker-Fletcher for their thoughtful analyses of the Million Man March as a popular religious movement. My aim is to share some of my own reactions and questions with reference to their reflections and to explore further the spiritual and ethical meaning of the Million Man March in light of two emergent themes in my own work as a Christian ethicist, exile and empowerment.

THE SERMON ON THE MALL: LOUIS FARRAKHAN, PREACHER

Dr. Butler's psycho-theological analysis of the Million Man March, and of the Sermon on the Mall in particular, is both provocative and wide-ranging. His major concern is to assess Minister Louis Farrakhan as a preacher. In my view, Minister Farrakhan's preaching cadence is very traditional. I have had occasion to tune in to his radio broadcast, only to struggle for a few minutes to identify his voice because in my hearing his preaching delivery is virtually indistinguishable from many other black religious broadcasters I have heard. On the radio, I can only discern Farrakhan by paying careful attention to his distinctive biblical interpretation and social-political analyses. Indeed, the notion of call-and-response is one of the key paradigms imposed upon the preaching event in the black context, one that brings great clarity to our understanding of why the Million Man March happened.

I am a bit confused by the proliferation of roles and images ascribed to Farrakhan in Dr. Butler's estimation—shaman, *griot*, intellectual, preacher, black nationalist, healer. From a strictly functional point of view, it would seem more helpful to devote greater attention to describing Farrakhan's effectiveness as healer, prophet, and reconciler.

I am intrigued especially by the suggestion that an ethos of nationalism shaped Farrakhan's message. My thought goes to Peter Paris's observation in *The Social Teaching of the Black Churches*:

A national dilemma reveals itself in the dual loyalties that black Americans have to the nation, on the one hand, and to the race, on the other—
conflicting loyalties because blacks have always felt a moral obligation to
both the nation and the race in spite of the moral conflicts between
them. . . . The major moral problem this dilemma has presented to black
Americans is that their respective loyalty to either race or nation implies
a lack of loyalty to the other.[1]

In my recollection, Farrakhan's sermon was informed at least as much by an
ethos of participation as an ethos of nationalism, as much by the principle of *e
pluribus unum* as by the tenets of "Nation Time." Why else would one choose
the nation's capital, at the site of America's most cherished monuments, to
assemble a million men to hear a manifesto of black nationalism?

Dr. Butler claims that Washington became "sacred space," and the Mall
became "hallowed ground." If this is true, was this sanctification effected by
Farrakhan's oratory alone or by the impressive appearance of a cloud of witnesses? Does the river to which these black men came bear any resemblance to
the Potomac River? If we have indeed witnessed a miracle of black male solidarity, of men giving testimony in XODUS SPACE, what further definition
can be given to the vision of fulfillment experienced by men "Xing the Jordan"?

PLEDGES AND RITUALS IN XODUS SPACE

Dr. Baker-Fletcher's critical evaluation of each aspect of the Pledge is instruc-
tive and insightful. As an ethicist, I have great interest in his effort to link the
Million Man Pledge to the principles of *Nguza Sabaa* associated with the
celebration of Kwanzaa. While I agree with much of what he has said, my own
interpretation of the reference to wives, and the implicit marginalization of
dates and girlfriends, would differ significantly from his. I would ascribe positive moral value to the affirmation of covenants of marriage and family as an
implicit frame of reference for the renunciation of abuse. I would support Dr.
Baker-Fletcher's call for a transition from March to Movement, but the ongoing value of an annual ritual enactment of the Pledge is not at all self-evident.

Dr. Baker-Fletcher's borrowing of the "decentering strategy of home sacredness" from the rabbinic wisdom tradition toward the end of establishing
"WHOLLY HOLY XODUS SPACE" raises some concerns in my thinking. If
America's most visible public square was ritually transformed into holy ground
during the March, is not this the same feat that Martin Luther King Jr. performed when he preached to 250,000 during the 1963 March on Washington for civil rights, and years before when Marian Anderson sang on the steps
of the Lincoln Memorial because she was denied access to the stage of Consti-
tution Hall by the Daughters of the American Revolution? I wonder if in this
case the ritual transformation actually works the other way around, that is,
that a million men brought to the Mall a transforming sense of the sacred they

had already cultivated in communion with God and with women and children in their own homes. I want to allow that at least some of them brought a prior experience of the sacred to the event; otherwise, they probably would not have come.

In an effort to enshrine this event into a ritual First Moment of Awakening, to memorialize this escape from "the psycho-cultural, economic, and spiritual 'captivity' of AmeriKKKa," the million men would be ill-advised to disregard the power and prominence of pre-existing spaces in our culture—family, church, and so forth—which offer a "habitus" and refuge from the assaults of a racist society.

EXODUS OR EXILE?

In my book *Saints in Exile* I have set forth my own rationale for promoting exile rather than exodus as a more fruitful and engaging theme for black ethical reflection. There I offer exile as a category of meaning for the interpretation of ethics and worship in African American religion and culture because it enables a more precise focus upon intragroup identity and ethics than the Exodus paradigm of black liberation theology affords by its analysis of victimization and suffering. Liberation theology emphasizes the moral obligation of the oppressor to set the oppressed free. An "exilic" theology would equally obligate the entire community of faith, inclusive of exiles and elites, to offer authentic liturgies of welcome and memory that enable the experience of liberation as homecoming.[2]

Exile functions alternately as a descriptive and normative concept. It is descriptive of the experience of African American people under the conditions of oppression and alienation. The "saints in exile" are religious communities of African Americans, inclusive of both Christians and Muslims, upon whom alien status is imposed on account of their race, culture, class, and, in some cases, their sex. The normative meaning of exile is most fully revealed in the expressions of personal and social ethics that come to light in the worship practices of black devotees who have further exiled themselves in significant ways by virtue of their strict codes of morality and by their peculiar liturgies of song, speech, and dance.

African Americans in the twentieth century have responded to the experience of exile and alienation in America by expressing their longing for some place or space—geographical, cultural, spiritual—where they can feel at home. To make oneself "at home" is not the same thing as being "liberated," especially if one's liberation has been effected by the initiative and action of one's oppressors. In my view, the gathering of one million black men on the Mall was an example of exilic ritual; that is, exiles making themselves at home in the sacred space demarcated by America's national monuments to New World manifestations of the political and cultural imperialism of Western civilization.

Regarding pledges, men seem more oriented to making pledges than women. Both Promise Keepers and Million Man March have invited men to make pledges to God and family—Promise Keepers publishes theirs on a wallet-sized card. I believe this pledge-orientation is related to the preoccupation some men have with roles. "What is my role?" they ask. Perhaps we are all familiar with the anxieties men have expressed in response to the rise of feminism because of the changing roles and expectations dictated by the liberation of women. But where is the program, the structure, the organization, that will guide these pledgees toward fulfillment of what they have promised?

A TESTAMENT OF INSTITUTIONAL EMPOWERMENT

Because I teach at a predominantly black university, I readily associate pledging with fraternities. While black fraternal organizations may have a spiritual and social element, as secret societies they have limited public visibility beyond the "step show." Mary McLeod Bethune, founder and president of Bethune-Cookman College, published a statement which was broadly circulated in *Ebony* magazine shortly before her death in 1955. "Last Will and Testament," a document of ethical teachings drawn from a lifetime of building educational institutions and women's coalitions, exemplifies an important alternative to the language of pledging:

> I LEAVE YOU LOVE. . . . Our aim must be to create a world of fellowship and justice where no man's color or religion is held against him.
> I LEAVE YOU HOPE. Yesterday, our ancestors endured the degradation of slavery, yet they retained their dignity. Today, we direct our economic and political strength toward winning a more abundant and secure life. Tomorrow, a new Negro, unhindered by race taboos and shackles, will benefit from this striving and struggling.
> I LEAVE YOU A THIRST FOR EDUCATION. More and more, Negroes are taking full advantage of hard-won opportunities for learning, and the educational level of the Negro population is at its highest point in history.
> I LEAVE YOU FAITH. . . . The measure of our progress as a race is in precise relation to the depth of our faith in our people held by our leaders.
> I LEAVE YOU RACIAL DIGNITY. . . . We, as Negroes, must recognize that we are the custodians as well as the heirs of a great civilization.
> I LEAVE YOU A DESIRE TO LIVE HARMONIOUSLY WITH YOUR FELLOW MEN. The problem of color is world wide, on every continent. I appeal to all to recognize their common problems, and unite to solve them.
> I LEAVE YOU FINALLY A RESPONSIBILITY TO OUR YOUNG PEOPLE. . . . We have a powerful potential in our youth, and we must have the courage to change old ideas and practices so that we may direct their power toward good ends.[3]

Bethune's exhortation to universal love, appreciation of the hope and dignity of struggle, view of education as a means of achieving personal ambition, insistence upon a positive sense of black identity and historical awareness, global consciousness of the reality of racism, and optimism with regard to the next generation, all testify of the engagement of black women in the pursuit of justice for all people.[4] Because Bethune was also a leader in the Black Women's Club Movement, her social ethics embodied a vital connection between academy and community. Her thought is documented in recent studies of the Black Women's Club Movement and of the role such organizations have played in "uplifting the race."[5]

IS THERE A PROGRAM IN THE HOUSE?

Thus far in our discussion of the Million Man March as a popular religious men's movement, we have lifted up the preacher and the pledge, but my question is, where is the program? In order to preach good news to the poor, the Christian churches must have in place a program of redemption that will guide men from their day of atonement toward a lifetime of purposeful achievement. If we challenge men to pledge new allegiances to family and community, we must also construct contexts that encourage them to honor these commitments. Moreover, it is somewhat disturbing to recall that although a massive offering was collected on the Mall from the million men, it is not clear that the organizers followed through on financial pledges made to the city of Washington and to further the cause of black economic empowerment.

In *Empowerment Ethics for a Liberated People* I coined the term *remoralization* to prescribe the process whereby demoralized people, and especially black men, can be empowered and redeemed.[6] In Webster's dictionary, *demoralize* has three meanings:

> 1. to corrupt the morals of: *The drug habit demoralizes its victims.* 2. To weaken the spirit, courage, discipline or staying power of; as hunger and cold *demoralized* the army. 3. to confuse or disorder mentally; as, the examiner's questions *demoralized* the applicant.[7]

Remoralization is my word for the process by which African American men and women can reverse the consequences and effects of *demoralization*. *Remoralize* means:

> 1. to restore to a morally sound condition: *The prayer habit remoralizes those who embrace it.* 2. to strengthen the spirit, courage, discipline, and staying power of: *Love and acceptance remoralized the men in the single fathers' support group.* 3. to enable creative problem-solving through restoration of mental clarity and order: *The adult mentor's close supervision remoralized the adolescent.*

Remoralization represents an approach to formulating a collective response to the alienated and self-destructive state of the disinherited African American male, that is, of those demoralized by poverty, its environment, and its effects. In order to be effective, the proposed remoralization process has to have an evangelistic strategy and a "lost-found" paradigm based upon a tandem principle of personal and social transformation. The challenge is to identify and nurture a new generation of morally empowered African American male leaders who can demonstrate to others that power is available to restore African American males to a morally sound condition; to strengthen them in spirit, courage, discipline, and staying power; to enable them to solve their problems through restoration of mental clarity; and to bring order to the chaos of their lives.

In my opinion, one of the most compelling examples of remoralized manhood for African Americans is the late Muslim leader El-Hajj Malik El-Shabazz (Malcolm X). He is remembered as a man who made a dramatic transition from a life of poverty and crime to become a great moral, religious, and cultural leader. Several aspects of Shabazz's leadership style and approach illustrate the remoralizing task, not least of which was his own testimony of personal transformation from a demoralized state under the power of religious faith within a structured religious community.[8] Moreover, it is with the strategy that Christians would call evangelism that Shabazz ministered to the disinherited—clearly, he was trying to save the souls, bodies, and spirits of an entire people. The Million Man March pointedly challenges the black Christian churches to develop paradigms that emphasize testimony, outreach, and spiritual nurture rather than speeches, marches, and political rhetoric, and to establish meaningful dialogue with other religious groups engaged in a common quest for community.

Dr. Butler quotes a text from the gospel of Matthew that implies that crowds of people crossed the Jordan in order to hear Jesus (Mt 4:25). Can it be that Farrakhan's prophetic call and proclamation effectively positioned a million black men for a mountaintop experience of ethical teaching and moral transformation at the feet of Jesus? If so, then the misguided opportunism of some black evangelical Christian preachers who denounced Farrakhan as the Anti-Christ and openly condemned the March and its participants may have resulted in missed opportunity, so that those best positioned to synchronize the most compelling claims of the gospel of Jesus Christ with an unprecedented mass spiritual pilgrimage of African American males effectively stymied themselves. Jesus concluded the Sermon on the Mount with a parable about hearing *vs.* doing the word of God, using the vivid imagery of construction (Mt 7:24-27). The wise man built his house upon a rock—we must realize that construction is seldom a solitary task. Proverbs 14:1 makes a similar declaration with reference to women: "Every woman buildeth her house: but the foolish plucketh it down with her hands." The Bible provides a foundation for planning and creating structures that will house men, women, and children as we journey together toward spiritual wholeness and fulfillment. In the absence of social structures established upon a bedrock of truthful proclamation, our preaching is so much huffing and puffing of wolves against hapless pigs. But in the fairy tale, even a pig had the wisdom to build his house with materials of sufficient strength to withstand the assault of hot air.

NETWORKING AND ORGANIZING

What organizational alternatives exist for implementation of a program that can sustain a Million Man Movement called into existence by preaching and pledging? I see several: (1) the original coalition that sponsored the March and collected the funds; (2) civil-rights organizations; (3) black fraternities; (4) black churches and denominations; (5) something new. I cast my vote for something new.

Farrakhan strongly urged the million men to join and to support a black organization of their own choosing, sound advice which should make a difference. However, if the preached word and the pledged word are to find meaningful fulfillment in our time, then someone has to develop and implement a new program that includes a strategy for long-term mobilization of human and financial resources. I cannot now foresee who among us has the integrity, credibility, and visibility to pull it off. I do not see the solution forthcoming from the program of racial reconciliation being pursued by Promise Keepers, but instead from the networking of men and women in a life-transforming witness of spiritual power and provision. One alternative would be for the organizers of the Million Man March to join forces with the National Council of Negro Women (NCNW). The NCNW convenes the Black Family Reunion each year on the Mall in Washington, not as a protest event but as a festival; it uses corporate sponsorships to provide information, entertainment, and cultural enrichment for black families. Perhaps the men could bring a prophetic and ritual element to the Reunion that would serve the purpose of enhancing the spiritual and cultural meaning of this event, particularly for the benefit of black children who are present. Another idea is for black men's organizations to join forces with Marian Wright Edelman and the Children's Defense Fund to support and participate in their annual Stand for Children, a political event convened also on the Mall in Washington.

In conclusion, it is my prayer that more black men like Lee Butler and Kasimu Baker-Fletcher with compelling vision and perspective regarding the plight of our community will have freedom to build collaborative relationships with others who are poised to follow up preaching and pledging with viable programs for action.

Notes

[1] Peter J. Paris, *The Social Teaching of the Black Churches* (Philadelphia: Fortress Press, 1985), p. 29.

[2] Cheryl J. Sanders, *Saints in Exile* (New York: Oxford University Press, 1996), p. 143.

[3] Mary McLeod Bethune, "My Last Will and Testament," quoted in Cheryl J. Sanders, *Empowerment Ethics for a Liberated People* (Minneapolis: Fortress Press, 1995), pp. 52-53.

[4] Sanders, *Empowerment Ethics for a Liberated People*, p. 53.

[5] On the Black Women's Club Movement, see Karen Baker-Fletcher, *A Singing Something: Womanist Reflections on Anna Julia Cooper* (New York: Crossroad, 1994);

Paula Giddings, *When and Where I Enter* (New York: Bantam Books, 1984); Evelyn Brooks Higginbotham, *Righteous Discontent: The Women's Movement in the Black Baptist Church, 1880-1920* (Cambridge: Harvard University Press, 1993); Marcia Y. Riggs, *Awake, Arise and Act: A Womanist Call for Black Liberation* (Cleveland: Pilgrim Press, 1994); Sanders, *Empowerment Ethics for a Liberated People*; Emilie M. Townes, *In a Blaze of Glory: Womanist Spirituality as Social Witness* (Nashville: Abingdon Press, 1995); and Theodore Walker Jr., *Empower the People* (Maryknoll, N.Y.: Orbis Books, 1991).

[6] Sanders, *Empowerment Ethics for a Liberated People*, pp. 104-13.

[7] From *Webster's New Universal Unabridged Dictionary*, 2d ed. (Dorset & Baber, 1983).

[8] See Malcolm X with Alex Haley, *The Autobiography of Malcolm X* (New York: Ballantine Books, 1964).

Chapter Twelve

GOD's Message, GOD's Call

Reflections on the Million Man March

IVORY L. LYONS JR.

I was not physically present at the Million Man March. However, spiritually I sensed that this was what was needed for Black men and women everywhere. The March made concrete for me God's presence and call even in the midst of troubling times. The presence of God enables us to endure the most difficult of circumstances, and God's call fills us with a sense of worthiness that is inescapable. The sense of urgency that led up to the March was evident in many facets of the African American community. Churches, mosques, temples, businesses, schools, and institutions were affected not just by the mass exodus of Black men but by the spiritual relocation of those who attended and those who wanted to be there.

As an ordained evangelical Black Baptist preacher, I am concerned about the spiritual message African Americans receive daily. I believe that Black men and women are deeply spiritual by nature. Spiritual messages have profound influences on our lives. These messages can be either positive or negative. Those spiritual messages we receive which question our humanity and our worth before God are negative and, unfortunately, bombard us daily. Messages which say that the only way to salvation is one particular way, messages that put down as "ungodly" the value of the voices of women, and messages that indicate anyone who has a different religion is damned to hell, inflict wounds that are difficult to treat and sometimes almost impossible to heal. These messages insinuate that because Black people are not the "chosen few" we somehow matter less in the sight of God, and that unless we accept another way of thinking as the right way of thinking we are not going to heaven. Furthermore, these messages say that even if we "believe" the right thing we still have to earn the right to be part of the chosen group. However, the hope the March brought about is the kind of positive message that we needed.

The message from the March hit a spiritual core lacking in many Black evangelical churches. The message from the March implied that the spirituality of Black men is important to God and that the spirituality of Black men has no denominational face. I know of at least one man who abstained from sexual relations prior to the March. I know of other men who looked at this like the season of Lent and also abstained from other activities. Despite popular belief, the March demonstrated that Black men can discipline themselves for the right reason. I think that this is what is feared about the March.

The spiritual implications for the March are vast and luminous and can be likened to what happened early in the Christian movement. Jews were oppressed like African Americans today. They too were deeply spiritual. However, many of their religious leaders thought that most of the Jews were outside the pale of God's love. Their lifestyle, so many religious leaders thought, was not only shoddy but reprehensible and an affront to all that is Holy. However, God still wanted to redeem the Jews. God still wanted the Jews to return to God, despite the persecution from within and without the community. God continued to send prophets, and finally God sent John the Baptist, the immediate forerunner of Jesus. John preached a message of the coming of God. He preached a message that was disconcerting to the religious aristocracy, because he preached a message of repentance. Many of them, smug in their attitude, did not think that they had anything from which to repent, and therefore they rejected God's message and messenger. However, many Jews repented, as evidenced by the baptisms John the Baptist performed. Then Jesus came, the unlikely one. He too had a message from God. His message was "God is love."

I am not going to liken Farrakhan or any of the main players involved in the March to Jesus. However, I want to discuss four aspects of the March that were similar to the call issued by Jesus, and the movement that developed from his call. The first aspect I would like to highlight is that the times were not much different then than now. The second aspect I would like to address is the spiritual disarray evident in the Jewish community then and in the African American community now. The third aspect I would like to lift up is that God had a plan for the Jews and God has a plan for all African Americans. The fourth aspect I would like to discuss is the tone of the message.

THE TIMES THEN AND NOW

The time now, as it relates to African Americans, and the time during Jesus' day, as it related to Jews, are broadly similar. The Jewish community was oppressed by Rome. Jews were heavily taxed and unfairly represented. Although there were some high-ranking Jews who held important political posts, their influence was overwhelmed by the Roman political and social structure and ultimately those leaders owed their allegiance to Rome. Today, there are more African Americans who hold political posts than there were Jews during the time of Jesus. However, the net result is the same economic and political exploitation; the influence of these leaders is dwarfed by the American political and social structure. African Americans, by and large, pay a higher percentage of their income in taxes and pay more for services they receive. It appears that the gains for which African Americans fought are being taken away. Persecution in its myriad forms persists.

SPIRITUAL DISARRAY

The spiritual dilemma among Jews during the time of Jesus was profound. The Temple, which was the center for the worship of God, had been rebuilt. The ceremonies had been carried out by the faithful. The religious laws were in place and followed by many. However, people still felt estranged from one another and God. Although the sacrifices were offered, oppression and fear were rampant among the people. Although there were trained teachers of the Law, it seemed that the religious leaders were more concerned about following the letter of the law than about helping people to establish or improve their relationship with God. Hatred for Rome and for Jewish traitors, such as tax collectors, abounded; contempt for Jewish leaders was pervasive. The spiritual situation in the African American community, as in its Jewish counterpart during the time of Jesus, is one of desperation. Many people attend church and try to live exemplary lives but still feel estranged from one another. In some places there is a church on every corner, yet many Blacks are oppressed and fearful—the presence of churches has not eased their burden. Although we have many preachers, it seems that many of them are more concerned about the church building than the people inside the church. Many denominations, churches, and religions are attempting to address the spiritual void in the lives of many people, particularly teenagers and children. Many Black Baptist churches have a youth pastor in the hopes of stemming the tide of teenage pregnancy, drug abuse, high-school dropout rate, low self-esteem, black-on-black violence, theft, and other problems. However, despite this and other sorts of efforts, many of these churches feel helpless in the face of this massive onslaught of crippling and debilitating circumstances. I contend that there are two reasons some of these efforts fail. The first reason is that the theology of many churches is one of exclusion—a we-against-them attitude. Second, most important and yet less tangible, there is a lack of nurturing/discipling spirit among the congregants, particularly among Black men. I want to elaborate this theology of exclusion in order to suggest a plan for mentoring in accordance with God's plan and call in the lives of Black men.

THE THEOLOGY OF EXCLUSION

Although most Black Baptist churches differ markedly from their white counterparts, there are some areas in which they are the same. In many Black churches there is a "we *vs.* them" attitude; the saints against the sinners. The attitude is that in order to be helped you must accept our way of thinking and believing. One of the ways in which this attitude of exclusion surfaces is in theology. Many churches are based on a theology that has as its model characteristics which exclude particularly African traits and a theology which excludes non-sanctioned forms of mysticism. Standards and modes of acceptable Christian behavior are actually those whites deem as good. For example, until recently "shouting" and "dancing" were not considered proper modes of Christian worship by most white churches and many Black churches, except in the "low" churches. However, the "shout" is an Africanism and a vital part of the African religious expression. Another example of the proper form of worship is exhibited in the music. For a long time many Black churches did not sing gospel music because it sounded too much like *juk'* (juke) music or music played in nightclubs. There was and still is marked disdain for gospel music in some Black churches. This distinction also indicated a division between what is considered sacred and what is considered profane. However, in many African traditions there *is* no real distinction between the secular and the sacred. Music is a viable expression of the human soul.

The theology of many Black Baptist churches, like their white counterpart, frowns on certain forms of mystical religious experiences. These churches imply, by their theology, that only those experiences that can be validated by "the Word" and "sound reason" are truly God-sanctioned religious encounters. Saints of God depend on the Word to sanctify their religion. However, the paradox comes across in at least one important dimension. While the Black church has accepted the invalidation of the mystical experiences, it has failed to note that it is by this "experience" that the slaves realized that what the slave-holders were preaching as the Bible was antithetical to their ethic. These slaves, therefore, reinterpreted scripture that was in line with their collective experience. It was the slaves' encounter with God in Africa and in America that sanctioned and validated their spirituality.

Although these are but two examples, they indicate a lack of faith in God and a lack of innovation or willingness to try something new on the part of many Black Baptist churches. Many churches believe that unless they worship in a particular way they will not be accepted by God. It is as if they doubt the fact that God loves them. These churches imply that somehow they merit God's love, which is contrary to what most of these churches preach. They believe that unless they do things (worship, use certain material, interpret the Bible, etc.) in a particular way, they will not only incur God's wrath but God will no longer love them. Furthermore, to exacerbate this schizophrenia, the standards many of these churches use to determine what God requires are standards that do not exist in the Bible and are antithetical to Blacks.

LACK OF MENTORING

Black male youth need Black men as mentors and role models. The kind of role models and mentors Black men need are not only celebrity-type people. Youth also need to see Black men working hard in their vocation to carry out their responsibilities. One of the major influences on young people today are peers and individuals who are close to them. Most Black church men do not get involved in the lives of Black male teenagers. Nor do many of these men see themselves as role models for the youth. They often forget that they too were teenagers and unrealistically expect teenagers to "act like they got sense."

Or some of these men believe that since they compromised when they were young, that these young men also need to "sow their wild oats"; therefore they fail to hold the young men personally accountable for anything. *The success of the Black Muslim movement is due, in large part, to the nurturing that the men receive once they convert.* Men receive the kind of attention that they want and need from other Black men. They are told that they are loved and that they are very important. They are challenged to live a style of life that demonstrates the dignity inherent in being Black. For many of them, the rhetoric matches the reality. Muslims demonstrate care for Black men by challenging them to rise above their insecurities and social status. They provide opportunities for young men to grow to be the men of God they are supposed to be. Black Muslims recognize and demonstrate that God is not only concerned about every aspect of an individual's life but that God expects that person to live with the belief that God cares. Minister Louis Farrakhan has much influence over many young Black men because he has shown this kind of nurturing and mentoring care for them.

GOD'S PLAN AND CALL

Just as God has a plan and a call for Jews, God has a plan and a call for all peoples of the Earth. There was a time when many Black Baptist churches believed that God had a plan for all Black people and not just the ones in the church. Black people readily identified with the Jews of the Hebrew Bible because of the similarity of slavery. Many Black folk believed just as God had chosen the Children of Israel for something special, God had also chosen them for something special. This "special task" was that *Black folk were to show white folks not only how to live but how to depend on God for everything.* We were to show that no matter what happened, God is reliable; although God may not come when you want, God is always on time. Many Black people now blandly accept a shoddy, narcissistic, and arrogant form of Black nationalism to the exclusion of other ethnicities. Many Blacks are just as "American" in their beliefs about other ethnic groups as whites are about Blacks. Admittedly, Black Muslims take a strong Black nationalist stance; however, their stance is within a global context. In other words, Black Muslims take a nationalist position understanding that they are connected with other people of African descent and with other people who are struggling against oppression. They believe that the Black man in America deserves what other people throughout the world struggle for—self-determination.

THE TONE OF THE MESSAGE

The tone of the message, like Jesus' message, was love. It was issued in love and those who received it in love benefited by it. It was a call for all Black men throughout America to come to terms with their lack of responsible action.

The message of Jesus mended broken relationships, healed wounded spirits, affirmed the outcast, and gave rest to the weary. Jesus also challenged the disinherited to take responsibility for their spiritual lives. Taking responsibility in this area will also affect other areas—our emotions, moral choices, financial decisions, and career decisions. The message of the March was a call to Black men not only to be our brother's keeper and our sister's keeper but to raise our children, nurture our wives, respect our elders, serve our neighbors, and to worship God with our style of living.

The message was a call to repentance. I believe that God called for the March and used Minister Louis Farrakhan as the vessel to carry God's plan for Black men. God used Farrakhan as God used Cyrus, who was king of Persia. God appointed Cyrus to protect the Israelites when they returned from captivity. God also called Cyrus the Anointed One or Messiah, which is the same title, according to Christian interpretation, used for Jesus.

THE IMPACT

The implications of this March are many. This March symbolized the power of Black men to take control of their lives through the grace and power of God. It says to a nation which imprisons more Black men than any other country in the world that these men are valuable to God, themselves, and their communities. The March also demonstrated the spiritual power that Black men have collectively. Even if just for a few days, Black men showed the world how to love, pray, sing, live, and praise God together. There were many who did not think that Black men could do this, that we were too unruly as a group to be able to command ourselves in such "civilized" decorum. However, the March was about love and male bonding in its highest sense. Such "civilized" decorum was what God had called Black men to be, at that moment, and every day. The March was a call from God.

It is important to affirm the spiritual significance of any leader of a religious movement because it has spiritual and social ramifications. In the case of Islam one must recognize the importance of the Prophet Mohammed to the Muslim and allow that Mohammed *was* a messenger of some sort from God. In the case of Buddhism one must do the same, and in Christianity one may also reserve a similar place for Jesus. The March was tremendously effective because it recognized and respected these different messengers as part of a much larger plan of God's call to Black men.

A call from God is an internal and spiritual matter among the individual, God, and the community. This call does not necessarily need an explicitly Christian reference. God speaks to the individual within the context of his or her life, and an individual's life may not involve being a Christian at the time of the call. The call is God speaking to that individual, calling forth the individual to a greater responsibility to himself or herself within the life of the community, and within the context of God's purpose for humanity. In other words, a call is a summons for a fuller relationship between God and the individual, which is acted out within the context of a community. God does not call an individual outside of a context of community; a call is not an isolated event. When an individual is called, he or she has to let someone know. Often God calls many people simultaneously. These individuals realize that what they are called to do is part of something much larger then they, but that they are an integral part of a whole.

The March was God's call to millions of Black men throughout the country. The call demanded greater responsibility on their part, to care more for themselves and communities. The call has spiritual ramifications which will become evident as those who heard the call, whether they were physically present or not, *act* on the call. It is unfortunate that many people focus on the fact that Louis Farrakhan "called" for the March. But I believe that he *was* God's messenger for that time. The question I think the rest of the country needs to ask itself is, What is God calling *me* to do?

Chapter Thirteen

A Shadow of Light Descended upon the Mall

BESSIE COLLINS

> *Now it happened that on the way to Jerusalem he was*
> *travelling in the borderlands of Samaria and Galilee.*
> *As he entered one of the villages, ten men suffering*
> *from a virulent skin-disease came to meet him. They*
> *stood some way off and called to him, "Jesus! Master!*
> *Take pity on us." When he saw them he said, "Go and*
> *show yourselves to the priests." Now as they were going*
> *away they were cleansed. Finding himself cured, one of*
> *them turned back praising God at the top of his voice*
> *and threw himself prostrate at the feet of Jesus and*
> *thanked him. The man was a Samaritan. This led Jesus*
> *to say, "Were not all ten made clean? . . . It seems that*
> *no one has come back to give praise to God, except this*
> *foreigner." And he said to the man, "Stand up and go*
> *on your way. Your faith has saved you."*
> —Luke 17:11-19, NJB

INTRODUCTION: THE BALM IS AVAILABLE, THE HEALING IS CONTINGENT

As a ritual, the Million Man March has the potential for individual, communal, and societal healing. The outcome of a ritual of healing is dependent upon one's attitude preceding and succeeding the event. From the Lukan text, I lift two points pertinent to this present discourse: (1) Jesus instructed the ten desiring to be healed to perform the ritual of going and showing themselves to the priests; and (2) one turned back, praised God, threw himself prostrate at the feet of Jesus and thanked him.

That all ten lepers have the desire to be healed from this "virulent skin-disease" becomes clear and is manifested in calling out to Jesus for help. When Jesus assigns them the ritualistic task of going to the priests, their response further indicates both the desire to be healed and the faith that Jesus is able to heal them. The critical difference between the one and the nine is an immedi-

127

ate acceptance of his "healed" condition visibly manifested in his gratitude. The comment "your faith has saved you" implies that the others are not—in essence—saved from their extant condition of brokenness. Somehow, at that moment in time, the one has set himself apart from the nine, a crucial point for my analogy to the March. The story does not reveal the ultimate status of the other nine.

Many attended the Million Man March with the expressed desire to be healed and reconciled to their community. The questions of the effectiveness of the March remain: How many have accepted their healing? How has that healing manifested itself within the community? While it is not within the scope of this chapter to assess, analyze, or concretely measure the effects of the March, I want to suggest that, as in the pericope from the Lukan text, we cannot and do not know the outcome of the story of each participant. I contend that the merit of the March is its ritualistic potential for healing and wholeness; healing is contingent upon action succeeding the ritual.

Being formed and transformed by ritual is not a startling phenomenon for Christians. Why then—in this predominantly Christian nation—was it so difficult to fathom the healing potential in the ritual of the March? Why was there such a mixture of excitement and ambivalence among Black Americans regarding this historic event?

Being a student of theology and personality immersed in a continuum of theological, theoretical, and rhetorical perspectives, I use a dialogical integrative approach to ponder the dynamics of the March. Utilizing womanist theology, Black psychology, and social and cultural analysis to examine and critique personality theories of human behavior, I address the following concerns: (1) mainstream America's difficulty in envisioning the event as a healing ritual; (2) Jungian archetypal figures and their relevance for individual, communal, and social healing; (3) a scene from my personal journey; and (4) the theological themes of sin, atonement, reconciliation, healing, and my concept of self. The conclusion expounds upon the March as ritual.

IN SEARCH OF STOLEN HUMANITY

Instinct . . . never operates as a force giving a momentary impact but always as a constant one. Moreover, since it impinges not from without but from within the organism, no flight can avail against it. A better term for an instinctual stimulus is a "need."[1]

The view—expressed publicly by General Colin Powell—which lauded the message of the March but rebuked the principal messenger generally prevailed in the African American communities. How can you separate the man from the movement? was a question directed from the mainstream toward a people proficient in separating the Christ of the Christian movement from the cultural imperialism of Western Christianity. The following news report indicates some concern among African Americans that the March would exacerbate racial resentment caused by the verdict of the O. J. Simpson criminal trial:

> The march's effort to use huge crowds to bring the capital to a halt, broadcast coast to coast and seen by white viewers and media analysts, may combine with strident rhetoric from march leaders to further inflame racial resentment. Those feelings were vividly expressed during the Simpson trial and could worsen if the Washington gathering is perceived as a threat, and further reason for whites to pull back along racial lines.[2]

Underlying this discourse is a psychodynamic theoretical presupposition[3] that the divergent reactions were caused by contrary needs on the part of each group. While seeking to understand the diverse response and divergent need surrounding the two events[4]—the Verdict and the March—I focus on the potential for healing in the Million Man March. Inherent in the discussion is the African American male's need to confess and atone for his condition in his personal, communal, and societal relationships.

The lingering presence of apprehension-laced celebration followed the Verdict and preceded the March. What motivated a million Black men to march on Washington? What need was there? Was it simply the horde instinct[5] described by Sigmund Freud? Horde instinct is an indiscriminate type of "follow the leader" rationale. The following is an example of this mainstream news media insinuation regarding the Verdict:

> No jury can render a verdict that isn't influenced by their own preservation and self-service. Jurors in such cases cannot simply melt back into their homes and neighborhoods and disappear. . . . It is not surprising in these cases that evidence is dismissed or ignored in favor of the path of least censure by the prying hordes and angry packs to which these jurors must answer.[6]

Black psychologist Wade W. Nobles critiques this Freudian notion of horde instinct:

> Even though Sigmund Freud never addressed in any of his major works the issue of African-American psychology, in *Totem and Taboo* (1950) he does attempt to explicate the psychology of contemporary society by examining and theorizing about the traditional practices of so-called primitive peoples. It needs to be pointed out in this regard that by interchangeable reference to the practices and behaviors of African peoples as "savage" or "primitive" Freud did more than attempt to find Darwinian justification for "his primal horde theory." He in effect gave historical credence (without any proof whatsoever) to the belief that African peoples held an inferior position to Whites on the evolutionary chain.[7]

Nobles further states that African American inferiority is an intellectual atmosphere which has permeated Western psychology. The above news media allusion illustrates this influence. I am convinced of this because I recall no media mention of "hordes" and "angry packs" when Simi Valley jurors justified the widely publicized violation of Rodney King's humanity.

In Freud's primal-horde theory "the individual gives up his ego ideal and substitutes for it the group ideal as embodied in the leader. . . . The other members of the group, whose ego ideal would not apart from this, have become embodied in his person without some correction, are then carried away with the rest by 'suggestion,' that is to say, by means of identification."[8] This explains, for me, the mainstream fixation with Louis Farrakhan as the leader of the movement. There was no consideration for the fact that, once initiated, movements can take on lives of their own and have separate and diverse motivations from those of the initiator. Perhaps the ego ideal for the movement was atonement, reconciliation, and healing.

While plausible, pyschodynamic theory makes me apprehensive. I agree with Nobles's critique regarding Western psychology's mathematical precision without spiritual illumination. It seems to be deterministic and leaves no room for grace. However, if we assume response is a result of need, what then were these respective needs? What need does white America have for O. J. Simpson's guilt; conversely, what need does Black America have for O. J. Simpson's innocence? Perhaps white America had a need to rid itself of collective community psychic guilt. Certainly the Black community has the need to continually claim and defend its humanity.

Carl G. Jung addressees this notion of community psychic guilt, which sounds very much like the Hebrew Bible concept of scapegoating. In a discussion of repression of instinctual desires he states: "None of us stand outside humanity's black collective shadow. . . . Projection carries the fear which we involuntarily and secretly feel for our own evil over to the other side and considerably increases the formidableness of this threat."[9] European crimes against Black people, suggests Jung, cause unconscious guilt in the collective psyche of the European race. He further states that it is both sinful and unwise not to be in touch with good and bad aspects of ourselves. Has the guilt in the collective psyche of the white community been projected onto Black men?

Nobles, in the following manner, illustrates the persuasiveness of this concept of projection:

> Freud's star pupil, Carl Gustav Jung, believed that certain psychological maladies found amongst Americans were due to the presence of Black people in America. He noted that "the causes for the American energetic sexual repression can be found in the specific American complex, namely to living together with 'lower races, especially with Negroes.'" . . . He went on to say that living together with "barbaric" races exerts a suggestive effect on the laboriously tamed instincts of the White race, and tends to pull it down.[10]

Black feminist and womanist theory supports similar incidences of such projection. In *Black Feminist Thought* Patricia Hill Collins refers to the controlling image of Jezebel as an example of an image projected on Black slave women in order to stereotype them and rationalize the rampant sexual assaults perpetrated on them by white men.[11] In *Sisters in the Wilderness*, Delores S. Williams's research concurs:

> One of the most prevalent images of black women today has its roots in the antebellum slave-woman/slave-master sexual liaison. Black women as "loose, over-sexed, erotic, readily responsive to the sexual advances of men, especially white men" derives from the antebellum southern way of putting the responsibility for this sexual liaison upon "immoral" slave women."[12]

This readily translates into the victim-blaming scenario that tends to surface in cases of abuse and assault: What did you do to provoke it? This need to project and find evil in others will continue until we are able to acknowledge our own evil.

Jung suggests the role of the counselor as facilitator, putting people in touch with their total being and empowering them to become self-critical, self-knowledgeable, and self-judgmental by owning their strengths and weaknesses.[13] We certainly have the ability to know, critique, and judge—others. Perhaps we can practice these skills on ourselves. In the March, one million Black men were willing to face their dark past performance, criticize and judge themselves in order to get to know their true selves.

Perhaps the assumption of O. J. Simpson's guilt arose out of a need to vindicate the sin of racism in the following manner: *See, I told you that Blacks were not human.* Conversely, were we as Black Americans in denial because such an inhumane crime could cause our humanity to again be challenged? Just as we cannot and do not know whether O. J. Simpson was guilty or innocent of this crime of murder, so too we cannot know what exactly prompted reactions which divided along the color line.

Given these scenarios, it becomes apparent that we have grossly misconceived the notion of what it is to be human. Guilt or innocence certainly does not add to or sever from us our humanity. Awareness of being created in God's image challenges us and reminds us of the awesome task of being like God. It sometimes even forces us to wear masks of pretense.[14]

Subsequent to the Verdict, the situation between Black and white America was taut. During and after the criminal trial, a divided America dropped the guarded persona of liberal acceptable moral behavior, exposing the problem of the color line.[15] Accusations of "playing the race card" emerged and collided with Blacks' awareness of the "race card"—white superiority, Black inferiority—built into the system.

A SHADOW OF LIGHT

In the video *The Wisdom of the Dream: Carl Gustav Jung*, the narrator elucidates a tradition in Basel, Switzerland, which is called Faust Night. It is a type of archetypal parade—a night in which participants wear masks that depict or express the repressed, inferior side of the psyche, the shadow. The shadow is one of the four archetypes of the inner self. Jung describes it as

> the most accessible . . . easiest to experience . . . for its nature can in large measure be inferred from the contents of the personal unconscious. The only exceptions to this rule are those rather rare cases where the positive qualities of the personality are repressed, and the ego in consequence plays an essentially negative or unfavourable role.[16]

From the perspective of the dominating culture in American society, Black men are often depicted as playing an essentially negative role. If I posit the analogy of a communal, extended, transpersonal self, Black men are cast as society's shadow. The positive aspect of their nature is perceived to be repressed! Their hidden side, then, would be their attributes.

An archetypal parade of redeemed Black men shedding their persona—the perception of violence—and getting in touch with the nurturing, supportive, spiritual, loving nature hidden behind that persona of what it means to be both Black and acceptably male in America converted the Mall into healing space. This is evidenced in reports of men who attended the March, reflecting their awe of brothers hugging and weeping for joy, happy to make internal and external connection with their true selves. When summoned, one million Black men responded in confession and atonement. I argue vehemently for the positive nature of this event. Therefore, I contend that on October 16, 1995, a shadow of light descended upon the Mall and transformed it into healing space.

LIVING WITH THE SCARS OF OPPRESSION

A few Black people may hide their scars, but most harbor the wounds of yesterday.[17]

> We carry too many scars from the past. Our past owns us. We wear our scars like armor . . . for protection. . . . Let's live our lives without living in the fold of old wounds.[18]

An image from Toni Morrison's novel *Beloved* will forever remain etched in my psyche; it is the image of the chokecherry tree on Sethe's back. The tree was actually a scar from wounds that resulted from her being brutally beaten for having broken the silence of her oppression.[19] Offering a provocative simile, Karen Baker-Fletcher asserts that voice is essential to womanism: "It is in song, in voice, that humankind is created in the image of God, or better, in the sound of God. . . . When Black women speak in the voice of equality and freedom . . . [they] echo the sounds and lyrics of God's voice."[20] Jacquelyn Grant proffers an interpretation of one's own reality.[21] A variety of techniques can be created to effect this juncture of interpretation; one popular mode is "sass," which, as described by M. Shawn Copeland, is a crucial form of resistance used to "guard, regain, and secure self-esteem; to obtain and hold psychological distance; to speak truth; to challenge; and to protect."[22]

There is something quite liberating about breaking the silence of oppression. It is difficult, however, adequately to articulate the pain of speaking the truth, to challenge unjust systems, and to endeavor to use your voice to protect, only to have it negated as though the deficiency is in your mouth and not in the ear of the hearer. Perhaps this hearing deficit can be attributed to the following revelation excerpted from Collins's *Black Feminist Thought*: "Now to white people your colored person is always a stranger. Not only that, we are supposed to be dumb strangers, so we can't tell them anything!"[23]

When I moved—with my daughter (12) and son (14)—to Denver to attend seminary, it was at a time street gangs were becoming a prominent threat to the area. As a result, young Black adolescents, under suspicion, were being regularly stopped by the police, photographed, and questioned to pad the city's emerging "gang file."

I found myself in the precarious position of rescinding my instruction to my children to respect the authority of police and having to amend this injunction by telling them not to divulge any information but rather request that I be contacted.[24]

One Sunday afternoon I was jarred from my sanctuary and sanctity when I discovered a police car parked on the curb in front of my house by my two children and three of their friends. My son frantically summoned me! The officer was soliciting and recording responses—from all five teens—to the following: "Have you ever been in juvenile detention? Do you belong to a gang? Do you have any scars or tattoos?"

He claimed that he was responding to a report of a break-in attempt at my house and that he was taking "contact reports." He could/would not adequately respond to why he did not contact me as the alleged victim of this crime. Claiming that he had received a report of two Black males attempting to break into my house, he continued taking "contact reports" in spite of the fact that I assured him that these two additional adolescents—who had knocked on my son's bedroom window to get his attention and were reported by a neighbor—were not burglars but visitors.

Eventually, a Black policeman joined the white policeman in taking these "contact reports" on my children and their friends. When I accosted the "Brother" concerning this flagrant violation of the right of these young people (three young Black males, one Black female, one white female), he retorted: "It is not like we held a gun on them!" It is my contention that the weapons they pulled—a pessimistic depreciative stance—were just as lethal to the psyche of these youths. Prior to that encounter, there were no visible scars; they now carry a psychic scar of a psychic violation.

In "mirroring," Heinz Kohut theorizes, we define ourselves through what is reflected in the eyes of others.[25] The vulnerability of African Americans, living with the scars of white superiority/Black inferiority, has manifested itself in self-hatred and rage. According to bell hooks,[26] Andrew Sung Park,[27] and others, this rage can be utilized positively to fight for justice; negatively, it can become internalized and toxic and cause a sinful condition. One contributing factor, white supremacy—as manifested in chattel slavery and systemic racism— causes pain and suffering which has both transformative and degenerative potential. In the Asian cultures this pain and suffering that can implode or explode is called *han*.[28] I appreciate Park's exposition, in *The Wounded Heart of God*, that traditional Christian theology has focused the doctrines of sin and salvation to the needs of oppressor with little attention to the oppressed. I am equally pleased with his following critique of the Newtonian mechanistic world view:

> Individualistic ways of thinking, egocentric ideas, and hierarchical attitudes are predominant in this world due to false worldviews. I suspect that the Newtonian worldview has contributed to the promulgation of such attitudes. . . . Against this Newtonian mechanistic worldview, a new idea has emerged in the contemporary scientific, philosophical, and religious world. That is the principle of interpenetration. Interconnectedness has been strongly espoused by quantum theory, process theology, and the Bible.[29]

SIN: A LACK OF "SELF" CONSCIOUSNESS

Carl Gustav Jung contends: "If the individual is not truly regenerated in spirit, society cannot be either, for society is the sum total of individuals in need of redemption."[30] Andrew Sung Park, along with womanist theologians and many others, posits a theory of relationality and interconnectedness crucial to my thesis of a communal rather than personal concept of self. My womanist thought is influenced by the communal concept of Christianity as well as the thought of the following African American practitioners and theorists: (1) Archie Smith[31]; (2) Wade W. Nobles, who writes, "The cardinal point, therefore, in understanding the traditional African conception of self, is the belief that *I am because We are, and because We are, therefore I am*. . . . Descriptively, we have defined this relationship (the interdependence of African peoples) as the 'extended-self'"[32]; and (3) Linda J. Myers, who notes: "Transpersonal psychology seeks to expand the field of psychological inquiry to include the study of optimal psychological health and well-being. The potential for experiencing a broad range of states of consciousness is recognized, allowing identity to extend beyond the usual limits of ego and personality."[33]

God, creation, and self are so intricately connected that the concept of "other" is moot.[34] When evil is that which thwarts well-being, and sin is perpetrated evil, then to sin against one's world is a sin against one's self and one's God. The cause of sin, then, is the lack of self consciousness.

Participation in the March was acknowledgment of this degenerative condition (sin/*han*),[35] and lack of self consciousness including a lack of awareness of who they are called and created to be. Healing begins with confession, acknowledgment of both desire and the need to be made whole. Black men expressed this desire in their articulation of expectations and realizations from the March[36]: to create cultural renaissance and community consciousness; to atone, reconcile, and rejuvenate spiritually; for former gang member to gain stability; to have an opportunity for intergenerational communication to share what it means to be a Black man in America; to send a political message that unified Black men can keep the nation moving or grind it to a halt; to come together and connect with Blackness, maleness, and spirituality; to spur more Black men to take responsibility for their families and jobs and to turn away from vice such as drugs, alcohol, and gambling; an opportunity for Black men to stand up and take their rightful place in society.

In interpreting my own reality regarding the March —an important tenet of womanist thought—I was aware of whispers and innuendo of sexism in the media regarding the invitation being extended to Black men only, I haven't heard such response from Black women. Throughout the community—which can be documented by the writings of womanist scholars—comments such as the following have flourished:

> We must acknowledge that "things as they are" are not serving the community well, and that clinging to prerogatives rooted in the oppression of women mitigate against the full personhood of us all. . . . Christian manhood does not consist of the capacity to rule. Christian womanhood does not consist of critical, silent collusion with the yoke of sexism. . . . Looking inward demands that women begin to realize that we do not serve the best interest of women, children, or men when we refuse to hold men accountable for oppressive behavior.[37]

Listen to the voice of a clergywoman as she reiterates prominent themes in womanist thought:

> I think it's absolutely necessary for African men in America to get together to pray, to meditate and re-evaluate their roles in society, in education, and most importantly, in the black family. It's something that's been needed for a very long time. . . . The day is a holy day and will mark an economic, spiritual and intellectual . . . revolution. As African-American women in America, we need to be supportive of any type of event that will cause healing and forgiveness of black men. We need this time for them to get together.[38]

A friend who attended the March reported that when he went through one airport he was encouraged by a group of women sporting t-shirts that read "We got your back!" In a borderless world view with a spirit of interconnectedness there is a liberating sense of omnipresence, an assurance that I am healed by your healing.[39]

BE PRESENT WITH THE PRIESTESS

Maya Angelou's presence and participation at the March caused me to re-member Baby Suggs, holy in the novel *Beloved,* and Townes's exposition of gathering at the Clearing:

> The gathering in the Clearing of Baby Suggs and "every black man, woman and child who could make it through" was a communal call to gather into wholeness away from the racist assaults of White folks. This could be a reinterpretation, if not a recasting, of Black separatism. The point in their gathering is not to create a separate identity—this was accomplished at their births. The people gathered themselves into a place of political and spiritual sanctuary. In that place, they began to re-mem-ber themselves through laughter and tears and dance and song. . . . To stand with Baby Suggs in the Clearing is to listen to the diversity of voices hearing her words of challenge, hope, and comfort. . . . They formed a community in the Clearing but each came with their own trail of living.[40]

Townes's commentary renders a prophetic analogy to the occurrence of the March. From several reports, the summons to March was experienced as a communal call to gather, to remember, to "re-member," which drew Black men from across the country; a place for political and spiritual sanctuary; a place or "re-membering" through laughter, tears, drumming, songs; a place of comfort, hope and challenge.

As I reflect, I recall the image of African baptism in Townes's *In a Blaze of Glory.* It is a beautiful portrait in my mind's eye—"The seas of the world below in the Kongo cosmogram resemble water in Christian baptism in which all sins are washed away and a 'new' person emerges from the water"[41]—and helps me envision another baptism of African men—a sea of men sweeping across the nation responding to the summons to be made whole, to repent and be baptized by immersion in a sea of Black men.

Excerpts from Maya Angelou's epic poem written for the occasion and her presence, as celebrant, lend the power of the same sacred space created in the Clearing by Baby Suggs. That which started with remembering, continues in celebration.

> Under a dead blue sky they dragged me by my braids
> beyond your reach . . .
> Through history you wore a badge of shame . . .
> The day has been long, the wounds have been deep
> Across the years
> Across the centuries
> Across the oceans
> Across the seas . . .

Memory is an important feature in Black psychology and womanist theology. Pastoral counselor Archie Smith Jr. refers to anamnesis—Ancient Israel used it in its rituals of confession—a "means to recollect the forgotten past and to participate in a common memory and a common hope . . . to call to mind again and again . . . some past events." Smith cites the mission and ministry of the Black church as helping to recover lost humanity.[42]

Frances Wood reminds us that "the first memory that must be claimed is that we were never meant to survive as human beings."[43] With this realization we must, with intent, remember the implosive and explosive factor involved in the pain and suffering of oppression. As African people once depreciated from humanity to property, in a nation not yet convinced or convicted of the fallacy of white superiority/Black inferiority, memory vitalizes and empowers us and is an essential source of resistance for "the recovery, the reconstitution of identity, culture, and self"; we are compelled to "name the burdens and claim the memories under which we struggle and labor." It is "an essential first step" in the march toward remembering, repenting, and doing the works.[44]

> Draw near to one another
> Save your race
> You have been paid for in a distant place
> The old ones remind us that slavery's chains
> Have paid for our freedom again and again.

Some central features of conversion are confession, atonement, and a desire to be changed. Change is a process. One can hear, within the litany, the redemptive tone and an implied behest to go and do likewise. Emilie M. Townes picks up the theme and adequately exposits that, from the perspective of the nineteenth-century slave, "human repentance and faith were not sufficient to guarantee salvation" and conversion was "not a pro forma ritual" but rather "a drama of personal salvation and freedom that demanded moral rectitude from the individual and the community of believers."[45] Salvation and healing are contingent upon how we utilize the balm to which we've been exposed and what we do with our healing becomes a cogent factor.

> Clap your hands, Let us come together to reveal our
>   hearts . . .
> Clap hands, Let's leave the preening and stop
>   imposturing in our history . . .
> Call the spirit back from the ledge
> Despite the history of pain
> We are a going-on people who will rise again.
> And still we rise![46]

Townes cites Bishop Daniel A. Payne in his description of the ring shout: "After the sermon they formed a ring, and with coats off sung, clapped their hands and stamped their feet. . . . Sinners won't get converted unless there is a ring."[47] The March was about sin, atonement, repentance, baptism, conversion, and salvation!

Like the ritual of holy communion, the litany calls us from brokenness into healing space. In the same manner that we partake of and can become the Body of Christ for the world, those who participated in the healing space can become healing space.[48]

A two-mile-park-like area between the Lincoln Memorial and the Capitol—where plans were made for a million men, a thousand drummers, a thousand singers to allow for five hours of prayer, speeches, and song—was transformed into the Clearing, and I can "re-member" hearing Baby Suggs telling them "that the only grace they could have was the grace they could imagine. That if they could not see it, they could not have it."[49]

The healing ritual of the March continues to offer an opportunity for spiritual reclamation and revitalization. In order to "re-member," we can remember, claim, and become that healing space that was afforded when a shadow of light descended upon the Mall, transforming it into healing space akin to the Clearing!

Notes

[1] Peter Gay, ed., *The Freud Reader* (New York: W. W. Norton, 1989), p. 565.

[2] Sam Fulwood III, "A Million Reasons for Hopes and Fears," *Los Angeles Times* (October 16, 1995), A1, A12.

[3] Wade W. Nobles identifies this psychodynamic view—that the structure of the mind is formed in childhood and that the child is a being with needs—as being problematic and further states that Black psychology is distinguished from general psychology in the following manner: "Psychology should be the study of the human spirit or the study of human illumination (understanding). Mankind in western psychology is however viewed as an 'object' and not a spiritual force. . . . It should be consequentially evident that the failure of contemporary western psychology is due, in part, to the legacy of its basic assumptions and narrow perception of what it means to be human" (*African Psychology: Toward Its Reclamation, Reascension, and Revitalization* [Oakland: Black Family Institute, 1986], p. 2).

[4] My view of the March has been influenced by my experience as an African American female Ph.D. student immersed in the theological and psychological rhetoric of the Theology and Personality Program at Claremont School of Theology, and by the media frenzy preceding, during, and following the O. J. Simpson criminal trial and verdict. Within this context I situate the March.

[5] Sigmund Freud, *Group Psychology and the Analysis of the Ego* (New York: W. W. Norton, 1959), pp. 69-71. "In 1912 I took up a conjecture of Darwin's to the effect that the primitive form of human society was that of a horde ruled over despotically by a powerful male. I attempted to show that the fortunes of this horde have left indestructible traces upon the history of human descent. . . . The psychology of such a group, as we know it from the descriptions to which we have so often referred—the dwindling of the conscious individual personality, the focusing of thoughts and feelings into a common direction . . . all this corresponds to a state of regression to a primitive mental activity, of just such a sort as we should be inclined to ascribe to the primal horde."

[6] "Letters to the Times," *Los Angeles Times* (October 16, 1995), B4.

[7] Nobles, *African Psychology*, p. 6.

[8] Sigmund Freud, *Group Psychology and the Analysis of the Ego* (New York: W. W. Norton & Co., 1959), pp. 78-79.

[9] Carl G. Jung, *The Undiscovered Self* (New York: Mentor Books, 1957), pp. 107-9.

[10] Nobles, *African Psychology*, p. 6.

[11] Patricia Hill Collins, *Black Feminist Thought* (New York: Routledge, 1990), pp. 68, 77. Of controlling images Collins asserts: "Portraying African-American women as stereotypical mammies, matriarchs, welfare recipients, and hot mommas has been essential to the political economy of domination fostering Black women's oppression. Challenging these controlling images has long been a core theme in Black feminist thought."

[12] Delores S. Williams, *Sisters in the Wilderness* (Maryknoll, N.Y.: Orbis Books, 1993), p. 70.

[13] Jung espoused self-knowledge as the solution to the problems that threaten civilization. Fearing that only a small percentage (40 percent) of the population was fairly intelligent and mentally stable, he suggests monitoring such forces as subversive minorities, State absolutism, hydrogen bombs, and spiritual and moral darkness. This small percentage was, he considered, the hope of threatened civilization. Jung feared that State rule and mass-mindedness were the primary threats to civilization and censured the use of scientific genius for destructive forces (e.g., the hydrogen bomb). He described the "mass" as being in a state of "collective possession." The starting point, for Jung, was getting in touch with the evil and dark forces that lurk within ourselves. These conditions he attributed to man's unwillingness to face his unconscious and some evil tenets within himself. Freud is chastised by Jung for his negligence or failure to deal significantly with the "black flood of occultism" of the unconscious—the archetypes—and is also accused of causing panic and fear of the unconscious and the devaluation of the psyche.

[14] Parodying God lends to our strengths and weaknesses yielding both positive and negative connotations. To have the following attributes is certainly desirable: being loving, self-giving, just, impartial, and compassionate. However, the acts of being partial, judgmental, fearsome, angry, and jealous are very seldom lauded, even though they are consistent with some images of God. Is it possible to be too loving, too compassionate, too justice-minded, too impartial, too self-giving, too partial, too judgmental, too fearsome, too angry, too jealous?

[15] W. E. B. Du Bois, *The Souls of Black Folk* (New York: Bantam Books, 1989), p. xxxi. At the turn of the century (1903) Du Bois offered critique that succinctly responds to this query even on the cusp of the turn of another century: "The problem of the Twentieth Century is the color line."

[16] Joseph Campbell, ed., *The Portable Jung* (New York: Penguin Books, 1971), p. 145.

[17] William H. Grier and Price M. Cobbs, *Black Rage* (New York: Basic Books, 1968), p. 24.

[18] Julie Dash, *The Making of an African American Woman's Film: Daughters of the Dust* (New York: The New Press, 1992), p. 157.

[19] Toni Morrison, *Beloved* (New York: Knopf, 1987), p. 17.

[20] Karen Baker-Fletcher, "Soprano Obligato," in *A Troubling in My Soul*, ed. Emilie M. Townes (Maryknoll, N.Y.: Orbis Books), p. 183.

[21] Jacquelyn Grant, "Womanist Theology," in *African American Religious Studies*, ed. Gayraud Wilmore (Durham, N.C.: Duke University Press, 1989), p. 213. In *Black*

Feminist Thought Patricia Hill Collins calls it self-definition, self-reliance, and self-determination.

²² M. Shawn Copeland, "Wading through Many Sorrows," in Townes, *A Troubling in My Soul*, p. 121.

²³ Collins, *Black Feminist Thought*, p. 68. Collins cites John Langston Gwaltney, *Drylongso: A Self-Portrait of Black America* (New York: Random House, 1980), p. 29.

²⁴ See Grier and Cobbs, *Black Rage*, p. 31: "We might attempt a retrospective construction of child-rearing among slaves between 1665 and 1865 in the United States. . . . Once the mother opts for her child's life she assumes the task of conveying to him the nature of the world in which he will live and teaching him how to survive in it. In effect, she had to take the role of slave master, treat the child with capricious cruelty, hurt him physically and emotionally, and demand that he respond in an obsequious helpless manner—a manner she knew would enhance his chances of survival. . . . He must, in fact learn to treat himself as chattel, his body and person as valuable only as the owner placed value on them. He must learn to fear and exalt the owner and to hate himself. . . . In order to survive as a slave, the child had to learn to abandon the usual narcissistic investment of self."

²⁵ Heinz Kohut, *The Analysis of Self: A Systematic Approach to the Psychoanalytic Treatment of Personality Disorders* (Madison, Conn: International Universities Press, 1995), pp. 115-99.

²⁶ bell hooks, *Killing Rage: Ending Racism* (New York: Henry Holt and Company, 1995).

²⁷ Andrew Sung Park, *The Wounded Heart of God* (Nashville: Abingdon Press, 1993), p. 138.

²⁸ Ibid., p. 138. Similarly, the positive and negative potential of the Asian concept of *han* appears to be pertinent to this discussion of the degenerative and transformative quality of rage inherent in the African American experience. *Han*, described by Park as "frozen energy that can be unraveled either negatively or positively," seems comparable to the experiences of pain and suffering in the African American community. Negatively, the *han*-ridden person may seek revenge or can slip into a fatalism that might develop into mental disorder or suicide. Positively, it can be converted into the fuel for transforming the social injustice and for community building.

²⁹ Ibid., p. 148.

³⁰ Jung, *The Undiscovered Self*, p. 68.

³¹ Archie Smith Jr., *The Relational Self* (Nashville: Abingdon Press, 1982), p. 56. Smith is a professor of pastoral psychology and counseling at Pacific School of Religion; he is also a practitioner of marriage, family, and child counseling. Smith credits George Herbert Mead for the concept of relational self—inseparably linked and dialectically interwoven mind, self, and society.

³² Wade W. Nobles, "Extended Self: Rethinking the So-Called Negro Self-Concept," in *Black Psychology*, 2d ed., ed. R. Jones (New York: Harper & Row, 1980).

³³ Linda J. Myers, "Transpersonal Psychology: The Role of the Afrocentric Paradigm," *The Journal of Black Psychology* 12:1 (August 1985), pp. 41-42.

³⁴ This is part of my philosophy of self that I am developing for current and future work. My point of departure is the convergence of womanist and African-centered thought. I hope to integrate my research in Black psychology, self-psychology (Heinz Kohut), and womanist theology to develop a workable concept of self-in-relations as a premise for developing therapeutic models of care and counseling in historically oppressed communities. My paradigmatic shift is evolving, and while I am striving for

diunital thought (joining of opposites, both/and), I am acutely aware of my dualistic (either/or) language.

[35] Andrew Hacker, *Two Nations: Black and White, Separate, Hostile, Unequal* (New York: Scribner, 1992). The following are examples of this degeneration: "the disgraceful condition of the black community . . . one third [Black males] 20-29 trapped in the jail industrial complex . . . the black community's economic standing and social opportunity depressed." African American men (12.5 percent of the population) were 45 percent of the inmate population in 1986. Disproportionate numbers of Black families (56 percent) are headed by women. Black families living below the poverty level—between 21 and 23 percent—compared to between 4 and 6 percent of white families. The 1990 unemployment rate of Black Americans was 11.3 percent compared to 4.1 percent for white Americans. Such conditions break one's spirit; brokenness necessitates healing.

[36] Ricky de la Torre, "1 Million Men, A Single Focus," *Daily Bulletin* (October 14, 1995), Inland Valley edition, A1, A4.

[37] Frances E. Wood, "Take My Yoke upon You," in Townes, *A Troubling in My Soul*, p. 44.

[38] Ricky de la Torre and LaTisa Strickland, "1 Million Men, A Single Focus," *Daily Bulletin* (October 16, 1995), Inland Valley edition, A4. The quotation is from Rev. LaQuetta Bush-Simmons, Associate Pastor, Antioch M.B. Church, Pomona.

[39] Nobles, *African Psychology*, p. 10. In the early 1900s with the emergence of American psychology, G. Stanley Hall did not break with the tradition of his European predecessors. As the founding father of the American Psychological Association, G. Stanley Hall (1846-1924) was also influenced by the Malthusian doctrine. His philosophy reflected the essence of the Machiavellian theory, which also deals with the dichotomy of white and black. He believed, for example, that "what is true and good for one (i.e. the Caucasian and the African) is often false and bad for the other."

[40] Emilie M. Townes, *In a Blaze of Glory* (Nashville: Abingdon Press, 1995), p. 64.

[41] Ibid., p. 22.

[42] Smith, *The Relational Self*, p. 19.

[43] Wood, "Take My Yoke upon You," p. 43. Wood quotes Revelation 2:2-5.

[44] Copeland, "Wading through Many Sorrows," p. 121.

[45] Townes, *In a Blaze of Glory*, p. 25.

[46] "Poet Adds her Voice to March," *Daily Bulletin* (October 17, 1995), A5.

[47] Townes, *In a Blaze of Glory*, p. 20. The citation is from Albert J. Raboteau, *Slave Religion: The "Invisible Institution" in the Antebellum South* (New York: Oxford University Press, 1978), pp. 68-69.

[48] Jung, *The Undiscovered Self*, p. 121. In the following Jung substantiates this possibility: "Anyone who has insight into his own action, and has thus found access to the unconscious, involuntarily exercises an influence on his environment. The deepening and broadening of his consciousness produce the kind of effect which the primitives call 'mana.' It is unintentional influence on the unconscious of others."

[49] Morrison, *Beloved*, p. 88.

Chapter Fourteen

A Ration of Compassion

A Sermonic Interlude

MARY MINOR REED

> *Live in harmony with one another; be sympathetic, love*
> *as brothers and sisters, be compassionate and humble.*
> —1 Peter 3:8

Read Psalms 34 and 1 Peter 3:8-12

Many people are hurting. They are lonely even though they are surrounded by large crowds.

They are hungry even though they have food to eat. They are thirsty even though they have water to drink. They are friendless even though they know many people.

People are hurting. Our sons and daughters are fatherless even though Dad may be around.

Our children are motherless even though Mom is in the home. Our families are loveless even though the home is filled with many offsprings. Our churches lack compassion even though the members are full of passion.

Jesus is driven by his compassion for others, not by self-serving desires. Louis Farrakhan is driven by his compassion for others. Farrakhan, out of his compassion for men of African descent, gathers in Washington, D.C., on October 16, 1995, one million men for an event called the Million Man March.

If you and I call ourselves children of God, we ought to act like a child of God. Farrakhan states in his speech, "Day of Atonement," that the men have "gathered . . . at the call of God. For it is only the call of the Almighty God, no matter through whom that call came, that could generate this kind of outpouring. God called us here to this point, at this time, for a very specific reason" (Madhubuti and Karenga 1996, p. 11).

If you and I call ourselves disciples of Christ, we ought to follow the ways of Jesus Christ. The "ought-ness" of our conversion experience says we should demonstrate a ration of compassion. The "ought-ness" of our compassion says that we strive to come into perfect union with God. In Farrakhan's "Day of Atonement" speech he states, "Atonement is the fifth step in an eight-stage process" in attaining perfect union with God. The process to bring a person into perfect union with God, according to Farrakhan:

Pointing out wrong faults
1. Acknowledge, admit the truth of some reality.
2. Confess your wrong to God and whomever you have offended.
3. Repent to God.
4. Atone or make amends for an injury or wrong.
5. Forgive.
6. Reconcile and restore.
7. The result is an improved position, or prefect union with God.

In 1 Peter 3:8-9 Peter writes originally to the Christian communities in Asia Minor. However, Peter also writes to the Christian communities of Los Angeles, Detroit, St. Louis, Philadelphia, Chicago, New York, Atlanta, Washington, D.C., wherever the people of God may live. Peter passionately urges his readers to seek those qualities that are essential to Christian life: unity of spirit, sympathy, love, humility, forgiveness, and compassion.

Farrakhan admonishes his listeners to "achieve a closer tie with the source of wisdom, knowledge, understanding and power," the Almighty God.

The "ought-ness" of the Christian's conversion experience demands that we demonstrate a ration of compassion. Yet the "is-ness" of our pseudo-altered lives says that we demonstrate absolute, self-serving passion. Let's talk about these two qualities, *passion* and *compassion*.

PASSION

Passion is the object of our own desire.

Often, when we speak about people's passon, we are referring to their individual desires, which are associated with some object of their desiring. Because of our ruling desires or passions, we spend our time trying to gain, attain, maintain, obtain, retain, ascertain, things, stuff, power, fortune, prestige, and fame. However, God wants us to desire a germane, pertained, sustained life in Jesus Christ. Farrakhan states it this way, "God wants us to humble ourselves to the message that will make us atone and come back to Him and make ourselves whole again" (Madhubuti and Karenga 1996, p. 17).

> A man always said he would retire,
> When he had made a million clear,
> And so he worked from
> "can't see in the morning to can't see at night,"
> From day to day, from year to year!
> At last he puts his ledgers up,
> And laid his stock reports aside,
> And when he started out to live,
> He found he had already died!

Tell me what you desire, and I'll show you what you love. The Bible tells you and me to "seek first the Kingdom of God and its righteousness, and all the other things will be given to you."

Many youths of today, Generation X (also known as the hip-hop generation), feel that the adults, the "baby boomers," have done them an injustice. They say, "The passion of the older generation has not been passionately passed on to the younger generation." Rappers like twenty-seven-year-old Ice Cube make statements like: "Nobody told me about the struggle, so I didn't know how to continue the struggle. . . . I just got that you have to get yours and don't worry about nobody" (*Newsweek*, 55).

Martin King's dream is a dream deferred.

Many of our youths possess a "gotta-get-mine" ethos. They do not understand the concept of delayed gratification. "Go to college, get a degree, start your career, by either getting a job or starting your own business, buy a car, buy a house, get married, start your family, in that order." They want it all, and they want it all now. It's not entirely their fault.

We, the baby boomers, have failed Generation X. The older generation has failed to be mentors. Therefore, some of our children turn to the criminal element. The criminal element is standing there on the street corner waiting to mentor and spend time with our children. Our churches are failing the youth. We cannot get men or women to make a commitment to mentor our youth, our children, your kids, for at least six months out of the year, three days out of the week, two hours out of each day. Our schools are failing our youth. Our homes are failing our youth. We have failed our youth, and they know that we have failed them.

Standing at the lectern of the Million Man March is fourteen-year-old Ayinde Jean-Baptiste of Chicago. With confidence and trepidation he proclaims, "When you stop making excuses, when you start standing with our mothers, when you stick it out with your families, when you start mentoring our young, when you start teaching us to be humane, then we can build a new nation of strong people. . . . Then your children will not join gangs, because they belong to a community" (Cottman 1996, 55-56).

People, don't you care?!

Louis Farrakhan and the Nation of Islam care. Farrakhan states, "We cannot continue the destruction of our lives and the destruction of our community." The men are instructed to return to their homes and communities and to make them decent and safe places to live. Our youths are filling their void with the rhetoric of Louis Farrakhan. Young black men make statements like,

I love Farrakhan without question or reservation. . . .
He's a strong, stand-up black man. . . .
I don't practice his religion, but I support him. . . .
He's never turned on us in the street. . . .
He's for turning us into men (*Newsweek*, 57).

People, don't you care?!

Whatever happened to the ethos of the National Association of Colored Women: Lifting as We Climb? Or Marcus Garvey, "To lift ourselves and to demand respect of all humanity." With integration we adopted the ethos of "I got mine. Now go and get yours." We substituted the American dream for Martin's dream. As a result, we are now living the African American nightmare: the abolishment of affirmative action, welfare reform, lack of financial aid, Proposition 209, double-digit unemployment.

In *Newsweek*'s March 1997 issue, the one with Shaquille O'Neal and Quincey Jones on the front cover, we read:

> In rapid succession, the civil-rights generation brought the collapse of legal segregation and the explosive rise of the black middle class. The hip-hop generation has been raised with progress, but also pain. For the rising middle classes, who benefited from integration and affirmative action, opportunities have never been better. The number of black families with incomes above $50,000 has more than quadrupled since 1967. But for those left behind, the world is measurably harder. Between 1967 and 1987, cities like New York, Detroit, Chicago, and Philadelphia lost more than half of their manufacturing jobs. By 1988, one in four black children lived below half the poverty level. Integration, which was supposed to be a pathway to equality, allowed successful blacks to flee the inner city, breaking down communities and leaving increased concentrations of poverty behind (*Newsweek*, 56).

This is the description of the African American nightmare driven by our passion. However, in the words of Booker T. Washington, "Success is not measured by how high you go, but the obstacles you've gone through to get where you are."

Often our passion separates us from God. Preoccupation with our own desires makes us unavailable to do the will of God. Maybe God wants you to stop and talk to your son, but you are too busy. So your son decides to join a gang. Or perhaps God wants you to talk to that frustrated teen mother who is hollering at her children. But you cannot stop what you are doing, or you will be late for your appointment. Or perhaps God would have you volunteer in a church or community program. But you are too tired because you have worked all week long on that job that God gave you.

You have become your object of desire. You desire the things of life more than the One who is the giver of life. But God wants to become our object of desire. And when God is the object of our desire, we can resolve to do what Farrakhan admonishes the men to do: "Go home and do something about what's going on in our lives and in our communities."

The phrase *the passion of Jesus* often refers to the suffering of Jesus. It is the last two days of Jesus' life, including the Last Supper, the agony in the Garden of Gethsemane, the arrest, trials, crucifixion, death, and burial.

The purpose of Jesus' passion is to do the will of God—reconcile you and me to God. Christians celebrate and remember the passion of Jesus at least once a month. The body of Jesus Christ is given to preserve the believer's soul and body to everlasting life; Jesus' blood of the covenant is poured out for you and me for the forgiveness of our sins. Jesus offers his life as ransom for you and me.

Human passion, on the other hand, is the object of our own desire. Its purpose is to carry out our own selfish desires. Lust is the perversion of human passion. Lust seeks to satisfy our own selfish desires. However, as people of God, we allow the passion of Jesus to dwell within us.

We are here to do the will of God. We say to God, "I'm available to you."

COMPASSION

Compassion is sympathetic consciousness of others' pain, misery, troubles, needs, heartaches, sufferings, together with a desire to alleviate them. Farrakhan says, "Black folk saw [the deaths of Ronald Goldman and Nicole Brown Simpson] with compassion."

It's not enough for you and me to know the distress of others. We must do something about it. It's not enough for you and me to feel the pain of others. We must help to ease their pain. God says to you and me, "It's not enough to love me whom you have not seen." God says to help those whom we see daily. "We must belong to some organization that is working for and in the interest of the uplift and the liberation of our people," purports Farrakhan.

Compassion contains two elements: sympathy and empathy.

Sympathy is a good emotional quality to possess. It shows that you care beyond yourself. It shows that your responsibilities lie beyond your purview.

A sympathetic person says, "I feel your pain." Sympathetic people are moved by their pathos. They are moved emotionally to pity a person. They say: "I feel for you. I know how you feel. I feel the same way. God will take care of you."

However, sympathy alone is not good. You and I also need to have empathy.

Empathy is the capacity for participation in another's feelings or ideas. It's not enough to say, "I feel for you, I think I love you."

Some young people believe that adults are not able to empathize with them. "Parents just don't understand." Parents respond, "Not true. Not true. Been there—done that."

Empathy says: "I feel for you. And I am going to do something about your situation. Let's go and get some food for you and your children. Here are a few dollars to buy some food. You want to go to college? Let me help you fill out the application. Let me help you find financial aid, write your essay, look for scholarships. You want to break that addiction? Come on, let's go to the Substance Abuse Program. You want a new life? Go to church with me today. I'll introduce you to a new way of life in Jesus Christ."

Sympathy allows us to feel. Empathy demands that we do more than just feel. Sympathy is the attitude we possess. Empathy is the action we demonstrate.

The Ten Commandments of Compassion:

1. Speak to people.
2. Smile at people.
3. Call people by their name.
4. Be friendly and helpful.
5. Be cordial.
6. Be genuinely interested in people.
7. Be generous with praise—cautious with criticism.
8. Be considerate of the feeling of others.
9. Be thoughtful of the opinions of others.
10. Be alert to give service.

When we possess sympathy and empathy, we are filled with compassion.

The Apostle Peter knows that while we may endure trials and unfair treatment, we are also called to a blessed life and abundant blessings. Peter illustrates this point by quoting Psalm 34:12-16, which is a veritable hymn of life for those who—though they may suffer—stand clearly in God's favor. Peter and the Psalmist both know that many afflictions may shatter our inner being; that is, break the heart of the righteous and crush their spirits. But our real existence and security are at a depth that suffering cannot reach, and, at that level, God's presence restores and preserves you and me.

> The wicked are those who are without God.
> Because they lack this depth,
> they are destroyed by the surface phenomenon of
> suffering.
> The absence of God in their lives is the real cause of
> their destruction.

All of us will suffer. But our level of suffering is determined by our relationship with God. Our personal relationship with God determines our ability to endure.

Have an attitude of compassion. Don't be led by your selfish passion. However, it's not enough to just possess an attitude of compassion. Our actions must mirror our attitudes. Have actions of compassion.

Many people think you have to be a millionaire before you can give to others. Therefore, many people do not give. They only get. They say things like, "I do not have enough to share with someone else." They make statements like that of the widow to Elijah, "I only have enough for me and mine." Oh, but God is waiting to bless them, just as God blesses the widow, if they would only give their all.

Give as the widow, who gave her mite. Give as the widow gave to the prophet Elijah. Give and watch God refill, and refill, and refill, and refill. Give your time, talent, and treasure to God.

An attitude of compassion plus actions of compassion equals the will of God.

Jesus had an attitude of compassion demonstrated by his compassionate actions. Compassion is the basic motivation of Jesus' ministry. Jesus knows the needs of the multitude of people who linger with him all day long. Jesus knows they are hungry. The disciples, like many of us, say, "Send them away. We don't have enough for them." Jesus feeds the people. In the words of Farrakhan, "We got to be more like Jesus, more like Mohammed, more like Moses, and become servants of the people in fulfilling their needs."

When we see our brother or sister who needs our help from afar, do we turn our head and look the other way? The prodigal son's father has compassion for his son. When the father sees the son from afar, he is moved with compassion. Can you do what Farrakhan commands, "Go to some jail or prison and adopt one inmate for the rest of his and your life to make them your personal friend—to help them through their incarceration, to be encouragement for them"? Are you willing to adopt one of the 25,000 black children waiting to be adopted? Are you willing to contribute to the economic development fund, "to build an economic infrastructure to nurture businesses within the Black community"?

Are you driven by your passion, or are you controlled by your compassion? As Jesus hangs on the cross, suffering, he is moved with compassion for his mother, Mary, and his friend John. "Woman, behold thy son. John, behold thy mother."

Can you say, as Jesus said in the Garden of Gethsemane, "Father, if you are willing, remove this cup from Me; yet, not my will but Thy will be done"?

> Can you truly say to God,
> Thy Way, O Lord, not mine,
> Thy will be done, not mine;
> Since Thou for me didst bleed,
> And now doth intercede,
> Each day I simply plead,
> Thy will be done.
>
> Thy way, O Lord, not mine,
> Let glory all be Thine;
> Keep me, lest I may stray,
> Near Thee from day to day;
> Teach me to watch and pray,
> Thy will be done.
>
> Thy will, Thy will be done,
> Thy will, Thy will be done;
> Incline my heart each day to say,
> Thy will be done.

Bibliography

Cottman, Michael H., ed. 1996. *The Million Man March: Our Youth/Our Future.* New York: Crown Trade Paperbacks.

Leland, John, and Allison Samuels. 1997. "The New Generation Gap," *Newsweek* 129, no. 11 (March 17): 52-60.

Madhubuti, Haki R., and Maulana Karenga, eds. 1996. *Million Man March/Day of Absence: A Commemorative Anthology.* Chicago: Third World Press / Los Angeles: University of Sankore Press.

Tan, Paul Lee. 1979. *Encyclopedia of 7700 Illustrations: Signs of the Times.* Chicago: R. R. Donnelly & Sons. Adaptation of #3589, "Ready to Retire," selected p. 836; adaptation of #6679, "Ten Commandments of Human Relations," selected p. 1477.

Toombs, Lawrence E. 1971. "Psalm 34." In *The Interpreter's One-Volume Commentary on the Bible.* Edited by Charles M. Laymon. Nashville: Abingdon Press.

Chapter Fifteen

Community, Solidarity, and Ecumenicity

Cornish Rogers

Several years ago, while touring in Tashkent of the former Soviet Union, I suddenly came across a courtyard of a mosque filled with 250 Muslim men bowing silently in prayer. I marveled at the sight of so many men in one place, bound by a common commitment. As a United Methodist pastor, I exclaimed to myself, "What a wonderful men's club this could be for the church!" Only in the military could one find such a large, disciplined group of Black men, I surmised.

That is why it took me by surprise that so many Black men, young and old, were willing to drop what they were doing and respond to a call to attend a vaguely summoned "Million Man March."

There wasn't much public relations hype about it in the media, Black or white. Nothing very attractive was promised to those attending except the dubious opportunity to "atone" and commit themselves to the best interests of Black people. The list of featured speakers was not overly attractive.

But they came, by the tens of thousands, "young and old, rich and poor, Muslim and Christian, straight and gay, educated and uneducated." [1]

It was apparent, in the remarkable response to such an ambiguous "call," that some fundamental chord in the self-understanding of African American men was struck. The nation's capital was not the target of the marchers, only the symbol of its nationwide assemblage. The marchers did not come to petition for a redress of grievances against the national government or to gear up for a unified national program for Black men. The marchers came together to *be* together in one place.

By all measurements it constituted an uncommon experience of commonness for Black men, a galvanizing of disparate features of the Black male experience in America into an ecumenical, interfaith, Pan-African expression of solidarity and "at-one-ment." And, as always, celebration.

Its ecumenical features were apparent. A broad variety of denominational affiliations was represented, which should come as no surprise for any mass Black assemblage. Black Americans have historically relegated their denominational identification to a secondary status behind their common Black Christian experience, an experience related to their common search for liberation. Many Black Christians allied themselves with denominations that missionized them or reached out to them with social-service resources; most doctrinal distinctions were glossed over. The vast majority of American Black Christians, however, are Baptists, an affiliation that provides maximum freedom for each local congregation to be autonomous. It was no coincidence, therefore, that the premier Black Christian civil-rights organization, the Southern Christian Leadership Conference, was largely peopled by Baptist clergy. Black Christians have generally ignored denominational lines to join together in quasi-religious social and political activities for the betterment of Black and poor people. Most NAACP meetings are held in Black churches and are often conducted in the form of loosely structured worship services. And, like the response to the Civil Rights Movement, Blacks of non-Christian faiths and even of no faith responded to the call. That is in part why there was an easy and amiable mix of Christian, Muslim, and atheist men assembling around the Christian doctrine of atonement. A deep and genuinely spiritual issue for all Black men was addressed by the call to the March, and many from all pathways of transcendence responded.

The overwhelming response to the call also revealed the readiness for a Pan-African demonstration of solidarity in the face of threatened nonexistence. It was Pan-African in the sense that the issues at stake were felt to be relevant to the African Diaspora throughout the world, not confined to African Americans. The call evoked the sense that what appears to be the African American predicament will, and in some instances, has already begun to be manifested in other African peoples from South Africa to Brazil. This oceanic sense of crisis submerged the issue of Louis Farrakhan's leadership role in the March. Indeed, it underlined the common predicament of Pan-Africans of all stripes.

This surge for survival is akin to the human body's chemistry. It seems the body has a way of marshalling all its resources to focus on rescuing its ailing member. It actually shuts off the rest of the body to focus all its powers on the infected area. Black men have sensed for years the sure destruction of their weaker brothers through prison, poverty, and AIDS; they were ready to respond to any call that might lead to their empowerment, however undefined.

That instinct for "circling the wagons" surfaced several decades ago when Angela Davis, a Black socialist scholar, was being viciously attacked for her political views and was in danger of losing an esteemed teaching position in the University of California system. The writer James Baldwin came to her defense in a *New York Review of Books* essay, in which he candidly disagreed with her political prescriptions for the United States but stoutly defended her right to state them openly without fear of unfair reprisal. He writes, "Angela, you are my sister, and I know that if they come for you in the morning, they'll be back for me at night." It is that kind of fine paranoia, a self-protective instinct developed over the years among Blacks for survival, that contributed to the massive response to the Call.

A major feature of the Call was a call to "atone," a richly variegated theological term that connotes expiation, reconciliation, making amends, and other nuanced feelings of not having done enough to be a responsible person. There was a strong sense of the need to do more for one's people, a sense of guilt for not having fulfilled one's responsibility, and a need to demonstrate in public one's determination to do more. Many Black men felt very strongly that they had failed to help their brothers and sisters and families and communities enough. T. S. Eliot in his play *The Cocktail Party* has Celia, a troubled young woman, remark, "It's not the feeling of anything I've ever *done*, which I might get away from, or any anything in me I could get rid of—but of emptiness, of failure towards someone, or something, outside of myself; and I feel I must . . . *atone*—is that the word?"[2]

That vague sense of the need to atone led to the moving "Million Man March Pledge," which all the men recited together in one place. That pledge brought to mind a turning point in the life of Claude Brown, recounted in his autobiography, *Manchild in the Promised Land*, in which he tells of his profligate early life on the mean streets of Harlem. One day, as he and his friend were on their way to get high on cocaine, a little boy with a dog smiled at him, told him that he had seen him several times, and declared that he wanted to be like him when he grew up. This rattled Claude so much that he told his friend that he couldn't go with him after all, explaining, "I don't have time for any cocaine right now. I've got to go and do something, and I've got to do it before another little boy with a dog comes up and asks me what I do." The call to atone struck a deeply felt sense of responsibility for the crisis in the Black community, and Black men responded en masse.

But the most dominant feature of the Million Man March was a mood of irrepressible joy and camaraderie among those in attendance. For such a large crowd there were few, if any, instances of misconduct or public disturbance. Strangers across economic and social class lines greeted one another as brothers, exchanged addresses and phone numbers. There was an unspoken awareness that everyone present was motivated to attend for the same general reasons, had some of the same experiences; therefore, they understood one another at a deep level. It was an atmosphere of welcome and familiarity, not unlike the words of the theme song in the TV series "Cheers": "Sometimes you want to go, where everybody knows your name, and they're always glad you came. You wanna be where you can see, everybody's troubles are all the same. You wanna go where everybody knows your name."

All those present knew the tremendous challenges ahead for the Black community, but all those present also knew that they were not alone in the march, wherein they were glad.

Notes

[1] Michael E. Dyson, ed., *Atonement: The Million Man March* (Cleveland: Pilgrim Press, 1996), p. xv.

[2] *T. S. Eliot: The Complete Poems and Plays* (New York: Harcourt, Brace, 1950), p. 362.

Chapter Sixteen

Summarizing New Ground

Liberation, Wholeness, and Power

G. KASIMU BAKER-FLETCHER

The cold, hard truth is that Black men and women living in the United States do not share identical experiences—but in some mysterious way they understand a common fate. While we are many, our sepia-mocha-*cafe au lait*-to-ebony-black skin-coloring has served as a social marker to delimit in the minds of all the "immigrant" peoples—from any of the many nations in Europe, Russia, China, Japan, the Philippines, or Korea—that *there,* located in *that darkness,* could be adequately contained all that is lower-than and less-than *anybody else!* This is cold, harsh, and brutal truth that African American religions—from the quietest "high church" Episcopal to the most exuberant effervescent "shouts" of Pentecostal worship, from the most secretive practitioner of Voudon to the disciplined austerity of a devoted Muslim—have both named and striven mightily to overthrow in the minds and hearts of each of their believers.

The cruelty of being isolated in the position of lowest-ranking human being, the viciousness of being held captive by glorious ideals of "democracy and freedom" while simultaneously being demeaned, the callousness of even the "educated" toward continued evidences of a "color-archy" by those who have benefited by the historically constructed ethos of "race"-consciousness—all these could drive a less resilient people over the brink into insanity. And yet we stand at the edge of a new millennium, still daring to hope, pray, and believe in a brighter tomorrow no matter how much past patterns of retrenchment and retreat threaten to subvert our joy. Such spirituality should not be relegated to tired Marxist prognostications about religion being "the opiate of the people." Opium dulls its addicts, numbing them from authentic experience of the external world by providing a means for an internalized escape from reality. African American religions, at their best, have offered neither escape from the present world nor an artificial experience so seductive as to allure its practitioners away from reality. Rather, they have provided world views, metaphysics, and spiritual disciplines capable of enabling Black religious folk to go away from times of worship with a transformed sense of what the Divine could fashion in their lives, even in the midst of torture, violence, abuse, and death. Rather than providing a steady and addictive form of "spiritual narcotic," African American religions have dared to transform Jeremiah's plaintive question "Is there no balm in Gilead?" into a declarative affirmation "There *is* a balm in Gilead." *That Balm is not a narcotic but a new vision of possibilities, an inner doorway opening hard-pressed minds and spirits toward positive possibilities in the midst of gut-wrenching sorrows.*

Black Religion after the Million Man March has dared to gather together testimonies about how the March affected various authors' religious understandings and sensibilities. As scholars, we have been bold to offer criticisms, even in the midst of measured praise, and sought for corrections to problems as engaged Black women and men. In the midst of addressing "cold truth," we have sought that Balm of religious genius which was slowly created over many generations, in the tears of our ancestors and their deepest longings for freedom. The Balm, in order to really work, must be applied to those areas of our collective Black "Body" in order for healing, wholeness, and power to be effected. In this way, while religious scholars in the technical sense, our words might be considered the ritual incantations of those Spirit-Workers of yore who knew how to summon the might and power of GOD to "visit" the Folk in unforgettable ways. We have not sought to criticize in order to show off our intellectual abilities. Rather, we have acted in the kind of passionately engaged fashion that the *Ngangas* (medicine men) and *Sangomas* (medicine women) of our Deep Ancestral Past would have been pleased to witness.

Somehow, in the midst of such richness, one can discern a concern to articulate certain themes. I have brought together several of these themes under three titles: *liberation, wholeness, and power.*

LIBERATION

Pioneering Black theologian James Cone once bluntly stated that the *sole reason* for ordering speech and thought about GOD, from a truly Christian perspective, was to enable the oppressed to recognize "that their inner thrust for liberation is not only *consistent* with the gospel but *is* the gospel of Jesus Christ."[1] Liberation, so understood, is a very *concrete* way of talking about what Christians have traditionally understood only in a *private and individualized fashion*, that is, the word *salvation*. To "be saved," then, is not only to confess one's personal "sins" before GOD and accompanying human beings, but also to *join a process of becoming free from both individual "sins" and oppressive/repressive socio-political, economic, and cultural conditions*. Contemporary Pan African theologian Jean-Marc Ela notes that, from his perspective as one from the tiny West African country of Cameroon, "salvation in Jesus Christ is liberation from every form of slavery."[2]

Can we speak of the Million Man March as a liberating event? Without qualification, Theodore Walker Jr. spoke of the March as part of the "perpetually good news" of GOD's saving/liberating activity. Walker defined the "perpetually good news" of GOD's activity as coterminous with Minister

Farrakhan's call and content of the March, noting that it is GOD who offers ongoing opportunity for "prayer, fasting, confession, forgiveness of sin, atonement, repentance, reconciliation, and responsibility." Walker's position exemplifies that of a classic Black theologian, clarifying how GOD's activity in the world is revealed in the actions of oppressed Black males who marched for their own liberation.

I noted that the March was a mixed event when interpreted within the framework of a second-generation Black liberation hermeneutic called XODUS theology and ethics. While it is easily confirmed that the massive gathering of Black males both produced and was indicative of an *XODUS SPACE,* it was not clear to me that it could be confirmed as an ongoing movement and process of psycho-spiritual and social transformation, or *XODUS JOURNEY.* As such, I found the March an expression of our deepest urges for liberation, but one that was unable to mount a sustained program and process whereby systematic *and* personal change could take place. As one concerned about Black males finding ways to name and stop abusive, disrespecting practices toward Black women and children, I was also extremely gratified that the March was the first public recognition by Black males that we have, in fact, been abusive and patriarchal. Such a confession I take to be a significant sign of a *liberated maturity and dignity.* It also is a powerful indication of the way in which the "battlefield" for liberation in this generation has moved from the pray-ins and sit-ins of the sixties to concrete relationship of family intimacy and into the marketplace of economic opportunity.

Victor Anderson, on the other hand, criticized that March for not promoting a liberating agenda toward gays and lesbians and for its silence on one of the primary health-care concerns for global Afrikans—HIV/AIDS. Anderson's concern was not to be a naysayer, but to pinpoint in what way such an important "symbolic event" can actually wind up repressing and silencing important members of Black communities, whose lives and contributions need to be uplifted, praised, and respected. I am certain that some will read Anderson as overstating his case by using the term *abomination* to describe the Million Man March. Nevertheless, his critique must be included in a genuinely *liberating* analysis of the March in order for one of the primary goals of any liberative agenda to be realized—*the insistence that inclusion of sometimes conflicting viewpoints makes for deeper realizations of freedom.* Anderson helps us to note that an emancipatory agenda for African Americans need not seek monolithic and imposed "agreement" to be effective. Measured and constructive self-criticism, even when it is aimed at such a popularly acclaimed Event as the March, may help us to name more accurately problems and to deploy strategies of transformation beyond a hearty chorus of "Amen!" for our achievements. The role of iconoclastic criticism, subversion of popular (and uncritically held) beliefs, is crucial in future developments of Black religion.

Salim Faraji described the March as a liberating Event for the entire Pan African Diaspora. He stressed its importance in signaling that African Americans have *awakened to a new consciousness and recognition of our need for unity, solidarity, and peace.* Further, Faraji carefully applied the Horus myth of ancient Kemet (Egypt), particularly in its long-standing role as a primary inspiration for resistance movements to foreign oppressors and evil throughout the thirty-five-hundred-year history of that revered civilization. Calling on African American churches to recognize that it is this liberative spirit of *Heruic Manhood* that binds *all* Black religions together, Faraji envisioned the rising of Black males as freedom-fighters embodying the spirit of Heru—by whatever Name each religion may call it!

Anthony Pinn wrote about liberation themes in relation to his analysis of Spike Lee's movie "Get on the Bus." Building on the notion "movement," Pinn utilized Victor Turner's triadic structuring of ritual process—*separation, liminal period,* and *reintegration*—as a way of interpreting the ontological development and humanizing movement of Black males depicted in "Get on the Bus" in relationship to the March itself. Pinn was concerned to reveal how liberation of African American males must wrestle with questions of *inclusion,* as did Anderson. He wrote about Spike Lee's admirable mentioning but problematic handling of issues of gay male inclusion, noting that Lee both names and subverts homophobic macho masculinity, on the one hand, and reinserts it through the device of a violent encounter. Pinn further interrogated the parameters of inclusion by asking whether all the really liberating "men" must be "left of center," seeing as the only genuinely conservative, Republican male is thrown off the bus! Pinn applauds the aims of the March toward building a vision of Black manhood around the themes of "renewed accountability and responsibility." His naming of the ambiguities in the process of coming into a fully inclusive understanding of masculinity were important markers toward what I would call a *mature understanding of liberation.*

WHOLENESS

Wholeness as a concept in *Black Religion after the Million Man March* has a very specific meaning for African American men and women. I define it as *a complex set of reactions, rituals, and behaviors developed against the ongoing existential psycho-spiritual state of fragmentation, ontological sense of incompleteness, biological dis-ease, and the socio-political and economic realities of rupture whereby selves seek to complete, heal, mend, and become reintegrated.* In the Million Man March/Day of Absence Black males sought to heal a lost and broken sense of both personal self and Communal Self. Before the entire world we confessed sinful ways, sought spiritual cleansing, and made public our intent to change ourselves and our behavior. We attempted to embody that ancient Christian concept of *metanoia—a complete change of heart demonstrated by a radical shift in values accompanied by changed behavior.* The theme of *atonement,* upon which the March was founded, was this seeking for wholeness for Black males. Such atonement could only be achieved through public confession and *metanoia.*

Lee Butler began his chapter elaborating the implications of Matthew 4:23–5:2, in which Jesus healed crowds of the ill while teaching them about "the good news of the kingdom" (Mt 4:23). Butler's focus on Louis Farrakhan was unique in this entire text, since my aim was to avoid getting into intellectual sparring about a controversial leader. Generally, Butler's analysis was positive in tone, setting Farrakhan into a historical Pan African context by revealing his connections to both traditional West African healing and communal rites, and the powerful healing legacy of Black preachers. Farrakhan was unveiled as a *Black Muslim Black preacher*, well within that venerable (predominantly *Christian*) tradition. As a preacher Butler further located Farrakhan as embodying those ancient storytelling gifts of the traditional *griot* in Africa, combined with the *shaman's gift* for practicing and eliciting from the community rites of healing and transformation. As an exemplar of an archetypal Black preacher, Louis Farrakhan's discourse at the March was reinterpreted as a "Sermon on the Mall," transforming mundane geography into Sacred Space. Comparing his insight with that of XODUS SPACE, Butler called for a revised understanding of Farrakhan's vision of wholeness by seeing his sermon as a "preaching cure" that embodied "liberative, transformative sound and word." Such a description ought to enable many of us to reexamine Farrakhan's contribution to the March with new eyes and revise his "place" as one contributing toward a positive future for African Americans.

Bessie Collins used the healing pericope of the ten lepers found in Luke 17:11-19 as a springboard for her reflections. Collins brought together notions of desire for healing with the possibility of living in a state of reconciliation to GOD's community. She did this by carefully deploying critical responses to the psychological theories of Freud and Jung—carefully noting the ways in which divergent psychological needs were expressed by African Americans and European Americans during the months leading directly to the March. Collins noted that Black people seemed to "need" O. J. Simpson to be innocent in order to bolster our sense of dignity against ongoing assaults. At the same time, she was particularly concerned with unveiling the embedded "collective . . . guilt" in the White community's reactions to the March in combination with the overall outrage of the majority population over the acquittal of O. J. Simpson in his criminal trial. She further uplifted the March as a potential symbolization of the shedding of typically negative stereotypes of Black males in the "parade of redeemed Black men . . . getting in touch with the nurturing, supportive, spiritual, loving nature hidden behind the persona of what it means to be both Black and acceptably male in America." What was particularly striking to me about Collins's analysis was the implication that wholeness for Black men was embodied in the *marching bodies of Black men who unabashedly moved toward a more vulnerable and open understanding of maleness*. I suggest that such a public affirmation of vulnerability, openness, nurture, and care reveals Collins's primary point, that *wholeness can be the potential for psychic transformation in a public display of subversive maleness*.

Collins ended her chapter evoking the healing space described in Toni Morrison's powerful novel *Beloved*—the Clearing. Like womanist ethicist and theologians Emilie Townes, and Karen Baker-Fletcher, Collins turns to the

Pan African spirituality expressed by Baby Suggs in that novel. It is a spirituality that calls for a *renewed love of one's heart/flesh/spirit and respectful recognition of the Other in the midst of a death-dealing social situation.* As Townes eloquently states it:

> To love one's heart is an individual and a communal call to question the radical nature of oppression and devaluation of the self and the community in the context of structural evil.[3]

The Clearing is that healing space, according to Emilie Townes, which teaches all African American women, men, and children gathered in sacred rituals that we have "learned to hate ourselves without ever realizing the level of our self-contempt."[4] In the language of the XODUS hermeneutic, the Clearing is a Space of Awakening from psycho-spiritual Sleep. Such an Awakening opens and enables one to experience deeply the healing power of "loving ourselves, developing our hearts," and simultaneously being "our best critics and our greatest cheerleaders for justice and hope.[5] Being both a critical and celebrative Moment, the Clearing (and XODUS SPACE) can bring together poetry with social analysis, scholarship with sermon, music with prose, all in service of bringing the Folk toward the *wholeness* of a healed life. Pointing beyond the Event of the March itself, Black religion after the March must find ways of re-creating in its rituals, words, and actions the Awakening wholeness of the Clearing, which for me resonates with the aim of XODUS. As in the Clearing, the XODUS is a SPACE and a JOURNEY wherein all the Folk speak words of Life in the midst of the "valley and shadow of death." In the Clearing the women's voices and spirituality call men to reconnection, wholeness, and delight. The March has begun to teach Black men the deepest lessons of the Clearing—that Black men must take responsibility for our own healing and create our own Sacred Spaces.

Womanist theologian of culture Karen Baker-Fletcher relies heavily on Alice Walker's definition of *womanist.* One of the points Walker makes is that a womanist is "not a separatist, except on occasion for reasons of health." Baker-Fletcher believes that just as occasional separate meetings and spaces for women exclusively is healthy, so Black males may require occasional separate times and spaces for getting in touch with their deepest, self-nurturing energies. She uplifted the March as a positive occasion for males to bond together without blaming or disrespecting women. Looking for ways in which African Americans can grow in mutual struggles for justice, Baker-Fletcher encouraged a "love that needs to grow." Paying attention, on the one hand, to *connections* between humanity and the environment, on the other, she was vitally concerned with enabling Black women and men to "love one another in all of our difference and diversity." Her contribution to a deeper understanding of wholeness involves the idea that *healing involves all reconnecting with the "earth, Spirit, and one another," one that can both recognize differences and grow in love and justice beyond the inherent separativeness that objectifying differences can produce.*

Cheryl Sanders also contributed a unique view of wholeness and moral power within the framework of a strong affirmation of traditional Christian values. Sanders interpreted the current condition within many Black communities as one of *demoralization requiring "remoralization."* For her, African American males require a process of empowerment and redemption. She challenged African American males to find current strategies of leadership on the secure ground of moral power.

Ivory L. Lyons Jr.'s section can also be seen as a call for wholeness directed toward conservative Black Christian theology and churches. Lyons believes that the Message and Call of the March reached a "spiritual core lacking in many Black evangelical churches." Like Sanders, Lyons speaks as an "insider," one whose life is aligned with an evangelical Christian interpretation of the Gospel. Lyons drew careful connection among the oppressive situation of Jews in first-century Palestine; the unconventional and radical call of Jesus with that of the March (and its messenger, Louis Farrakhan); and the centrality of love and repentance in both Jesus' Gospel and Message of the March. Lyons criticized exclusionary and divisive aspects of evangelical theology within conservative Christian Black Churches that disengage African Americans from acquiring a global view toward our subordination and disable the possibility of collective action across religious and doctrinal differences. Lyons's work reveals a hope that the deep divisions of religious dogma and practice within Black communities may find ways in which to transcend arrogant and self-serving doctrinaire hermeneutics in order to seek a more holistic approach to both our spiritualities and our capacity for love.

With regard to that very specific construction of masculinity based on literalist readings of certain "household codes" within the New Testament, Pastor Jack Sullivan and I sought to deconstruct the domination and control practices inherent in Headship models of manhood, which we see as inimical to the healing of our communities. We discussed the possibility of developing new understandings of those ancient and revered terms like *brotherhood* and *friendship*, with a stress on ethical character traits such as vulnerability, trust, dependability, accountability, responsibility, and interdependence. Sullivan called such a new understanding of male relationship a *"Quilted Community" wherein each man could envision himself to be an interconnected thread essential to the entire fabric of the Community.* Like those designed by the "senior sisters" of his church, Sullivan suggests that the Quilted Community would be comprised of those fragments and discarded pieces of clothes no longer seen as "useful"—a potent simile of the Quilted Community that *was* the March! The March could be viewed as a symbol of that Wholeness experienced only when the vast diversity of African American/Pan African male humanity—in all our difference, conflicts, strengths, weaknesses, sinfulness, and sanctity—came together as a living Quilt. All that could be considered broken and fragmented about Black males was woven together in songs, prayers, speeches, Word, and Colors that day. The March was a Quilt representing the possibility for healing to the entire world, broadcast by the media as a vision of what our wholeness could be with the Spirit's help.

POWER

Power has been defined as "coercive force that only a privileged and dominating minority can hoard, accumulate, and use to preserve its own interests."[6] The very fact of bringing together a million Black males—signifiers of societal disempowerment—reveals that such a view of power could be subverted by a "transformed understanding of power [which] names *intimate communal interaction as genuine and creative power.*"[7] With the eloquent language of their accumulated and determined numbers, Black males marked American society with a transformed understanding of power by showing that a *communal, cooperative, and interactive understanding of power* ought to be the *cultural norm of masculinity* and *humanity.*

Such a view of power was expressed with particular poignancy by Theodore Walker in his articulation of the "calm-prayerful-peaceful-joyful-loving spirit of the March." Such spirit pervaded the massive outpouring of men, women, and children that Walker noted the confident witness of one man who was separated from his fifteen-year-old son by the press of men. The man, Lawrence Oliver Hall, initially felt alarm for his son's safety but also sensed in his heart that all would turn out well: "My son would be fine in the hands of God and in the company of brothers committed to spiritual renewal and atonement."[8]

What I find moving about this story is what Walker described as a "sense of security in the loving embrace of a million-plus keepers of one another." By becoming *our brothers' Keeper* to one another, at least for that day, we ascribe to it a *sacred separateness* quite different from "normal" days. I remember that my own family *fasted from consumerism*—from buying and selling goods—on that day as we participated in the Day of Absence. Salim Faraji noted that he fasted in preparation for the March. A brother from the Atlanta area who elegantly hosted me for a Men's Revival at his church, Leon Frazier, spoke about fasting from food and abstaining from intimate relations with his wife during that period as preparation for the March.[9] It is clear that African American males took seriously the Mission Statement of the March, written by Maulana Karenga: "We call then for a Holy Day of Atonement on this October 16, 1995, a day to meditate on and seek right relationship with the Creator, with each other and with nature."[10]

We ought to ask ourselves about the relationship between the ethos of fasting and sanctifying of a particular Day, which we separate from other days as Holy, and critical discourse about the kinds of words, issues, and ideas we include as a part of that day. Anderson's condemnation of the March as forwarding an "abomination of a million men" distinctively dislodged laudatory comments about that day precisely because he suggested that *silencing an oppressed minority within an oppressed minority can corrupt the sanctity of an Event—even one as significant as the Million Man March.* I take Anderson to be challenging us *to be extremely careful* about such important Events as the March because *spiritual power can be used, and often is utilized to silence dissent.* Karen Baker-Fletcher noted that the strong criticisms of Black feminists like Angela Davis probably had a salutary effect on the promoters of the March, perhaps even compelling them to include at least some important women as representatives on the platform. Yet Anderson noted, correctly, that *no gay or lesbian* representative was heard from on that Day from the platform. If a new and communal-cooperative-interactive form of power is to follow from the March, then leaders like Louis Farrakhan, Ben Chavis Muhammad, Jesse Jackson, and others may need to seek out Black gays like Keith Boykin, whom Victor Anderson mentioned. It would be a powerful sign of the development of a radically new and creative form of communal-cooperative-interactive power if the Million Families March currently being planned sought out gay and lesbian participation in its planning, especially in light of the *fact* that gays and lesbians are part of our families as uncles, aunts, mothers, fathers, sisters, and brothers—whether they are "in the closet" or not!

BLACK POWER, HOLY POWER

Walker also noted that the March's concern with "population-specific [in this case *African American*] social-ethical prescriptions" as being consistent with the ongoing Black Christian "appropriation of black power/nationalism." In our multicultural era mention of Black Power can degenerate into calls about "black provincialism," "reverse racism," and condemnations of what some consider an anachronistic strategy of the sixties. In an era when African Americans have been targeted politically as recipients of unfair "discriminatory practices" in the campaign to end a generation of so-called "affirmative action policies," we must be careful to publicly interrogate what Black Power means for our generation. The Black theology of James Cone in the late 1960s conflated GOD's struggle against oppression with the ongoing struggle of Blacks against repression. As one located in the Los Angeles Basin, I am increasingly reminded of the need for Brown Power, Red Power, and Yellow Power. All such constructions, however, *presuppose White Power* as the normative condition. Anderson's *Beyond Ontological Blackness* radically subverts such understandings by naming them as *reactionary and dependent on the existence of White Power.*

Is Black Power for our time the bringing together of a million Black males, or is it gaining more Black-owned and operated companies on the Fortune 500 list? Are massive gatherings the true sign of Black Power, or has the time for such gatherings faded? House Speaker Newt Gingrich loudly declaimed that such gatherings were anachronistic when asked for his response to the March on October 16, 1995, on CNN. I would submit that most African Americans still need massive gatherings both to promote our interests in the public sphere and to renew our commitment to struggling for dignity in a country still rife with beliefs and practices inimical to African American flourishing. Massive outpourings of support, solidarity, and community like the Million Man March most likely will continue to be a part of Black religious experience.

At the same time that events like the March meet our psycho-spiritual needs, economic development and opportunity must continue to be key indicators of concrete progress toward Black Power. *Power* as "the capacity to decide, to act, and to do"[11] will continue in the foreseeable future to be measured in capitalist terms. The ability to amass, control, manipulate, influence, and determine the course of institutions, communities, and peoples is judged by economic clout.

African American entrepreneurial adventures—under the influence of the community and family principles of *Ujima* (collective work and responsibility) and *Ujamaa* (cooperative economics) that were presented in the Third and Ninth Pledges (see chapter 10, "Keeping the Promises of the Million Man March")—have a unique opportunity to advance both the *particular interests* of African American communities and the *general interest* of the United States economy. Black Power might now revise the maxim What is good for the market is good for the country (a dictum that has previously excluded the interests of almost everyone except a very tiny elite of fabulously wealthy individuals!), to **What is economically healthy for Black Americans is good for all Americans.**

At the same time, because the March called on Africans from throughout the Diaspora to become aware of one another's economic, social, and political plight, the deeper message of the March may be **What is good for relatively privileged American Africans must be shared for the betterment of Africans throughout the world.** Such a challenge would expand provincial notions of Blackness beyond the shores of the United States and subvert selfish tendencies, which in the end would undermine the grand rhetoric of "African solidarity" often used in the discourse of Black nationalism.[12] African American capitalists must be encouraged to find new ways of *contributing* to others and thereby expand narrow definitions of "self-interest," which tend to collapse into lifeless "bottom-line" profit margins.

Power, according to Martin Luther King Jr., must be understood in its context with love and justice. King noted that love and power need one another to realize themselves fully, for "power without love is reckless and abusive," while "love without power is sentimental and anemic."[13] Further, King combined love, power, and justice in the next two sentences: "Power at its best is love implementing the demands of justice. Justice at its best is love correcting everything that stands against love."[14]

In an admirable fashion, barring the silence on issues of AIDS/HIV and homosexuals, the March brought together under the banner of a Holy Day concerns about economics with those of religious zeal and idealism. This was no small feat, especially for African American males who have been under-identified with economic power (as bankers and CEOs) while being over-identified with religious power (as preachers). Yet all of us deeply acquainted with Black Churches recognize that this public "marriage" of economics with religion is typical of many of our most progressive churches. Churches like First A.M.E. in Los Angeles are economic powerhouses for poor African Americans by not only aiding the community in start-up monies but also providing job fairs every year.[15] While not every church can provide the massive economic assistance that the ten-thousand-member First A.M.E. can—or its comparably sized neighbor West Angeles Church of God in Christ (which also has a thriving economic development ministry)—all Black Churches can find ways to form coalitions and alliances with various businesses and agencies interested in fostering economic growth. Previous strategies of looking for government assistance seem to have outgrown their effectiveness in an era of cut-backs and the politics of balancing budgets by slashing programs that benefit the poor.

The importance of fashioning a new understanding of Black Power for Black Religion might best be understood if we take seriously Rev. Mary Minor Reed's prophetic summons to *compassion*. As a Christian, Reed's call for African American men and women to embody the "sympathetic *consciousness* of others' pain, misery, troubles, needs, heartaches, sufferings, together with a *desire* to *alleviate* them" that she calls "compassion." Compassion combines into action powerful qualities of human interaction in Rev. Reed's view: sympathy and empathy. As a consciousness wedded to action, compassion's attitude "plus actions of compassion equals the will of God." Learning from the spirit of the March, Reed saw the March as an important object lesson in how African American males can take active responsibility for each other, and, by showing compassion, become truly powerful men.

Cheryl Sanders provided a powerful Christian interpretation of true power. Sanders focused on the Exodus paradigm, noting that her work looks toward the *exilic theology* in which the entire community of faith—oppressors and the oppressed—"inclusive of exiles and elites . . . offer[s] authentic liturgies of welcome and memory that enable the experience of liberation as homecoming." Exile is a life-choice pervaded by "strict codes of morality" and by the "peculiar liturgies of song, speech, and dance" practiced by the "sanctified" or "saints." Her interpretation of African American alienation in the United States emphasizes a *longing for some place or space—geographical, cultural, spiritual—where they can feel at home.* She differentiated being at "home" from being "liberated" because the outcome of being "liberated" might be affected by those who are one's oppressors. She interpreted the Million Man March as an *Exilic Ritual* in which "exiles making themselves at home in the sacred space demarcated by America's national monuments to New World manifestations of the political and cultural imperialism of Western civilization" experienced Home-Coming.

In response, I would note that XODUS shares Sanders's profound appreciation for rituals in which that which has previously been "everyday" and mundane is charged with the Spirit/spirit-possibilities of transcendence/immanence. In XODUS rhetoric I take this moment to be a moment of Self-Liberation, in which one psycho-spiritually and culturally "Re-Turns" to an Afrikan self. This Re-Turn is a kind of Home-Coming but is self-critical of oppressive Afrikan traditions of patriarchy and abuse inimical to Black survival here in the "New World." As New World Africans, I believe that we need both Liberation and Home-Coming. I see Sanders using both words, but we see their relationship differently. I suspect, however, that both of us believe that by participating in an Act/Event/Ritual of the proportions of the Million Man March, New World Africans demonstrated a *POWER TO BE OUR-SELVES, IN THE SPIRIT OF GOD, NO MATTER WHAT "OPPRESSORS" THOUGHT OF THE EVENT!* Such power is a "Black Power" of the SPIRIT, a **Holy Power** rooted in GOD. Expressing such a Holy Power transcends the "Gaze"[16] and whims of oppressive forces—forces both external and internal, individual and communal. *It is a "Black" power of the SPIRIT because we, in our dark-skinned "Black" bodies, revalorized and* (to borrow Sanders's term) *began the process of remoralizing ourselves with prayers, words, drumming, and song.*

We do not have to confine Holy Power to a Christian framework. The March included the ancient Pan African religious tradition of *pouring a libation for the ancestors.*[17] A Pan African religious vision of Holy Power might involve some important retrieval of traditional African religion's understanding of **homecoming and reconnection with the Village.** Malidoma Patrice Some's *Of Water and the Spirit* addresses his painful reinitiation after having been "taken" from his Dagara village for many years of "training" in a French seminary. Upon his initial return, Some' experienced himself as a stranger, alienated from previous ways, uncomfortably living in two worlds—one of ritual, magic, and spirit (traditional Dagara), and the other a rationalized world of doctrine (what he calls "Christian"). After a painful and self-revealing "initiation," Some' writes of the joy of his *homecoming,* in which he experienced a "melody never experienced before, so peaceful that it produced within me a joy beyond definition."[18] Some' noted that this experience was one of *profound connection with everything—humanity and nature:* "I understood that what makes a village a village is the underlying presence of the unfathomable joy of being connected to everyone and everything."[19]

For many Black males the March provided something of this mystical sense of connection, *the Village writ large.* This Village was a million-plus members marching on ground hallowed by their tears, deferred dreams, prayers, fasting, and all of those encoded hopes, bold words, prayers, and dreams of those ancestors who had marched there before. The spiritual sense of connection those brothers experienced was further enriched by the fact that in the Mall (despite the fact that it was on the Capitol side and not the Lincoln Memorial side) the ground itself resonated with all of the spiritual Memory of previous marches and speeches—as both Karen Baker-Fletcher and Cheryl Sanders suggested. Being connected to a Village, Homecoming is a vital part of an ecumenical understanding of Black Religion—the kind that transforms dreams by its Holy Power into real power.

PROPHETIC CHALLENGE TO BLACK CHURCHES

Black Churches are challenged in this volume to become more progressive and committed to concrete social activism. From the most conservative voices to the most liberal, no matter how much their positions disagreed, authors in this volume spoke with one accord about the dangerous overall laxity in social activism that has lured many Black Churches into an individualistic, privatized, and quietistic faith. With backs pressed against the wall of hard times, many Black Churches have resorted to the quick and easy absolutism of a "fast-food approach" (as Jack Sullivan called it) to both biblical interpretation and preaching.

If the "conversion" of Rev. Ben Chavis to Minister Benjamin Muhammad of the Nation of Islam is any indication, other genuinely frustrated Christian progressives may also switch to other religious alternatives. Yet we have reminded the reader of the historical mission of Black Churches, which at their best have been *leaders* of social change and not followers. While the cold, hard truth of the matter has perhaps been best described in Gayraud Wilmore's *Black Religion and Black Radicalism* as a *dialectic between periods of radicalism balanced with periods of retreat into privatist Christianity*, I would contend that **this current period of retreat must find the spiritual power and moral courage to advance into a new era of radicalism**.

Farrakhan's call for a March ought to be viewed as an alarm bell calling for the "real" Black Churches to Wake Up! The call was so successful in reaching the hearts of spiritually hungry Black males that they responded to the call, not necessarily to Farrakhan. With great discussion and discernment, Black males felt *inspired to a new vision of themselves*. As one male activist against sexism who attended the March, Victor Lewis of Oakland, California, told me, "There is a difference between being *inspired* by Farrakhan, and *following* his leadership."[20] Contrary to the demonization strategy of a few radically conservative and fundamentalist Black Christians, the conservative Christian voices in this volume (Sanders and Lyons) found ways to incorporate the themes, substance, and calling of the March into their faith framework. Like many who attended the March *without* any sense of a Christian faith framework, both Sanders and Lyons found some inspiration from the March, even as they disagreed strongly with Farrakhan.

If XODUS Christians, womanist Christians, and evangelical Christians can all agree with humanists (Anthony Pinn) and activists like Victor Lewis about the necessity for a radically new activism, then let Black Churches arise to our summons. Let Black Churches, as many as have the muster, draw on those deep well-springs of righteousness we learned about at the feet of our ancestors and elders. Let their cries for GOD's mercy and justice flow through our veins, fill our minds, and be uttered from our lips. Let a New Church arise from the ashes of Civil Rights X-Scapism and Fast-Food, Me-First Christianity. Let a new Day come forth in which the cutting edge of social change is drawn and defined by Black Churches in coalition with progressives of other religions. The cutting edge cannot be confined to good preaching and a large membership roster, because those are not enough for people who have lost their ability to believe in themselves. The cutting edge must be located by the bringing together of our strengths into an organized and disciplined coalition, which the Apostle Paul (and Cornish Rogers) calls the *Body of Christ*.

The March was a foretaste of what can happen ecumenically when all the committed Folk of faith rise to the challenges of our time.

A NEW ACTIVISM

In the end I hope that the March, and our discussions and critical reactions to it, will provide concerned and committed religious persons, leaders, teachers, parents, and business persons with an inspiration to breathe the fresh air of a new kind of activism. Ultimately, such an Activism will be measured in the powerful ways in which Black males returned to their homes and took on the hard tasks of loving, nurturing, and cooperating with their families and communities. This New Activism is an activation of the spirit. It is an activism achieved by getting back in touch with the Creator—by whatever Name we Name the Divine—and then living our life in accordance with life-affirming values. Such a New Activism is both *interior* and thereby cultural, and *exterior*, and thereby socio-political and economic.

The Million Man March taught us that we have power from bonding together that no experience of racism, poverty, or injustice can quench. We have a wholeness that comes from cleansing ourselves of unnecessary and sinful ways, irresponsibility, and a lack of accountability. Such a wholeness comes from gathering together, praying together, and working together toward a new vision of Dr. King's Beloved Community. Like threads in a beautiful, precious Kente cloth, we are a Quilted Community, each unique and yet interdependent. Freeing ourselves mentally, Black men have told the world that we are now, finally, AWAKE! Not begging, not groveling, not crying, we nevertheless wept for joy on that day because we had summoned a new strength from inside ourselves we had not previously known. A mass of loving, caring, and powerful Black males, calling forth from an ancient part of ourselves, "Long Live the Spirit of the Million Man March!"

Notes

[1] James Cone, *A Black Theology of Liberation*, The C. Eric Lincoln Series in Black Religion (Philadelphia and New York: J. P. Lippincott, 1970), p. 17.

[2] Jean-Marc Ela, "Christianity and Liberation in Africa," in *Paths of African Theology*, ed. Rosino Gibellini (Maryknoll, N.Y.: Orbis Books, 1994), p. 142.

[3] Emilie Townes, *In a Blaze of Glory: Womanist Spirituality as Social Witness* (Nashville: Abingdon Press, 1995), p. 48.

[4] Ibid., p. 63.

[5] Ibid.

[6] G. Kasimu Baker-Fletcher, *XODUS: An African American Male Journey* (Minneapolis: Fortress Press, 1996), p. 22.

[7] Ibid., p. 23.

[8] Taken from *Atonement: The Million Man March*, ed. Kim Martin Sadler (Cleveland: Pilgrim Press, 1996), pp. 99-100; fuller version quoted by Theodore Walker in "Can a Million Black Men Be Good News?" above.

[9] Brother Frazier shared this with me more than once during my stay with him and his family (Gloria, his wife, Myron and Michael, his sons), noting that his son Myron

and "many other brothers" had done similar things the days and weeks before the March (First African Presbyterian Church, Lithonia, Georgia, June 11-June 14, 1997).

[10] Maulana Karenga "The Million Man March/Day of Absence Mission Statement," in *Million Man March/Day of Absence: A Commemorative Anthology,* ed. Haki R. Madhubuti and Maulana Karenga (Chicago: Third World Press; Los Angeles: The University of Sankore Press, 1996), p. 143.

[11] This is the "neutral definition" Martin Luther King Jr. gave to *power* in many of his speeches.

[12] Calls for "Black solidarity" or "Africans Unite!" are as ubiquitous as Bob Marley's song "Africa Unite" on his *Survival* album, and as specific as the speeches and writings of Kwame Ture (formerly Stokely Carmichael).

[13] This definition is King's unique twist on Paul Tillich's *Love, Power, and Justice,* as found in his *Where Do We Go from Here: Chaos or Community?* (Boston: Beacon Press, 1967), p. 37.

[14] Ibid.

[15] The F.A.M.E. job fairs have been massively attended in the last few years, with well over six thousand people coming from all over the L.A. Basin to look for jobs, be interviewed by representatives of companies, and learn skills for acquiring work. The F.A.M.E. Renaissance Program is a $10 million-plus enterprise created to negotiate economic recovery after the April 1992 Uprising/Riots.

[16] *Gaze* is a term I developed in *XODUS*, p. 88.

[17] The Official Program of the Million Man March started with an invocation or Islamic Adan by Sheik Ahmed Tijani Ben-Omar of Accra, Ghana, followed by a Christian prayer by Rev. Fred Haynes of Friendship West Baptist Church of Dallas, Texas. Then a "Salute to Our Ancestors Libation Ceremony" was performed by Melvin Deal and The Heritage African Dancers and Drummers and others (Sadler, *Million Man March/Day of Absence,* p. 159).

[18] Malidoma Patrice Some', *Of Water and the Spirit: Ritual, Magic, and Initiation in the Life of an African Shaman* (New York: Jeremy P. Tarcher/Putnam Books, 1994), p. 301.

[19] Ibid.

[20] Conversation with Victor Lewis; the Rev. Marjorie Bowens-Wheatley, pastor of Community Church of New York City; and the Rev. Dr. Sharon Lewis, pastor of the South Shore Community Church of Chicago, April 28, 1997, Black Church and Domestic Violence Task Force meeting, Seattle, Washington.

Contributors

Victor Anderson teaches ethics, critical theory, American philosophy, and philosophy of religion at Vanderbilt Divinity School. Recipient of numerous prestigious academic fellowships, he has also served as a Reformed minister. Anderson is author of *Beyond Ontological Blackness: An Essay on African American Religious and Cultural Criticism* (New York: Continuum, 1995), *Pragmatic Theology: Negotiating the Intersections of an American Philosophy of Religion and Public Theology* (Albany: State University of New York Press, 1997), and numerous articles.

Garth Kasimu Baker-Fletcher teaches Christian ethics, moral philosophy, critical theory, and deconstruction at both Claremont School of Theology and Claremont Graduate University. Editor of *Black Religion after the Million Man March*, Kasimu is the co-author of *My Sister, My Brother: Womanist and XODUS God-Talk* (Maryknoll, N.Y.: Orbis Books, 1997); author of *XODUS: An African American Male Journey* (Minneapolis: Fortress Press, 1996) and *Somebodyness: Martin Luther King Jr. and the Theory of Dignity* (Minneapolis: Fortress Press, 1993). He has contributed to various books and journals. Kasimu is an ecumenical ordained Baptist minister.

Karen Baker-Fletcher is a womanist theologian and ethicist who is an associate professor of theology of culture. She teaches womanist and feminist theory, theology, and ethics at both Claremont School of Theology and Claremont Graduate University. Co-author of *My Sister, My Brother: Womanist and XODUS God-Talk* (Maryknoll, N.Y.: Orbis Books, 1997), and author of *A Singing Something: Womanist Reflections on Anna Julia Cooper* (New York: Crossroad, 1994), she is currently working on a book of womanist reflections on creation-centered spirituality to be titled *Sisters of Dust, Sisters of Spirit: Womanist Wordings on God and Creation* (Minneapolis: Fortress Press, forthcoming).

Lee H. Butler Jr. is an assistant professor of theology and psychology at the Chicago Theological Seminary. His recent publications include "More Than Sensual Healing: African American Pastoral Psychology in the 21st Century," *The Journal of Religious Thought;* and "The Evolution of Shamanism within the African American Christian Church," *Shamanic Applications Review.*

Bessie Collins is an ordained United Methodist deacon recently appointed an associate minister at Hamilton U.M.C. of Los Angeles. Studying to become a certified pastoral psychotherapist in the Personality and Theology Program at

Claremont School of Theology, she combines womanist literature, Black women's sacred song, and various psychological theories in her work.

Salim Faraji is an Afrikan-centered master's degree student at Claremont School of Theology; he attended the March. Faraji has worked as an activist, drug-rehabilitation counselor, and grass-roots organizer. Deeply schooled in a variety of African-American religions, such as the Ausar Auset Society, Ife' divination, Islam, and Black Baptist roots, Faraji's work seeks to articulate common threads of culture and spirituality among these varieties of religions in order to foster resistance to oppression.

Ivory L. Lyons Jr. is an ordained Baptist minister and student at Claremont Graduate University. His dissertation, "The Idea of Sin in the Work of Reinhold Niebuhr and Howard Thurman: A Confluence Toward Justice," critically sifts the two primary authors for ways of forwarding justice. As a Black Christian, Lyons's work seeks to open Black evangelicals to new ways of being faithful Christians in dialogue with others.

Anthony B. Pinn is an assistant professor of religious studies and director of the African American Studies Program at Macalester College in St. Paul, Minnesota. He has published with *The Journal of African American Men* and *The Journal of the Interdenominational Theological Center*. His book *Why Lord?: Suffering and Evil in Black Theology*, was published in 1995 by Continuum, New York. He is currently working on four book projects, including *Varieties of Black Religious Experience: A Theological Introduction* (Minneapolis: Fortress Press, forthcoming 1998).

Mary Minor Reed is a staff minister of First African Methodist Church, special assistant to the bishop. An alumna of Claremont School of Theology, her ministry work with youth in South Los Angeles has gained her an excellent reputation in the city of Los Angeles.

Cornish Rogers is professor of evangelism, ecumenism, and mission at the Claremont School of Theology. In his twenty-five years of pastoring to multi-ethnic congregations, he also has served as a full-time editor of *Christian Century*. A member of the World Council of Churches, Professor Rogers's vast experience in ecumenical outreach and dialogue is unparalleled.

Cheryl J. Sanders is professor of Christian ethics at the Divinity School of Howard University. She is author of *Empowerment Ethics* (Minneapolis: Fortress Press, 1995) and *Saints in Exile* (New York: Oxford, 1996). Recently installed as pastor of the Third Street Church of God, Sanders's work reflects her vocation as a dedicated pastor-scholar.

Jack Sullivan Jr. is the pastor of the United Christian Church of Detroit, Michigan. He attended the Million Man March. He contributed "Our Collective Responsibility" as a chapter in *Atonement: The Million Man March*, ed. Kim Martin Sadler (Cleveland: The Pilgrim Press, 1996).

Theodore Walker Jr. is professor of ethics and society at the Perkins School of Theology, Southern Methodist University, Dallas, Texas. He is author of *Empower the People: Social Ethics for the African-American Church* (Maryknoll, N.Y.: Orbis Books, 1991) and a contributor to other books and journals.